The Future of Law in

a Multicultural World

PRINCETON UNIVERSITY PRESS

PRINCETON, NEW JERSEY

1971

The Future of Law in
a Multicultural World

By Adda B. Bozeman

This book is sold subject to the condition that
it shall not, by way of trade, be lent, resold,
hired out, or otherwise disposed of without the
publisher's consent, in any form of binding or
cover other than that in which it is published.

This book has been composed in Linotype Baskerville

Publication of this book has been aided by
the Whitney Darrow Publication Reserve Fund of
Princeton University Press

PRINTED IN THE UNITED STATES OF AMERICA
BY PRINCETON UNIVERSITY PRESS

PREFACE

THIS book was originally prepared as a paper for presentation at the Fifth Maxwell Institute sponsored by the International Relations Program of the Maxwell School of Citizenship and Public Affairs, Syracuse University, August 25-30, 1968. Its major theme was suggested by Professor Michael Barkun, the conference coordinator, who thought that I might best contribute to the Symposium on "The United Nations and International Law" at Kasteel Oud-Wassenaar by developing some of the themes that had preoccupied me in two earlier compositions, namely: "Representative Systems of Public Order Today" (a brief comment upon Professor Harold Lasswell's address at the Annual Meeting of the American Society of International Law in 1959), and *Politics and Culture in International History* (Princeton University Press, 1960). The present volume, then, is conceptually closely related to my earlier work. However, whereas the latter is most concerned with the historical records of the world's major literate civilizations, particularly as these had accrued up to ca. 1500 AD, the present analysis is focused upon the present and the future of law and organization in the world. Furthermore, the range of cultures and political systems is expanded here so as to include Africa south of the Sahara and Southeast Asia; and next, the discussion of the subject matter is carried by certain structuring ideas not developed previously.

The process of transforming the manuscript into a book was aided greatly by the comments I received from

v

Professor Barkun and all other members of the Syracuse conference. To them I hereby express my deep gratitude. Two friends gave invaluable assistance: Arne Barkhuus, M.D., who supplied numerous and significant bibliographical references, and Mr. Joseph Campbell who gave needed advice on some sections of the work. I am greatly indebted to Mrs. Martyn Hitchcock for editing the book, and to Miss Delight Ansley for composing the index. Now, as ten years ago, I want to thank the Princeton University Press—this time especially Miss R. Miriam Brokaw, Mr. William J. McClung, and Mr. Sanford G. Thatcher—for their thoughtful guidance and support.

The system of transliteration for Arabic words corresponds to that used by the Library of Congress; but words commonly used in English are given in their anglicized form.

Bronxville, New York
1970

CONTENTS

INTRODUCTION

THIS book attempts to clarify the meanings carried by references to law in the political systems of certain selected culture zones; to estimate the durability of these meanings in times to come; to compare the locally and regionally valid references, and to see them in the global context of culture-transcendent schemes of law and organization.

The thought directing this endeavor originates in Occidental approaches to knowledge. Furthermore, it is biassed in favor of the assumption that differences between cultures and political systems are functions primarily of different modes of perceiving and evaluating reality. This means for purposes of the following sets of interlocking inquiries that the particular connotations carried by law in the West, the Middle East, Africa, Indianized Asia, and China are appreciated best if the general thoughtways and value systems in each of these realms are studied on their own local merits.

Knowing by in-dwelling, to borrow Michael Polanyi's phrase,[1] is theoretically possible for each aspiring individual, irrespective of his education or specialized training. In the framework of academic disciplines, however, such a challenge can probably never be wholly met, if only because a given thought world is always vaster and more intricate than the sum total of its intellectual categories or divisions. And this limitation carries added weight if one remembers that non-Western societies

[1] "On the Modern Mind," *Encounter*, XXIV (May 1965), 16-17.

have not brought forth equivalents either to our general structured universe of knowledge, or to the particular academic disciplines and methodologies of which it is composed, just as they have not produced "Occidentalists" or other foreign area specialists to match the legions of Orientalists and Africanists that have for centuries been at work in our civilization.

In these confining circumstances, only the philologist or linguist appears ideally equipped to understand "the other" in his authenticity since he can go to the heart of the matter that counts. And yet, even he would be hard pressed to meet the challenge if confronted with a plurality of collective "others," for no *one* philologist can be presumed to master the scores of complex languages represented by the diverse speech communities of which the world has been composed throughout the known millennia. It is true, of course, that each of the other recognized branches of learning also offers possibilities for the analysis of foreign realms. However, experience shows that none is self-reliant or sufficient to supply an equal measure of discernment in respect of all cultures and political systems. History, for example, may be said to supply the most fitting key if the door to the Arab realm is to be unlocked, but it is of limited use in a study of Negro Africa where anthropology offers greatest rewards. That is to say, in each case the individual scholar must make a decision (and it may appear arbitrary to others) as to which of the many charted roads is most likely to lead to understanding in a given field of inquiry. Indeed, faced with a broad spectrum of societies and interested in the isolation of diverse patterns of thought in each of them, he cannot be bound by any one academic discipline, but must instead accept the entire range of the humanities and social sciences as his field of operations; and this means that he must often rely on wisdom gathered by others, be they predecessors or contemporaries. The present book, then, while unified in its design, is not unified in terms of methodology. Furthermore, not being written either by a philologist or a person with a lifelong immersion in each of the societies here considered, it is not based on original discoveries but rather on insights derived in the main from what are commonly called secondary sources.

The matter of "law," more particularly as it relates to public order systems, exemplifies most, if not all, of the aforementioned problems. The course of Western thought and history, and the evolution and establishment of Western forms of political organization would be incomprehensible were one to ignore either the existence of law, or the consistent efforts of successive generations, beginning with those guided by the Roman jurists, to abstract law from other categories of thought and from such normative controls as custom and religion.[2] But this has not been the case in either Africa or Asia where human groupings have been held together effectively in comprehensive orders dominated by respect for religion, etiquette, the stabilizing function of war and conflict, or the superior wisdom regularly imputed to selected men. In short, law is not recognized everywhere as a distinct idea or a paramount reference. As Barkun rightly remarks in the course of his searching analysis of the subject, if it is true that organization or public order is assured primarily by religion, then it is futile, indeed misleading, to approach the organizational

[2] Sir Henry Sumner Maine, *Dissertations on Early Law and Custom* (New York, 1883), p. 5, to the effect that there is no system of recorded law from China to Peru which is not entangled with religious ritual and observance when it first emerges into notice.

scheme as if it revolved around law.[3] For not only would
the identity of these societies be critically deformed were
one to read the Occidental meaning of law into the
native records, or to incorporate the ruling native norms
into the framework of jurisprudence and legal history as
built in the West, but the converse, too, would be true:
namely, that law would forfeit its trusted meanings in
the West.

Certain verbal formulations covering broad concord-
ances between the function of Occidental law on the one
hand, and that of Asian and African concepts and rules
on the other, may of course be advanced in behalf of
the cause of uniformity. However, it is doubtful whether
compound definitions that overlook or excise locally
crucial particulars can be conducive, in the long run, to
clarity and precision in intercultural discourse. As it is,
one may well have to admit that the word "law" is today
overworked or overstretched, but in the absence of ade-
quate alternative, sufficiently simple, yet meaningful,
words, it is not surprising to find that the Chinese *fa*
is being rendered rather consistently as "law"; and the
same holds for the Indian term *dharma*, and the tribal
customs of Negro Africa. However, the most sensitive
translators of foreign idea systems have made it abun-
dantly clear that this Western verbal symbol does not
really cover the non-Western substance of which it
speaks, and that it therefore needs extensive annotations
in each case. It is this lead that will be followed in the
present discussion.

Whether viewed as a set of concepts, norms, or social
institutions, law everywhere is linked, explicitly or im-

[3] Michael Barkun, *Law Without Sanctions: Order in Primitive Societies and the World Community* (New Haven and London, 1968),
pp. 29ff.

plicitly, with schemes of social and political organization. Given the meanings carried by law in the West, the public order system here—whether subsumed in the city, the kingdom, the empire, the nation state; or the international society—has been cast traditionally in terms of the supremacy of law. Moreover, since European law has been associated from its beginnings with the need felt on the one hand to isolate and protect individual rights, and on the other to define the responsibilities of citizenship, government has been viewed preferentially as a compact or contract between men. That is to say, in this civilization in which the individual human being has been disengaged from the group, it is possible to assume that men, be they governors or governed, are capable of entering into binding obligations.

Neither of these norms, nor any of the values, beliefs, or perceptions upon which they rest, can be presumed to exist in other systems of public order, most of them also trusted by the people they enclose, even though they may appear overtly coercive from the Occidental point of view. In the context of local and regional organization as in that of law, then, one and the same word will be found to evoke uniquely different associations and to cover a multitude of diverse realities. Unless the latter are revealed and steadily kept in mind, cross-cultural comparisons of such organizational devices as "corporation," "state," "empire," and "constitution," are bound to be misleading; and "diplomacy," "alliance," "treaty," and such structuring principles as "order," "peace," "justice," or "war," will carry different meanings.[4]

4 This warning was sounded by T. E. Holland when he pointed out, by way of some critical comment on the theories of Sir Henry Maine,

The time perspective in the service of which the twin causes of law and organization are here considered is the future—a concept as enigmatic as that of time itself, and one least capable of rallying multicultural accord. For not only must one realize that the mysteries and ambiguities of time have possessed the human imagination everywhere and in all periods of recorded history, and that there exist therefore as many orders of time as speech communities and cultures, but one can also hold with J. G. von Herder that everything everywhere carries within itself its own measure of time, and that two different things will never have the same measure of time. Time, then, is relative in many senses, and its partition into present, past, and future may be no more than a convention.

Working in the context of this convention, it is possible to say that all societies share a strong commitment to the present and the past, or, as Ortega y Gasset suggests,[5] that society *is* primarily the past. For since society itself cannot think, remember, or plan ahead, it must stand everywhere for order, constancy, and preservation. No human grouping can overcome this primary disposi-

---

that Asian societies cannot be judged by European criteria. See *Elements of Jurisprudence*, 13th ed. (Oxford, 1928), p. 52. It has found a recent echo in Scott A. Boorman's work, *The Protracted Game: A Wei-ch'i Interpretation of Maoist Revolutionary Strategy* (New York, 1969), p. 3, where the author introduces a comparison of Chinese Communist and Western strategic thinking: "For the Western historian, the degree of which strategic preconceptions hinder interpretive analysis of Western military history is, of course, minimal: the historian is dealing with a portion of his own cultural and intellectual heritage. A similar observation is true of the attitudes and actions of a Western soldier or statesman dealing with an essentially Western conflict situation. The applicability of Western analytic criteria vanishes, however, when the Western analyst, lay or governmental, attempts to confront the strategic techniques of a culture different from his own."

[5] *History as a System and Other Essays Toward a Philosophy of History* (New York, 1941), p. 210.

tion toward time unless it becomes somehow receptive to the individual and his innovating thought. Cultures, whether literate or nonliterate, in which the communal element is absolutely dominant over the principle of individuation, as it has long been in most African and Asian areas, will therefore tend to remain fixed to that which is. And since the past is trusted here as the abode of truth as well as authority, it will perforce instruct or dominate the present. In this connection, then, the notion of "the future" cannot be said to have intrinsic meaning.

The European peoples escaped the restrictions which came to bind societies in China, India, the Near East, and Africa because they have been continuously responsive to the unsettling forces emanating from biography. The impulse for this departure from the norm is due to their inheritance and steady use of certain classical, especially Greek, traditions, among them most particularly the commitment to cultivate rational yet daring thought. Contrary to the adjoining Near East, where early adventurous races had staged the neolithic revolution and invented writing, but where all later societies converged upon the view that there is nothing new under the sun, curiosity was progressive in Greek society,[6] thus opening up unbounded future time for the investment of aspiration and achievement. Under the impact of this new principle of humanized time which makes for the expectation that the uncertain future may be partially divested of its unpredictability by human effort, whole societies in the West have aimed at a mastery of time by distinguishing consciously between present, past, and future, and by striving on the one

[6] See A. N. Whitehead, *Adventures of Ideas* (New York: 1933), pp. 99ff, 108f.

hand for "development" and on the other, simultaneously, for "stability."

No Occidental institution exemplifies the organic complementarity of these two dispositions toward time more tellingly than contract—the core of all associational life in this civilization and, as suggested earlier, the source of constitutional government. What makes contract a unique expression of the European time sense is the theory of confidence that it encloses: confidence not only in the ability of men to preempt and order time that lies ahead of them by means of promises to do or refrain from doing something, but confidence also in the binding nature of obligations assumed in the past. All Western constitutions, bills of rights, and acts of legislation that are normative rather than merely formal or rhetorically demonstrative, are in the final analysis emanations of this mode of thinking. That is to say, they cannot be transplanted effectively into other civilizations, ruled by totally different political traditions and philosophies of time.

Other aspects of the linkage between political organization and time that require brief mention here in the interest of clarifying the intent of subsequent discussions, particularly the stress upon certain records of the past, concern the concepts, respectively, of "progress" and "political development." Both words are future-directed, and both suggest that the future will be an advance over the past. This proposition is of course perfectly tenable as long as the passage of time is being viewed sequentially or mechanistically, but it does not necessarily hold in an evaluation of the forms of human life and thought that are being revealed in the "progressions" of millennia, centuries, or epochs. Thus, to give but one example, European thought in the twentieth century may be said to have developed steadily in the course of two and a half thousand years, but it is debatable whether it is more "progressive" than that registered in ancient Greece. Similarly, aspiration may be a constant motif in the West, but it does not always or invariably lead to achievement either intellectually, politically, or economically,[7] nor does it inevitably aim at fashioning a "future" that is different from the "past." Indeed in certain circumstances—and here the period of the European Renaissance comes to mind—the most "progressive development" may actually consist of a return to the culture's past. Such thoughts may be out of season in the modern Atlantic community of nations, but the present situation in all non-Western societies reveals quite unequivocally that the future is being fashioned—often by means of revolutions[8]—in terms of resurrecting trusted ancient orders. The references to the past in the following discussion of the future of law and organization in a multicultural world should be viewed in the light of these considerations.

[7] Cp., David McClelland, *The Achieving Society* (Princeton, 1961), p. 202, for the conclusion that societies are apt to lose interest in achievement when their dreams and visions change, and that economic growth is determined ultimately not by material forces but rather by values and motives. Also H. W. Singer, *International Development: Growth and Change* (New York, 1964), chaps. 6, 7, that brainpower and people are the real clue to "development" even in the economic sense of the term.

[8] Cp. H.A.R. Gibb's reminder in *Studies on the Civilization of Islam*, ed. Stanford J. Shaw and William R. Polk (Boston, 1962), p. 44, that revolutions, as history seems to show, rarely change the essential character of basic institutions, but only emphasize the tendencies which are already shaping them in a given direction.

The Future of Law in

a Multicultural World

CHAPTER ONE

INTERCULTURAL DISCOURSE AND THE PROBLEM OF UNDERSTANDING

Words and Ideas

WORDS often assume an existence of their own, separate from the ideas in conjunction with which they first appeared. One particular term may come to stand for a variety of concepts, sometimes only loosely related to each other; it may shed a meaning with which it has long been closely associated; it may attract an idea formerly carried by a different term; or it may come to convey an entirely new intellectual construction. Some of these metamorphoses are barely perceptible while occurring; others by contrast are willful manipulations. For, whereas the development of the relation between thought and its expression is sometimes allowed to take place at random, it is at other times and in other places the object of watchful scrutiny.

For example, in the formative period of classical Roman jurisprudence, law and Latin were cultivated in close alignment to each other with the result that legally and politically crucial concepts were conveyed reliably to successive generations. The elaboration of theories of natural law and natural rights in the seventeenth and eighteenth centuries, on the other hand—admirable and fruitful as it may have been in the context of philosophy—impaired the integrity of "law" and "rights" as juristic concepts because the language of legal symbolization was permitted to move away from the meanings it had originally held. Furthermore, these two words, "law" and "rights," had at that time become particularly active precisely because they were being widely trusted in all sectors of Western civilization as summary symbols for major value orientations, and in the light of this fact, their careers suggest that culturally strategic terms may also be particularly vulnerable terms. Every civilization or human grouping, unified by its own language and traditions and rallying around its own preferred concepts and symbols, must have had to face, at one time or another, similar problems in relation to the relevance of thought to word. But what in any case is clear from the records is that the integrity of the thinking process, and therefore also the integrity of the culture itself, is greatly dependent upon the careful use of words.

In a multicultural environment and in periods marked by intense international discourse and cultural borrowing, the association between ideas and the symbols denoting ideas presents special complexities and challenges.

India and China, for example, had coexisted for centuries in virtual ignorance of each other until certain extraordinarily talented linguists and translators began to adapt Buddhism, an originally Indian faith, to Chinese needs. These intellectual go-betweens translated numerous texts and compiled elaborate dictionaries of Sanskrit-Tibetan-Chinese terms in behalf of the cause they served. However, in their painstaking labors they presently came to realize firstly, that whole categories of Sanskrit terms could not be rendered into Chinese at all; secondly, that entire concepts had no equivalents in Chinese patterns of thought; and finally, that India and China had developed different ways of thinking and lived by totally different values. What was required, they thus found, was not a mere translation of words but rather an interpretation of the images and experiences that had originally inspired the words; and this meant in the final analysis that all of India and all of China had to be understood before the separate aspects of Buddhism could be made meaningful to the Chinese.[1]

This bold intellectual process (upon which several generations of scholars engaged) of adjusting to each other two very different vocabularies of words and ideas conduced eventually to the establishment of a purely Chinese kind of Buddhism; and the operation was so successful that India and China became strangers again, as they had been before Buddhism had linked their spiritual destinies.[2] Furthermore, in the extended context of the history of cultures and intercultural relations, the remainder is in order that Indian Buddhism was finally to wither away in its confrontation with the orthodox Hindu order, while Chinese Buddhism did not long maintain itself in the face of Confucianism. The original roots of the two civilizations had evidently

[1] This was realized already in the fifth century AD when Fa Hsien left on his pilgrimage to India, determined to study the general habits of the people rather than merely stored texts of religious wisdom.

[2] For this chapter in intellectual history see in particular the works of Arthur F. Wright and Daisetz T. Suzuki. Cp. also the conclusion reached by Oswald Spengler, *Der Untergang des Abendlandes*, 2 vols. (Munich, 1923), II, 64ff. For a brief summary of some of the issues here involved, see Adda B. Bozeman, *Politics and Culture in International History* (Princeton, 1960), pp. 146-61, and authorities there cited.

not been disturbed. And in the light of this well-known record, it is ironical, to say the least, that twentieth-century representatives of India and China should have "borrowed" Buddhism as the official guiding reference, not only for the establishment of amicable political relations between their own two countries, but also as the major informing principle of their project for an all-Asian solidarity bloc that might defy the West. Yet this is what was arranged by means of accords and conferences, notably in 1954, when Communist China and India agreed to incorporate references to Buddhist ethics—i.e., the *panca-śīla*—in a treaty recognizing China's military acquisition of Tibet under the guise of regulating trade in this unfortunate Buddhist land.

It would be difficult to find a more instructive example of what can happen when the organic relation between words and ideas is deliberately severed or otherwise allowed to lapse, and when ideas stand suddenly emptied of their intrinsic meanings. The original system of Buddhist ethics had been aimed at developing a nonpolitical mentality, withdrawn from the concerns of acquisitive and self-defensive action. The Buddha, with this end in mind, had laid down ten precepts for "right conduct," of which the first five—the *panca-śīla*—admonished every Buddhist to avoid: 1) the destruction of life; 2) theft; 3) unchastity; 4) lying; and 5) the use of intoxicating liquor. Sino-Indian diplomacy, however, 2,500 years later, took over this hallowed Buddhist formula in the full knowledge that it had carried through the centuries exclusively religious connotations, and enumerated, then, for the conduct of international relations, five "norms" that had been recognized in Occidental international law and politics even before they were inserted in the Charter of the United Nations

6

(which itself was a product, not of Eastern, but of Western political thought), namely: 1) mutual respect for each other's territorial integrity and sovereignty; 2) nonaggression; 3) noninterference in each other's internal affairs; 4) equality and mutual advantage; 5) peaceful coexistence and economic cooperation. In other words, the implied reference to Buddhist ethics was from every point of view entirely spurious—and especially since Chou En Lai and Nehru, the architects of this Asian house of friendship, were openly scornful of all religion. Subsequent events—including a Chinese invasion of India made possible by the prior occupation of Tibet—were to prove that China had outwitted and enfeebled its Asian collaborator by creating illusions through artful verbalizations—which is a mode of psychological warfare that had been common not only in Confucian China but in Hindu India as well, where *māyā* (deceit, trick, the display of an illusion) and *sāman* (the way of appeasement) had long been recognized as primary tools of statecraft. Lulled to sleep by Chinese rhetoric, Indian thought was unable to recall in time the actual meaning of the Buddhist value-language of its own heritage.[3]

The borrowings engaged in by the Muslim elites of

[3] Maoist China is using Buddhism overtly as a political tool in the management of neighboring peoples. Buddhist associations and congresses designed to control Buddhist activities on the mainland have been sponsored as props for the operation of the Communist Party, and indigenous Buddhist organizations in e.g. South Asia are being subverted methodically so as to align them with the policy interests of China. The present manipulation of the faith has strong precedents in Confucian China, especially in the Sui and T'ang dynasties, when Buddhism was reduced to the status of a "barbarian" creed. Then, as now, China succeeded in persuading Buddhists that their religion was perfectly compatible with resort to violence. For a recent discussion of the political aspects of Buddhism today see Jerrold Schecter, *The New Face of Buddha* (New York, 1967), especially the chapters dealing with Buddhism and political power in Southeast Asia.

7

the Near East during the first centuries of the Islamic era were carried out under circumstances and by human dispositions significantly different from those of the early interchanges between India and China; and yet they, too, illustrate the proposition that cultural borrowing is a creative act that does not necessarily lead to intercultural understanding. Mohammed had fashioned his new faith by openly accepting religious propositions that had been fundamental to the older rival religions of Judaism and Christianity, and successive Muslim governing and scholarly elites drew freely from Persian, Indian, and Byzantine knowledge, taking only what could be absorbed and ignoring what appeared to be incompatible with their basic domestic value system. None of these encounters with the highly developed Oriental civilizations was felt to threaten the integrity of the "new" Islamic culture world. However, a crisis came with the onslaught of Greek thought, which presented not only new ideas for which native equivalents were missing, but, more importantly, a revolutionary way of thought that invited the inquisitive to rely rather upon the reasoning powers inherent in their own imagination than on the authority of established religion and tradition. The areas of knowledge in which the encounter between the two systems of thought was most intense were philosophy and the natural sciences.[4] Here we

---

[4] Other parts of the Hellenic legacy, notably tragedy, comedy, and history, went largely unnoticed. Homer and Socrates represented ideas that were incomprehensible here, as they were throughout the Orient, as Hans Heinrich Schaeder notes in *Der Mensch in Orient und Okzident: Grundzuege einer eurasiatischen Geschichte* (Munich, 1960), p. 122. See also Louis Gardet, "L'Humanisme Greco-Arabe: Avicenne," in *Journal of World History* II, no. 4 (1955); J. J. Saunders, "The Problem of Islamic Decadence," in *ibid.*, VII, no. 3 (1963); and above all the rich and varied analyses of Islamic culture by H.A.R. Gibb, Gustave Von Grunebaum, and Wilfred Cantwell Smith.

find the towering intellects of Fārābi (c. 870-950) and Avicenna (979-1037) fearlessly immersed in the substantive aspects of Greek philosophy, and capable, moreover, of correlating and fusing Hellenic and Islamic, as well as Persian, concepts, so as to fashion imposing philosophical structures of their own. Yet these great but isolated men were not allowed to set the tone of the intercultural dialogue. The consensus of the dominant theological guardians of knowledge had it that divine revelation was the exclusive source of truth and that Greek thinking was a threat to the faith; or, as Ghazāli (1058-1111), one of the greatest and most influential of orthodox thinkers, held, reliance on reason was bound to lead to unbelief. In the face of a continuously uncompromising administration of sacred law as the exclusive carefully bounded context for speculative thought, Greek philosophy in its conceptual integrity simply could not be understood after the eleventh century AD, no matter how dedicated the labors of the translators may have been. Relegated to the category of "alien sciences," it never inspired the kind of concerted effort toward the further discovery of assimilable ideas that had sent the early Chinese Buddhist scholars on comprehensive quests to understand all of India. What we observe instead is a massive but uncoordinated and somewhat shallow movement aimed only at excerpting formulations and dialectical devices from the body of substantive thought in the service of which the devices had been developed by the Greeks.

For example, as Von Grunebaum points out, Islamic hellenizing philosophers could accept many of Plato's doctrines but none of his ontological premises, with the result that Platonic theorems could never become

9

really operative in the Muslim world after their trans-plantation.[5] Obliged to defend their own tenets not only against the sophisticated adversaries of Islam in the newly conquered, formerly Christian territories, but also against rival orthodox defenders of the faith, the hellenizers freely helped themselves to a great deal of Aristotelian logic while evading conceptually threaten-ing philosophical propositions—just as others in their midst were drawing extensively on Hindu mathematics while bypassing Hindu philosophy.[6] In short, Greek philosophy was useful to Islam mainly as an auxiliary science capable of supporting what was to all intents and purposes its opposite, namely the monolithic con-trol of knowledge by religion. One can even say that the integrity of Islamic culture and society, as originally defined, was preserved by this carefully limited associa-tion with the vocabularies of non-Islamic and non-Arabic thought and values. And one may say, further, that these generations of arabized and islamized Near Eastern peoples were actually remaining faithful to tra-ditions set by very much earlier generations in the re-gion; for the Greek factor had, after all, been a con-tinually challenging presence from about the fourth century BC onward, i.e., in pre-Islamic times, without inducing any radical questioning of prevalent thought patterns in the then existing Semitic societies.

Further West, meanwhile, the Romans had estab-lished for Europe an altogether different precedent by insisting on learning all that there was to learn from Greece; and their approach was followed by the Euro-pean Christians, hesitatingly at first yet stubbornly,

[5] G. E. Von Grunebaum, *Modern Islam: The Search for Cultural Identity* (Berkeley and Los Angeles, 1962), pp. 138-39; also Schaeder, *op.cit.*, p. 124.

[6] Saunders, *loc.cit.*, p. 807.

until they were intellectually capable—thanks in large measure to translations of Greek texts by Nestorian Christians and other residents of the Arabic-Islamic realm—of examining rationally the relation between classical and Christian systems of knowledge. In the course of a series of intellectual movements known collectively as the Renaissance, they were able finally to develop entirely new vocabularies of thought and discourse: yet these—it was soon realized—could be used profitably only by minds freely committed to the processes of rational thinking invented by the Greeks.

In contrast, the Mohammedan intellect, which in the early Islamic era had amazed contemporaries with its adventurous spirit, was prohibited from going that far. From about the eleventh century onward, it was held in check by ecclesiastical theories of law and government[7] and forced to operate in a cultural environment from which foreign influences were banned unless found compatible with the faith as interpreted by theological jurists. "Renaissances" here were consequently mere returns to familiar grounds, which had been temporarily vacated or neglected: for the conviction reigned that all the great problems of knowledge had been solved, once and for all, by the revealed word of God.

In the course of his masterful analysis of this intellectual impasse and its historic effects upon subsequent Islamic thought, as well as upon all the later relations between Islam and the European West, Gibb writes as follows:

> The struggle between rationalism and intuitive thought for control of the Muslim mind was fought out, for the first time, over the postulates of Greek speculative philosophy in the early centuries of Islam.

7 See *infra*, pp. 53ff, 62ff.

11

The intellectual consequences of that conflict were decisive. They not only conditioned the formulation of the traditional Muslim theology but set a permanent stamp upon Islamic culture.[8]

In sum: by rejecting rational modes of thought, the Arabs—and Muslims in general—rendered themselves constitutionally distrustful of all abstract or a priori universal concepts, such as "the law of nature," "ideal justice," and the like, which have had such a decisive normative effect on the evolution of secular legal systems in the West. These concepts, Gibb continues, were branded in the Near Eastern realm as "dualistic" or "materialistic," emanating from false modes of thought. "It is therefore," he writes, "not to be wondered at that to the generality of the Muslim ulema the West came to stand for pure materialism: they do not know what lies behind all the external manifestations of Western material civilization, and they judge it mainly by its reflections in Muslim life and Muslim writings—manifestations which are often fantastically divorced from the spirit of Western culture."[9]

The discourse with the West, which had commenced so promisingly in the shared context of Greek learning, was thus cut off in a decisive manner. Even Muslim "modernists" in the twentieth century, eager to loosen or even to shake off the fetters of traditional thought, appear to be doomed to failure in their efforts. "Baked in the same oven of which the medieval 'Greece-ridden' theologian was the product,"[10] the Islamic modernist

---

[8] H.A.R. Gibb, *Modern Trends in Islam: A Critique of Islamic Modernism* (Chicago, 1947), pp. 7ff.

[9] *Ibid.*, p. 48.

[10] F. Rahman, "Internal Religious Developments in the Present Century Islam," *Journal of World History*, II, no. 4 (1955).

attempts "to adopt European practice without accepting the theory of the human presupposition, or the attitude to the world lying at the basis of it."[11] One of the few contemporary Arab thinkers who has had the courage to address himself to the essential problem of Islam today is Ṭāhā Husayn (b. 1889). In his *Future of Culture in Egypt,* he points to Greek thought as the source of the West's vitality and as the one possible bridge between his own civilization and that of the modern Occident. "Europe is Christian," he writes, "and I do not call for the adoption of Christianity, but for the motive forces of European civilization. Without them Egypt cannot live, let alone progress and govern herself."[12] But on the other hand, another writer of the same generation, Tawfīq al-Hakīm, writes that an understanding of the human ideal of the Greeks would be a powerful weapon in Arab hands, which would enable them to overcome the destructive human concept of the West.[13]

Thus a tradition of ignoring or misunderstanding ideas emanating from "the other," notably the Occidental counterplayer, whether represented by ancient Greece or by the modern West, had become so firmly settled in the formative period of the Islamic civilization as to prove unshakeable in subsequent centuries— except perhaps in Turkey and Iran. Due probably to both an insecure self-view and a basic fear of the Occidental impact upon the local political scene, it has had

[11] Von Grunebaum, "Westernization and Self-View," in *Modern Islam*, p. 139f; see in particular the comments on a speech by Gamal Abdel Nasser, and see also "Nationalism and Cultural Trends" in the same volume.

[12] Ṭāhā Husayn, *The Future of Culture in Egypt* (Washington, D.C., 1954), pp. 17ff.

[13] Quoted in Von Grunebaum, *Modern Islam*, pp. 232ff.

the effect of stunting intellectual growth and blocking the evolution of interculturally valid norms and institutions—effects which have been most poignantly manifested in the general sphere of law and order, as a subsequent discussion will show.

B.

Cultures and Modes of Thought

THE foregoing references to two complex sets of records of intellectual relations between adjacent civilizations clearly show that ideas, even under the best of auspices, are not transferable in their authenticity, and that reliable intercultural accords are therefore difficult to reach, even when assiduously prepared by specialists in the art of translating words and ideas. More importantly, the same case studies reveal that in the final analysis cultures are different because they are associated with different modes of thought. In fact, it even appears that the very meaning of the word "thinking" is likely to vary from one cultural tradition to the next. The successive generations of any given society will be inclined to think in traditionally preferred grooves, to congregate around certain constant, change-resistant themes, and to rebut, whether intentionally or unconsciously, contrary ideas intruding from without. And it is in just this way that the signature of a civilization becomes gradually fixed and legible to others.

14

The reading of these signatures, variously developed by scholars from Herodotus onward, has become a major concern in all modern intellectual disciplines,[1] for

[1] This is not the place for a review of all that has been written in these respects. The following modern authorities are cited because their works contain particularly succinct discussions of the relation between thought and culture.

One of the most original thinkers on the subject and the first to study Africa in depth as a living cultural organism was Leo Frobenius (b. 1873). See *Erlebte Erdteile, Ergebnisse eines deutschen Forscherlebens* (Frankfurt am Main, 1928, 1929), 7 vols., especially vol. IV, *Vom Völkerstudium zur Philosophie*, in which he develops the concept of *paideuma* in relation to the traditional culture of a people—be it in primitive or high-culture areas; and vol. V, *Das Sterbende Africa: Die Seele eines Erdteils.*

Alexander Goldenweiser writes in *History, Psychology and Culture* (New York, 1933), p. 59: "If we had the knowledge and patience to analyze a culture retrospectively, every element of it would be found to have had its beginning in the creative act of an individual mind. There is, of course, no other source for culture to come from, for what culture is made of is but the raw stuff of experience, whether material or spiritual, transformed into culture by the creativeness of man. An analysis of culture, if fully carried out, leads back to the individual mind. . . . The content of any particular mind, on the other hand, comes from culture. No individual can ever originate his culture—it comes to him from without, in the process of education. . . . As an integral entity, culture is cumulative, historical, extra-individual."

See also *ibid.*, pp. 66ff, to the effect that there is such a thing as the primitive mind, just as there is a French or German mind, even though explanations for this phenomenon must be sought in history rather than in biology.

And Clyde Kluckhohn, "Values and Value Orientations in the Theory of Action," in Talcott Parsons *et al.*, *Toward a General Theory of Action* (Cambridge, Mass., 1951), pp. 409-10: "There is a 'philosophy' behind the way of life of each individual and of every relatively homogeneous group at any given point in their histories. This gives, with varying degrees of explicitness or implicitness, some sense of coherence or unity to living both in cognitive and affective dimensions. Each personality gives to this 'philosophy' an idiosyncratic coloring, and creative individuals will markedly reshape it. However, the main outlines of the fundamental values, existential assumptions, and basic abstractions have only exceptionally been created out of the stuff of unique biological heredity and peculiar life experience. The underlying principles arise out of, or are limited by, the givens of biological human nature and the universalities of social interaction. The specific formulation is ordinarily a cultural product. In the immediate sense, it is from the life-ways which constitute the designs for living of their

15

not only have most cultures—the living as well as the dead—been now defined as separate organisms, but "the Greek mind," "the European mind," "the American mind," "the Communist mind," "the Hindu mind," "the Chinese mind," "the Arab mind," "the African mind," have become the separate objects of distinct and often meticulous treatments, albeit on a variety of grounds, as the profusion of such rubrics in the learned literatures of history, psychology, ethnography, linguistics, philology, philosophy, and sociology shows. In the general fields of the sociology and psychology of knowledge, meanwhile, scholars have successfully isolated thought patterns and types of causality by distinguishing, for example, mythical thinking from speculative or adventurous thinking, and by contrasting that which is specifically "modern" in the human mind with that which is "primitive," "archaic," or "savage." As a result of these findings it should be possible today—at least in the West where most of the research has originated—to perceive "the other" realistically on his own terms.

This was the task that I. A. Richards set himself in his exhaustive analysis of the traditional Chinese mind,[2] and according to his findings Chinese thinking operates within unquestioned limits, seeking a conception of the mind that should be "a good servant to the accepted

community or tribe or region or socio-economic class or nation or civilization that most individuals derive their 'mental-feeling outlook.' "

Likewise, I. A. Richards, *Mencius on the Mind* (London, 1932), p. 80, asks: "How deep may differences between human minds go? If we grant that the general physiology and neurology of the Chinese and Western races are the same, might there not still be room for important psychological differences? Peoples who have lived for great periods of time in different cultural settings, developing different social structures and institutions—might they not really differ vastly in their mental constitutions?"

[2] Richards, *op.cit.*

moral system." Only such conceptual distinctions are allowed as are useful in supporting social aims, and only such facts are recognized as are compatible with an approved social order.[3] Furthermore, whereas the Western tradition provides an elaborate apparatus of universals, particulars, substances, attributes, abstracts, and concretes, Mencius gets along without any of these.[4] Consequently, if we were to apply our own system of differentiation to the process of understanding Mencius, we would succeed only in deforming his thinking.[5] Addressing himself in the 1930's to the task of preparing for the twentieth-century dialogue between China and the West, Richards suggests that we must first reconstruct the traditional Chinese mind in order then to compare the purposes and limitations of thought of the two civilizations. It is in this connection that he proposes a technique for comparative studies that would establish multiple definitions of the ranges of possible meanings carried by our chief pivotal terms such as knowledge, truth, order, nature, principle, thought, feeling, mind, datum, law, reason, cause, and good.[6]

[3] *Ibid.*, pp. 62ff.   [4] *Ibid.*, pp. 89ff.

[5] Conversely, if Aristotle had spoken Chinese or Dacotan, he would have had to adopt an entirely different logic, or at any rate an entirely different theory of categories. See C. K. Ogden and I. A. Richards, *The Meaning of Meaning* (New York, 1959), p. 35. Attempts to express ancient Chinese thinking with English as an instrument would be worth making, even if they did no more than demonstrate the disaccord between the two methods of thought and language. See *Mencius on the Mind*, p. 9. See Marcel Granet, *La Pensée Chinoise* (Paris, 1934), for one of the most exhaustive definitions of the Chinese mode of thinking.

[6] *Mencius*, pp. 92ff, for Richards' explanation and justification of this proposal. *Ibid.*, p. 125: "With well-planned maps of even a few groups of meanings, many kinds of comparative study would become possible that are impossible at present. For example, that 'Love' has for Europeans a certain range of meanings . . . is a cardinal fact for any student of our mentality. Such differences as may hold between sections of the European peoples in this respect are also of great in-

This proposal was made in the field of linguistics and with reference to China only, but its basic assumptions, methods, and goals are valid for all disciplines, as well as for interdisciplinary research. Furthermore, they hold good also on the level of actual foreign affairs. For example, unless it can be known what meanings the terms "order" and "law" might carry in each of the states currently composing the world society, it will be impossible to understand any of the local governments on their own merits, to structure relations between different governments, or even to assess the factors that might make, or not make, for a reliable world order.

The task of perceiving the other in his authenticity, or of identifying the essential "configuration" (Kluckhohn's term) of a given culture, is more difficult in the twentieth century than it was in earlier epochs, and more complex today than it was thirty years ago, the most obvious reason being the interpenetration of multiple modes of thought and discourse that has attended the swift expansion and intensification of international relations on every level of human activity throughout the world. To know, in the tangle of separate idioms found within one and the same society, just which vocabulary supplies the governing value references, and which, on the other hand, is preferred only for reasons of rhetoric or expediency; to discern which grafts are likely to be rejected and which, by contrast, are fit to be accommodated in some form or another—these and the like are questions of major significance, which require an-

---

terest. But whatever these differences may be they probably vanish in comparison with the differences between the ranges of 'Love' (and its equivalents in European languages) and the ranges of any of the Chinese terms that may be proposed as equivalents."

swers if the general goal of order and understanding in international communications is ever to be approximated. Modern sinologists appear to agree, for example, that it is important to discover just what is Maoist, what traditionally Chinese, and what Western in contemporary Chinese patterns of politically significant thought. And in respect of Maoist thought again (especially insofar as it bears on war) it will be necessary to disentangle the influences of Marx and Lenin on the one hand, and of the Chinese martial classics, notably the Sun Tzu, on the other, before attempting to speculate profitably upon the long range implications of the striking convergence between these two "operational codes," conceived in different millennia and in the contexts of altogether different cultures and political systems.[7]

The "gulf of discontinuity" between past and present China, upon which John K. Fairbank has commented

[7] See in particular Sun Tzu, *The Art of War*, trans. Samuel B. Griffith (Oxford, 1963). This work is the first of a number of such classics. Composed between 400 and 320 BC, revived and reissued under the auspices of many later dynasties, it had been profoundly influential throughout Chinese history before it became the main source of Mao Tse-tung's thinking on military strategy and tactics, on the role of war in society, on the organization and use of intelligence, and on psychologically effective methods for enfeebling and disorienting an enemy. See Mao Tse-tung, *Selected Works*, new ed., 4 vols. (London, 1958), in particular the following essays: "Strategic Problems of China's Revolutionary War"; "Strategic Problems in the Anti-Japanese Guerrilla War"; "On the Protracted War"; and "Problems of War and Strategy"; also Mao Tse-tung, *On Guerrilla Warfare* (New York, 1961), cp. *infra*, pp. 153ff.

As Griffith points out, *The Art of War* was known well to the military circles of both Russia and Japan, and if the Americans had been aware of its influence, particularly if they had remembered that the Japanese strike first and declare war later, Pearl Harbor might not have happened. *Op.cit.*, p. 177.

See also: Wei Yang, *The Book of Lord Shang: A Classic of the Chinese School of Law*, trans. Dr. J.J.L. Duyvendak (London, 1928); and Han Fei Tzu (d. 233 BC), *Basic Writings*, trans. Burton Watson (New York, 1963).

19

so instructively,[8] might not have appeared to be so great—at least in respect of China's approaches to international relations—if the classics on military and psychological warfare and the use made of them by successive Chinese dynasties had been as widely known in the West as the classical Confucian maxims on peace and harmony. Ignorant of that other aspect, the Occident proceeded to build for itself a highly idealized version, and it was this somewhat contrived shape that controlled the imagination in the crucial decades of the twentieth century, when China appeared to accede not only to the developed techniques of Western logic,[9] but also to the West's preferred notions of law and order. Had European and Chinese scholars cooperated in verifying the actual meanings carried by the terms "peace," "war," "order," "law," "sincerity," etc., in their respective civilizations, misunderstandings in intellectual discourse and miscalculations in policy might have been prevented or at least minimized. As it was, the idealized shape established itself as the real shape in Occidental consciousness, even as China was proceeding to accept into its vocabulary yet another alien frame of conceptual reference—that of Communist words and ideas, which itself was already a hybrid of culturally diverse strands.[10]

[8] John K. Fairbank, "China's World Order: The Tradition of Chinese Foreign Relations," *Encounter*, XXVII (December, 1966). On the relationship between Confucianism, Western Civilization, and Communism, see also Joseph R. Levenson, *Confucian China and Its Modern Fate*, 3 vols. (Berkeley and Los Angeles, 1958-1965), esp. I, 146f, 160f; p. 59 to the effect that borrowed Western knowledge was to be used only to defend the core of Chinese civilization.

[9] See Richards, *op.cit.*

[10] The present Maoist regime appears to be fully aware of the risks implicit in the coexistence of competitive, often mutually exclusive, idioms of thought and communication. At any rate, its linguistic policy is designed to simplify the classical Chinese language by eliminating words that traditionally carry clusters of often ambiguous meanings and thus assure a certain freedom of reflection. Once removed from these

Some of the most intricate patterns in the relation between words and ideas are found today in the syncretic cultures of Southeast Asia,[11] where value references to multiple, often seemingly contradictory, belief systems have been interacting continuously for centuries in ever-changing, yet locally effective, vocabularies of discourse. Just as elites administering the ancient Khmer Empire were imbued with the knowledge that pre-Indian forces were operative underneath the dazzling surface of the indianized Khmer society (where monarchs were Buddhists in their personal capacity, while exercising their royal functions in strict accordance with Hindu rites), so did Prince Norodom Sihanouk in modern Cambodia know when to speak in the voice of a God-King, when to activate the heritage of the *arthaśāstra*, and when to resort to the language either of Marxism-Leninism or of French democracy. And an even more complex register of tones was at the disposal of President Sukarno and his ideological assistants, who built a unifying mystique for thousands of separate islands by borrowing eclectically from incantations, symbols, and formulations originally identified variously with animistic magic, Mohammedanism, Hinduism, Buddhism, Confucianism, Christianity, Fascism, and Marxism, and by introducing a new synthetic "national" language, based on Malay, but writ-

linguistic opportunities for uncontrolled thinking, Chinese minds may well lose touch with their own classical heritage and end up knowing and meaning only what their current rulers want them to know.

[11] These cultures may be less syncretic than is commonly assumed. Recent archaeological discoveries near the Burmese border of northern Thailand (as announced in January 1970 by Dr. Wilhelm G. Solheim, II, of the University of Hawaii) appear to reverse the long-held view that the Thais and other peoples in the area borrowed their technology from the Chinese and the Indians. Now it looks as if it may be just the opposite, for the findings have revealed not only that the Thais were farming long before the ancestors of the Babylonians, but also that they used bronze for weapons and tools 1000 years before the Chinese.

ten in Latin characters and enriched by elements drawn indiscriminately from all the technological and ideological jargons of the modern world. Western minds, holding fast to the meanings with which they associate the separate terms here strung together, may find little or no coherence in this kind of mechanical integration, or in the hodgepodge of rhetoric that marked most of President Sukarno's major policy statements. But the Indonesian, notably Javanese, mind seems to have been fully satisfied with a logic that purported to join Gandhism, militant Islamism, the American Declaration of Independence, the Rights of Man, and the Communist Manifesto in one magical "constitution" designed to confirm Indonesia's "guided democracy" even while exorcizing "the demon of federalism."[12] Moreover, the "Manifest Politik" (MANIPOL) which Sukarno developed as he went along—officiating either as the carrier of "the mandate of Heaven," as the executor of "the mandate of the people's suffering," as the expert interpreting the science of Marxism, or as the heir to the masters of Javanese magic—was linked by him to the traditional vision of an all-powerful cosmic order, as well as to the eventual creation of what he called a "pax humanica." Conveniently epitomized in *panca-śīlas*, *tri-śīlas* and various other slogans, such as NA-SA-KOM (the union of nationalism-religion-communism), and RE-SO-PIM (the union of revolution-socialism-leadership), these verbalizations combined to form a catechism as it were, the mere invocation of which was widely trusted to assure the glory of the nation:

12 See Herbert Luethy, "Indonesia Confronted" in *Encounter*, xxv (December 1965), and xxvi (January 1966), for a close analysis of these borrowing processes and their effects. See *ibid.*, xxv, 86, and xxvi, 79, for some unconventional Indonesian renditions of Marxism. See also *infra*, pp. 54, n. 12, 59, 61.

How lucky the Indonesian people are! Other nations have only a Proclamation *or* a Declaration of Independence. We have both a Proclamation and a Declaration. . . . Now, the mental conditions for our struggle are really complete. This Trinity (RE-SO-PIM) is the law of all nations, it is a universal law. . . .[13]

Simpler than the amalgams of interlocking but not necessarily congruous references produced in the Orient have been those recently appearing in the new states of sub-Saharan Africa. Here where indigenous traditions of literate thought are missing, and where the native culture world has been exceptionally resistant to all outside influences (including by and large those of Islam), the borrowings of the past fifty years or so had to be hasty if the African peoples were to participate in a civilization that had been fashioned by literate thought. The primary needs were felt in the area of politics and economics, and the obvious sources for the required grafts were the vocabularies of Occidental nationalism and constitutionalism on the one hand, and of Marxism-Leninism on the other. Throughout this preliminary period of their conceptual takeoff toward an attainment of identity, the governing and theorizing elites have swung freely between the two disparate frames of thought and discourse, speaking in mixed and mingling metaphors, without evident regard for the integrity either of "the operational code of the Soviet" or of the language of Western democracy.[14] In some cases the borrowings have been scarcely more than linguistic echoes of non-African speech communities, devoid of

[13] From a speech of 17 August 1961, as quoted by Luethy, *loc.cit.*, January 1966.
[14] For illustrations of this admixture see the publications of Kwame Nkrumah.

intrinsic political significance.[15] In others they have served as psychologically satisfying rationalizations of ambivalent states of mind. For example, the Leninist dogma of imperialism has been valued chiefly because it entitles all non-Western peoples, especially those in formerly colonial areas, to be simultaneously resentful, envious, and imitative of the West.[16] Furthermore, and most importantly in the context of this discussion, certain alien words and concepts have been proven increasingly useful as solid yet mobile platforms upon which to solidify acquired positions and from which to project desired objectives. Thus is bears remembering that modern African societies derived their new identities as states from the original meanings with which the West had invested the words "self-determination" and "sovereignty," whereas today, by contrast, when the sovereignty and territorial integrity of the new nation-state is being contested by tribalism, often precisely in the name of self-determination, these concepts have forfeited their utility value in Africa—at least in the estimation of those who are currently in power. Yet this demise of meanings has not been permitted to dislodge the words themselves, as Ali A. Mazrui convincingly shows.[17] Having proved their potency once, they are now being "re-tooled" to stand for other things, often the opposites of the meanings they carried before. For example, in the practice of numerous African leaders and publicists "sovereignty" and "self-determination," having been officially severed from the parental normative system of

15 See Thomas Hodgkin, "A Note on the Language of African Nationalism," in St. Antony's Papers, No. 10, *African Affairs No. One*, ed. Kenneth Kirkwood (London, 1961), p. 30.

16 See Alfred G. Meyer, *Leninism* (New York, 1963), pp. 257, for a discussion of "The Dialectics of Backwardness."

17 Ali A. Mazrui, *Towards a Pax Africana, A Study of Ideology and Ambition* (Chicago, 1967).

24

the West, and from Wilsonian thought and usage in particular, are now being made to serve the cause of the Negro race. The new references are to "pigmentational self-determination" and "racial sovereignty"—notions designed to sanction foreign and domestic policies aimed at transforming Africa into a reservation for black peoples only. And similar destinies have attended the careers of words lifted from the vocabularies of communism.[18]

Africans, having no deeply rooted interest in theory and philosophy—fields of mental concentration that presuppose a well-developed relationship to writing—may be readier than the literate peoples of the Near and Far East to reject or ignore the implications of ideas, just as, on the other hand, they may have a more pronounced sense than literate folk of the requirements of the actual moment. However, the tendency to fit a thought to a word, rather than a word to a thought, is shared with them not only by such an "esperanto" culture as that of the Indonesians, but also by such a linguistically authentic community as that of the Arabic-speaking world. In Shouby's view,[19] Arabic, deeply revered as the inimitable language of poetry and religion, has gradually conduced among those who speak it, to a general vagueness of thought; an overemphasis on the psychological significance of linguistic symbols at the expense of their meanings; overassertiveness and exaggeration in discourse; and a general disregard for "mere factuality." By comparison with Western literatures and languages, it is suggested, words there tend to become substitutes for, rather than representatives of, thoughts. Furthermore,

[18] Hodgkin, *loc.cit.*, pp. 38ff, commenting in particular on the pronouncements of M. Sékou Touré.

[19] E. Shouby, "The Influence of the Arabic Language on the Psychology of the Arabs," *Middle East Journal*, Summer 1951, pp. 284ff.

25

and for the same reasons, they have a way of replacing or postponing acts and accomplishments. These very qualities, according to Hisham B. Sharabi, make Arabic eminently suited for diplomacy: intention is easily concealed, and meaning need be revealed only obliquely. But by the same token, this commentator continues, Arabic is in many contexts incapable of precision, thus promoting long-windedness, inconclusiveness, and often misunderstanding in political deliberations.[20] In the Middle East and North Africa, as elsewhere in the non-Western world, the language of modern politics has certainly been borrowed from the West, yet some of its most significant ideas cannot be readily rendered in the face of culturally different realities. The Arabic versions of "the state," "nationalism," "sovereignty," "federalism," "imperialism," "communism," and "revolution," are incomprehensible to outsiders, Sharabi suggests, unless the psychological and historical associations carried by each of these terms are clearly borne in mind:

> STATE, *al-dawlah*, may also mean government, regime, power, administration. The state, in the na-

[20] Hisham B. Sharabi, *Nationalism and Revolution in the Arab World* (Princeton, N.J., 1966), p. 94. But see Charles Issawi, "The Arabic Language and Arab Psychology," *Middle East Journal*, Autumn 1951, pp. 525-26, and Abou Hadeed, "Psychology and the Arabic Language," *ibid.*, Winter 1952, pp. 112ff. See also G. E. Von Grunebaum, *Medieval Islam: A Study in Cultural Orientation* (Chicago, 1946), p. 37, on the unparalleled vastness of the Arabic vocabulary and the possibility of rendering thoughts with great precision: "Where Greek frequently has but one word to denote many objects, Arabic offers many words to denote one. Phonetic beauty is added to its staggering richness in synonyms. Precision and concision of expression adorn Arabic speech. While it is true that thoughts can also be rendered in foreign languages, Arabic will render them with greater exactitude and more briefly." Further qualities stressed by this scholar are unrivalled possibilities in the use of figurative speech and stylistic and grammatical peculiarities to which no corresponding features can be discovered elsewhere. Satisfactory translation from and into Arabic is thus rendered impossible in his view.

tional sense, did not come into being in the Arab world until very recent times. The state is seen in terms of its political leadership and its power of coercion rather than as an independent structure represented by institutions and laws that have permanence and validity outside individuals and considerations of power used by government. The state has as its most permanent circumstance the bureaucracy, the only institution that has resisted change and survived upheaval and coup d'état. Still, especially in revolutionary regimes, there is no clear distinction in popular consciousness between the state and the individual or individuals who wield the powers of the state.[21]

The foregoing illustrations (deliberately selected from both the past and the present records of a world that has always been multicultural) suggest that cross-cultural communications lead to misunderstandings by virtue of their very nature. They also confirm the conclusion that the selection of traits of the "giving culture" by a "taking culture" is determined by forces and tendencies present in the latter, and that a society will reinterpret the cultural traits that it borrows in accordance with the order and demands made by its own mind system. These findings corroborate Spengler's general thesis, where he states that:

[21] *Op.cit.*, pp. 102-103; cp. also H.A.R. Gibb, *Studies on the Civilization of Islam*, ed. Stanford J. Shaw and William R. Polk (Boston, 1962), pp. 44ff to the effect that there is no word to denote "state" as a general concept.

On the difficulty of translating Western political and economic concepts into Swahili and the arbitrary increase in the denotations of certain terms that are apt to result from the renditions thus given, see Wilfred H. Whiteley, "Political Concepts and Connotations—Observations on the Use of Some Political Terms in Swahili," in Kirkwood, ed., *op.cit.*, pp. 11ff.

Two Cultures may touch between man and man, or the man of one Culture may be confronted by the dead form-world of another as presented in its communicable relics. In both cases the agent is man himself. The closed-off act of A can be vivified by B only out of his own being, and *eo ipso* it becomes B's, his inward property, his work, and part of himself.[22]

On the particular subject of law they also bring to mind Montesquieu's dicta in accordance with which the laws of one nation can never be suited to the wants of another nation, for laws must harmonize with the nature and the principle of government that is established.[23]

Due allowance having been made for misunderstanding as an organic or inevitable aspect of all intercultural relations, it remains to be remarked that on the political level communications are today in an inexcusable state of disarray, and that the intellectual failure here is clearly that of the scholarly and political elites of the West. For whereas the non-Western societies, non-Communist as well as Communist, are fast recovering their native voices—having recognized, often in stridently aggressive ways, that the mainsprings of their thoughts and actions are, after all, not to be found in the conceptual system through the medium of which they attained status in the international system—the Western leaders

[22] Spengler, "Perspectives of World History," *The Decline of the West*, 2 vols. (New York, 1930), 57.

[23] Charles Louis de Secondat, Baron de Montesquieu, *De l'Esprit des Lois* (Paris, 1869), bk. I, chap. 3, pp. 8-9. In this connection see also William Searle Holdsworth, *Some Lessons from Our Legal History* (New York, 1928), pp. 84ff. Commenting on French and English experiences with the jury system, Holdsworth states that, while it is easy to transplant an institution like the jury, it is not possible to transplant the environment in which it was developed and in which it flourishes; for "institutions are tender plants, and depend upon a congenial soil and atmosphere."

are holding fast to the illusion that their own vocabularies and values in the sphere of politically significant behavior and organization are still meaningful in the rest of the world. Acquiescing in short-lived semantic victories and the establishment of pseudo-orders, they are programmatically ignoring a truth richly documented in history and society: namely, that political systems are, in the final analysis, carried and informed by substratal cultural forces.[24] Complacent in their posture, they witness passively the faulting of cherished policies, the crumbling of trusted orders, and the reduction of fundamental beliefs to mere clichés—in fact, the slow erosion of their cultural substance. In sum, the main casualty in these modern borrowing processes is the very civilization whose power and inventiveness called forth the worldwide dialogues in the first place.[25]

The swift devaluation of that part of the Occidental vocabulary for which worldwide applicability has been claimed suggests that we have relied and are relying much too heavily still upon the wealth of universals that distinguish Western science, Western philosophy, and Western political thinking from non-Western systems of thought. Obsessed with the task of creating an egalitarian, world-spanning conceptual order, reluctant to face up to natural diversity and disorder in human affairs, we have tended to force our preferred structures and typologies upon institutions and modes of thinking which, as I. A. Richards noted in his presentation of

[24] Compare in this respect Alfred North Whitehead's conclusion that political systems are transient expedients on the surface of civilization. *Adventures of Ideas* (New York, 1933), p. 101.

[25] For a perceptive discussion of this modern phenomenon see Peregrine Worsthorne, "Trouble in the Air—Letter from Ghana," *Encounter*, XII (May 1959), pp. 3ff. The theme here is the rapid denaturing of the English parliamentary system after its transplantation to Gold Coast and Ashanti.

Chinese thought, "may very well not have any such structures at all, and which may not be capable of being analyzed by means of this kind of logical machinery."[26] To level rather than to differentiate has thus become the fashion in our politically crucial academic disciplines— notably political science, psychology, and sociology— even in a period when such trends have been conspicuously absent from literature, the arts, and (non-Marxist) history: fields of thought in which uniqueness and diversity have been celebrated consistently.[27] Differences between Western and non-Western societies that simply could not be ignored have been ascribed whenever possible to the particular stage of growth and development in which the "new" organism is presumed to find itself, the implication being that, once finished, developed, or mature, the local system would fit snugly into the category to which it had been assigned in the first place. That is to say, here again the projected norm has been lifted from the experience of the West.

Certain tendencies, always latent in the social sciences, have thus become accentuated as scholars have scrambled to integrate Africa and Asia in existing patterns so as to maintain their concept of a universal order, if only in the neatly structured cardhouse of private cerebrations and filing cases. Among them one notes in particular an overriding concern with methodology and a passion for building models and expounding general laws of human behavior supposed to be valid everywhere, both of which exercises have too often had the effect of deflecting attention from the heart of the

26 Richards, op.cit., p. 92.

27 However, there are strong indications in many intellectual circles that history is gradually being consigned to "les oubliettes," as Marc Bloch, himself a Marxist historian, feared it would be if sociology were given too free a rein.

matter that was to be processed, and of protecting the processing (i.e., the Western) mind from the realization that the newly discovered life either had been captured prematurely in a formula, or had already escaped the stranglehold, to evolve in very different channels, leaving empty forms.

Recent developments in non-Western areas support these conclusions and cast doubt upon some of the approaches favored in the recent past. For it must be recognized that many of these approaches led to evaluations of the newly created political societies of Africa and Asia that have, on the whole, been wide of the mark, whether pointing to an end of tribalism and the attainment of national consciousness in Nigeria, the bright prospects for democracy in Nkrumah's Ghana, the sound foundations for federalism of the Western type in East Africa, or the decay of indigenous principles of statecraft in South Asia. Similarly, the language of economic planning and development which grew in the future-directed lifestyle of the West and presupposes certain human qualities, such as the willingness to accept long-range responsibilities, steadfastness of will, and self-restraint, has proved misleading or even meaningless in many essentially past- and present-oriented societies of the Orient and Africa. There the locally preferred time perspectives cannot readily accommodate such concepts as "development," "aspiration," and "planning," and the prevalent normative systems are unfavorable to the cultivation of those mental and mechanical disciplines without which viable national economies cannot be sustained.[28] Many of these errors in projection might

[28] See Luethy, loc.cit., for valuable comments on the disdain with which all matters pertaining to economics, including bookkeeping, are commonly viewed in Indonesia. Cp. also Bernard K. Gordon, *The Dimensions of Conflict in Southeast Asia* (Englewood Cliffs, N.J.,

have been avoided had scholars been less bound by classificatory schemes which had been conceived, after all, on the basis of insights and experiences accumulated in an earlier age when only Western states were engaged in continuous interactions; or had the scholars been

---

1966), pp. 32, 68ff, 88. See Gunnar Myrdal's study of South Asia's problems and prospects in Gunnar Myrdal and Associates, *Asian Drama: An Inquiry into the Poverty of Nations* (New York, 1967). Commenting on basic Asian character traits and attitudes, he lists "low levels of work discipline, punctuality and orderliness; superstitious beliefs and irrational outlook; lack of alertness, adaptability, ambition and general readiness for change and experiment; contempt for manual work; submissiveness to authority and exploitation; low aptitude for cooperation," as the fundamental impediments to economic and social growth (vol. III, p. 1,862).

On the dubious value of certain kinds of models and of socioeconomic comparisons carried out without regard to cultural factors, see Frederick Harbison, "Human Resources and Development," in UNESCO, *Economic and Social Aspects of Educational Planning* (Paris, 1964), especially pp. 122, 125. Speaking of the Tinbergen-Correa model and similar approaches, Harbison writes that this model, although giving the appearance of methodological precision, is actually no less dependent upon guesswork and no more objective than any other approach, largely because the assumptions are not supported by empirical evidence.

See also Theodor Geiger, *The Conflicted Relationship: The West and the Transformation of Asia, Africa and Latin America* (New York, 1964), pp. 84ff, to the effect that social science models inevitably oversimplify the phenomena they purport to explain.

Harold D. Lasswell, "The Relevance of International Law to the Development Process," in *Proceedings of the Sixtieth Annual Meeting, American Society of International Law* (April 28-30, 1966), notes that in the broad context of world affairs the whole notion of development is expected to be ephemeral. "The theoretical model holds that at some discernible future every nation on the globe will achieve a minimum threshold sufficient to support a self-sustaining level of accumulation of values in modern institutional forms" (p. 3). These values, he writes, are not limited to wealth and health, safety and comfort; developing countries also reach for power and respect, and other value assets and opportunities (p. 2). But in this respect it must be noted that the practical question whether, and if so, how these goals can be reached, and whether the entire developing process can be linked meaningfully on the one hand to existing international law and the ethics of mutual aid, and on the other to existing value systems in the developing nations themselves, has received rather discouraging answers "in the field."

more open in their interpretation of the ancient Oriental and African orders whose recent upsurge has either washed away or diluted beyond recognition most of the colonially implanted European institutions. Today, when the myth of sameness is fast evaporating and the rhetoric of unity ceases to screen existing discords as to the meaning and purport of internationally crucial concepts, it is important to identify the configuration of each active culture and political system as authentically as possible, and to locate its major and most trusted terms of reference, compare the findings, and insist on clarity in all international communications. Such an exploration may at times become a quasi-archaeological activity; for layer after layer of accrued borrowings may have to be analyzed before it becomes possible to distinguish the genuine from the counterfeit, the constant and indestructible from the merely passing. Only after the cultural map of the world has been brought up to date— and this will require intense interdisciplinary research— shall we be able to proceed, first, to a comparison of the different tables of enduring culturally preferred values, words, and meanings, and then to the formulation of an internationally shared vocabulary capable of assuring clarity in discourse.[29]

[29] My approach here owes much to Leo Frobenius, *op.cit.*, and "Early African Culture as an Indication of Present Negro Potentialities," *Annals of the American Academy of Political and Social Science*, CXI (November, 1928), 153-65; also to Ezra Pound's theory of "understanding error." As Guy Davenport shows in "Pound and Frobenius," in *Motive and Method in The Cantos of Ezra Pound*, ed. Lewis Leary (New York, 1954), pp. 38-39, Frobenius's study of Africa "stands as Pound's ideal of historic method: to see through the debris of a civilization its paideumic structure, which somehow is never lost and which is ripe for rejuvenation and influence from the best of other cultures, provided the nature of error which ruined it can be known and removed."

CHAPTER TWO

POLITICAL SYSTEMS AND
THE ROLE OF LAW

THE following discussion, while informed by the general thoughts and assumptions set out in the preceding pages,[1] has two limited purposes: to consider the various meanings carried by law in the actual and normative political systems of the West, the Islamic Middle East, Africa south of Sahara, Indianized Asia, and China; and to compare these findings with a view to determining whether there are actually any significant points of accord that might justify undifferentiated cross-cultural references to "law" and so be fit to provide a secure foundation for the organization of relations between these realms.[2]

Since the applicability or efficacy of law is being openly questioned today in all local scenes (not excluding those of the West) as well as in the arena of world affairs, such a limited inventory of legal and law-related orientations may assume some of the aspects of a much-

[1] The general approach is briefly sketched in Bozeman, "Representative Systems of Public Order Today," *Proceedings of the American Society of International Law*, 1959. But see also Myres S. McDougal and Harold D. Lasswell, "The Identification and Appraisal of Diverse Systems of Public Order," *American Journal of International Law*, vol. 53 (January 1959), and Charles McClelland, "The Function of Theory in International Relations," *Journal of Conflict Resolution* (December 1960).

[2] As Thurman W. Arnold observes in *The Symbols of Government* (New Haven and London, 1935), p. 36, law can obviously never be defined; but it is equally obvious, he continues, that adherents of legal institutions must never give up the struggle to define it. No definition is intended in the present discussion.

34

needed general reappraisal or stocktaking of existing forms of political organization. However, the base or measure of comparison for such a discussion as this must be "law" as the concept is understood specifically in the West, since it is the Western system that has supplied the major words and concepts in terms of which the political organizations of non-Western peoples have not only been analyzed but also, in more recent times, revised. Furthermore, it is this system, too, that has brought forth the prevailing international order for the conduct of relations between the greatly various political entities in the present-day world.

1.

THE WEST

NO WORD in the political vocabulary of the West has exercised the imagination as consistently as "law." From the times of classical Greece to the middle of the twentieth century, men in this civilization have tried not only to catch in a durable definition the essence of what has been generally known as law, but also to discover its sources and to delineate its functions. They have speculated ceaselessly about the relations between law and nature, law and reason, law and tradition, law and religion, law and justice, law and power, and law and

35

society, and have been profusely inventive in creating a great variety of actual legal processes and institutions. From the maze of recorded systems and beliefs that have resulted from these activities it is impossible to draw very many incontrovertible conclusions concerning the place of law in Western societies. And yet, there are a few constant and fundamental principles that appear to have been generally acknowledged, implicitly or explicitly, throughout the centuries.

First of all, it is clear that law as here understood presupposes literacy, expressing in particular a mode of literate thinking that inclines the mind to abstract reasoning. Conversely, it is apparent from the general history of pre-Christian and Christian Europe that all Western thought patterns have been profoundly affected by legal thinking. What comes across, transcending epochs, linguistic communities, and nations, is the fact that the language of law is essentially a symbolic code of precise concepts that had to be abstracted from a multitude of facts, concrete human experiences, and complex chains of reasoning, before they could be fixed in word systems already marked by an unusually high degree of conceptualization.

Secondly, then, it appears that this mode of rational thought could have evolved only because in the West the individual mind was recognized as the exclusive source of the human imagination. Western approaches to thinking in general, and to legal thinking in particular, are inseparable from a style of life in which the individual is expected to function not only as a member of a tribe, city, polis, class, guild, religious group, state, or other association, but also—and indeed primarily—as an autonomous human being. It is this assumption that explains the convergence of all European legal systems

36

upon "the person" as the primary and fundamental legal concept; for with it goes the acknowledgement that the person is capable of suffering and inflicting wrongs, assuming rights, and discharging responsibilities. Furthermore, it is explicitly recognized in this view that the individual can commit himself voluntarily and rationally in associations with others. And nowhere is this particular assumption so clearly abstracted and formulated as in the contract law of the Romans that in time became the frame of reference for most of Christian Europe, and the source, therefore, of the myriads of associations, partnerships, and corporations, through which, in each century, men chose to join their wills and interests. In the West, that is to say, human relations were shaped contractually in the exercise of self-regulation before they were defined in the public political charters that established states, governments, and greater unions on a contractual basis.

Public and private patterns of organizing society have always been greatly dependent upon the prevalence of certain human dispositions. For example, the pledge, the promise, and the obligation, which are pivotal references in the law of contract, imply confidence in "the other" and confidence also in the future. In other words, law, order, and organization are closely linked on the one hand with a time perspective that accommodates the notion of the future, and on the other with an ethic that enjoins good faith. These two concepts, it is important to remark, were given a secure place in all Western systems of law, but only after they had been legalized in the form of contract. Their integration serves to illustrate one of the most characteristic aspects of Occidental legal history; namely, the systematic, deliberate way in which legally crucial norms have been borrowed from ethics, philosophy, or religion, to be carefully transposed into reliable maxims of law. Other examples are to be seen in the embodiment of the elusive ideal of justice in reliable legal rules of equity and fairness, the acceptance of the Christian ideal that all men are equal in the eyes of God and the gradual elaboration of this concept in the value language of secular law, and the methodical sifting of accumulated customs and conventions with a view to determining just which of them should properly be regarded as law. In no case was the interplay between law and the other normative systems left to chance. The influence, indeed the need, of philosophical, religious, and ethical considerations was usually affirmed as helping to keep law in touch with life. Yet these considerations were not allowed to supplant law, or to disturb the integrity of law as an autonomous, separate, and, in the field of public order, superior, normative reference. Nor, for that matter, could law be kept from decisively moulding religion and morality in return, as the history of canon law shows. In short, it would be difficult not to conclude from the records that law has been consistently trusted in the West as the main carrier of shared values, the most effective agent of social control, and the only reliable principle capable of moderating and reducing the reign of passion, arbitrariness, and caprice in human life.

None of these aspects of "the rule of law" can be appreciated, however, unless it is borne in mind that Western society is dynamic and promethean, almost by definition, and that forms of social order have here been called into being for the express purpose of accommodating individualism and its corollary, the principle of development. That is to say, the task of organizing human relations in appropriate forms of government

38

has presented certain challenges in this civilization that have been absent in cultures geared to the maintenance of the status quo and to the general expectation that nothing new or different is to occur in life. What must be stressed, then, in any discussion of the answers to these challenges, whether given in theories or in practices, is the fact that political organization in the West cannot easily be separated either from that peculiar sense of the distinctness of law that has permeated all sectors of the culture for more than two millennia, or from the actual secular legal orders that have both antedated and transcended the particular passing forms of state and government. True to a lifestyle that favors diversity and flexibility, these last have been infinitely various and forever changing in the West; whereas the juridical systems, by contrast—being synopses of fundamental convictions and commitments—have stoutly survived the turmoil of the times. Brilliantly administered by law-minded yet life-conscious elites, they have sustained the integrity of the civilization as a whole and decisively informed the art of government.

Some of these intricate relations between law and political organization are well illustrated by the history of England, as Goodhart shows in his penetrating essay on the Magna Carta. Neither parliament nor the legislative process could have been conceived in medieval England, he declares, had the people—the governed as well as those in control of government—not been possessed of a deeply rooted disposition to be law-abiding. Lord Bryce, commenting on the same point, once remarked that "the declaration [in Magna Carta] of the supremacy of the 'Lex Terrae' are the critical words on which the fabric of British freedom was solidly set before a representative Parliament had come into existence."

And Sir Frederick Pollock is quoted by Goodhart to a similar effect:

> The time was not ripe for Parliaments till there was a fairly settled, strong, and regular system of order and justice. And the needful settlement and strengthening were brought about chiefly by measures which we should now call law reform.[3]

Comparable examples are to be found also in the histories of Western civil law countries, all pointing to the fact that law and order must exist, fully appreciated by the general public, before representative government can be expected to work. The modern practice which has become general since the close of the Second World War, of endowing newly independent non-Western states with parliamentary institutions without first ascertaining whether their populations have been accustomed to think and act in terms of the kind of law subsumed in these institutions, can thus not be said to be sanctioned either by logic or by experience.

Certain other typical aspects of Occidental political organization deserve brief mention at this point, if only because they attest to the organic connection between a culture's style and mode of thought on the one hand, and its preferred norms of government on the other. The general European conviction that the state is a creature of law and that government should be structured in accordance with a higher law, has found common expression in the symbolic language conveyed by the law of contract and law of property—legal categories particularly responsive to the implications of individual-

---

[3] See James Bryce, *Magna Carta Commemoration Essays*, ed. H. E. Malden (London, 1917), Preface, p. xvii; and Arthur L. Goodhart, "Law of the Land," published for the Magna Carta Commission of Virginia (Charlottesville, Va., 1966), pp. 33-36.

ism, as earlier references have suggested. The state was defined in ancient Rome as a partnership or bond in law, and in eighteenth-century English literature as a compact between successive generations meant to endure through time. In such states men are supposed to function as citizens: that is to say, not merely as subjects doing the bidding of those who happen to hold power, nor as private persons following callings of their choice. This idea of citizenship certainly derives from the general realization that individualism, whether directed to the fulfillment of the inner self or to the control of the outer environment, is the driving force in society, and that government should protect the individual in his personal activities even while preventing him from infringing on the liberties of others or from jeopardizing the interests of the community as a whole. Yet it also reaches beyond these objectives in its presumption that the individual must be able to transcend private associations and beliefs, whether based on religion, class, caste, age, or occupation, and assume civil obligations as well as civil rights within the context of his political status as a member of the state. And this same contractual symbolism, with its stress on reciprocal promises, inhabits the idea of legislation. It is entirely possible, of course, to liken the enactment of a law to the giving of an order, in the sense that both are deliberate acts and both are sanctioned by coercive force. Yet in any legislation there is also implicit a set of mutual promises and the expectation, shared by government and governed, that these engagements will be kept.[4]

[4] For a discussion of the idea of obligation in government see in particular H.L.A. Hart, *The Concept of Law* (Oxford, 1961), pp. 40ff, 79ff. See Charles Howard McIlwain, *Constitutionalism Ancient and Modern* (Ithaca, N.Y., 1940), p. 71, on the convergence of Roman and medieval English and French constitutionalism in the dictum of Papinian: "Lex is a common engagement of the republic."

These are some of the understandings of the nature of political organization that explain why the Occident has traditionally dreaded lawlessness, and cannot easily acquiesce in the rule of an absolute power unmitigated by respect for law. History does not deny that every part of Europe and America has had its times of trouble during which law has been flouted and suspended, the inventive individual spirit held captive, or the community coerced into quiescence. Yet one of the strongest leading motifs, vividly documented for every Occidental state, is the disposition to contest the use of illegal power, disestablish tyranny, return communities to the rule of law, and perfect legal remedies for infringements of the law. Furthermore and most importantly, the records attest to an abiding preoccupation—and this on all levels of political association, from cities and cantons to empires and commonwealths—with forms of representative democracy in which the powers of government and the rights of the governed are expressly circumscribed in a constitution. But such an Occidental constitution, whether found in the common law of the land, as in England, or in a special written covenant, as in most other political societies of the West, is itself a derivative of general legal propositions and understandings, even as it is the most effective mechanism for the continuous refinement of both the concept of law and the reality of political organization.

For the classical Roman, medieval European, and modern Atlantic societies, constitutionalism has been continuously attractive for two additional reasons. Just as it was known to promote unity and cooperation within a particular realm by neutralizing the natural tension always present in relations between the individual and society, so was it trusted whenever a number of self-governing communities decided to join their destinies or special interests in greater unions. Throughout Europe, especially on the continent, and most notably in Germany, one finds recorded a wide spectrum of different corporate entities fostering the common religious, economic, political, or intellectual concerns of their diversified memberships within the secure framework of constitutional principles. Both before and after the "modern nation state" was recognized as the primary political organization, the West was covered with leagues of cities, communities of cantons, companies of merchants, concerts of self-governing faculties and universities, commonwealths of abbeys, and all sorts of other collectivities, sodalities, and "Gemeinschaften," each functioning in accordance with its own charter and corporate law, yet usually also encompassed in some higher or vaster constitutionally structured union: whether, in medieval times, the Catholic Church and the Holy Roman Empire, or in later centuries, one of the great political federations, confederations, or empires. The second continuous attraction of law and political organization has been their close association with the maintenance of peace. What needs to be briefly noticed here in this connection, apart from the fact that peace is a corollary of unity between like-minded people, is the historical circumstance that in Europe local declarations of a special, often temporary, "peace"—as for example the King's Peace, initially limited to a monarch's reign, the Peace of the City, the Peace of the Fair, the Peace of God, the Truce of God—were habitually entrusted to the objective, equalizing language of the law; they were allowed, furthermore, to accumulate and merge until they came to constitute durable and general systems of public order, breaches of which could be viewed as violations of criminal or constitutional law. In other words, both concepts, that of peace and that of unity, which had been carried into general consciousness by the memory of the Roman Empire and the tenets of Christian ethics and religion, were deliberately and rationally concretized through contact with secular law and constitutional thinking. Moreover, neither of these intellectual activities and achievements on the plane of political and legal organization would have been possible if the West had not held fast to its peculiar sense of time and history, and developed literate thought the way it did.[5]

Just as constitutionalism rather than despotism was generally accepted as the superior normative reference on local levels, so it became, in time, the source also of preferred standards for the conduct and organization of interstate relations within the culturally unified Occidental realm. The commitment to processes of orderly parliamentary deliberation, and the recognition within each self-governing community of the need for unity and

[5] Commenting on the properties that distinguish Occidental thought in general and legal thought in particular, Max Weber observed that the West had developed a method which cannot be found in any other civilization. This method he called "logical formalism." Its characteristics are that law making and law finding proceed rationally and logically, i.e., upon the basis of generic rules that are not determined by any religious, ethical, political, or other system of ideology, but are formulated, instead, by the use of generic concepts. In classical Rome, he notes (pp. 219ff) some of these concepts were formulated in such a way that they afforded the practitioners the opportunity to subsume an extraordinarily diverse range of life situations under one single concept. Such a method, Weber concluded, is the peculiar product of Western civilization and one which cannot be found in other legal systems, notably not in those of the Orient. See Max Weber on *Law in Economy and Society*, ed. Max Rheinstein, trans. Edward Shils and Max Rheinstein, 20th Century Legal Philosophy Series, vol. VI (Cambridge, Mass., 1954). For brief comments on contrasting versions of "law" and "organization" in the Orient on the one hand and the traditional Occidental order on the other, see *ibid.*, pp. 184-85.

peace, gave rise to the belief that governments should resolve their disputes and reach accords by resorting to the same methods of discussion and negotiation that they respected in their internal jurisdictions. The methodological elaboration of these principles began officially in the seventeenth century with the creation of what may be called the Grotian system and ended in the mid-twentieth century with the establishment of the United Nations system. Since the latter is thus a direct outgrowth of the earlier inter-European scheme of organization, the former must be reviewed briefly in its essentials before one can proceed to estimate the prospects of law and organization in a multicultural environment.

Grotius thought only of Europe when he cast about for reliable principles of international order. Confronted with a devastating intra-European war, he buried himself in the records of Europe's cultural legacies. Greeks and Romans, Jews, Essenes and Christians, Goths, Franks, Angles and Saxons are found cited in *The Rights of War and Peace* as exponents of this heritage. Their modes of thought and reasoning, their definitions of what is rational and natural, their judgments of what is just or unjust, were studied and compared by Grotius in order to find concordant answers to the fundamental question of how war might be justly conducted and peace justly maintained between independent states. History, religion, political philosophy, ethics, law—and above all Roman law—supplied the representative precedents and pronouncements from which he deduced his law of nations. The equities of neighborliness observed by Roman property owners suggested to him the rules for coexistence between states; the rules of the Roman law of contract he applied to treaties between states;

45

and Roman definitions of crimes and wrongs were followed in his classification of permissible and impermissible injuries to life and property during war. In short, Grotius seems to have realized, consciously or unconsciously, that an international system is as solid only as the linkage relating it to the component local systems. And actual developments subsequently confirmed the logic of this position, when the Occidental political order evolved into a pluralistic society of equal sovereign states, all in substantial agreement on certain normative values, among which the following were the most important.

"Peace" was clearly differentiated from "war" and regarded as ethically superior and politically preferable; yet "war" was accepted as a legitimate exercise of sovereignty—at least before 1920—provided it were lawfully conducted. "Power" was given due recognition as a political fact of life, but it was always suspect and considered subject to the same kind of legal and moral restraints that might also be invoked against any form of absolutism within the state. "Unity" and "understanding" between separate states were valued above discord and division. "Diplomacy," viewed as the natural ally of law and democracy, was supposed to serve the ends of peace rather than those of war, and the code required that it should be conducted "honestly" and "in good faith." Furthermore, the entire vocabulary of internationally significant values was commonly rendered in the language of law. Indeed, "international law"—a collection of norms adapted from the laws, ethics, religion, and customs of a number of nations related to the Occidental culture realm—was commonly viewed as the cornerstone of the entire international system.

It goes without saying that in the practice of Occi-

46

dental states these normative principles were often violated or ignored. However, lapses and failures were usually expected to elicit a sense of "guilt" on the part of the offending state, and on the part of others a demand for "retribution." In brief, the Western approach to international politics was impregnated with principles of ethics, morality, and law that generations of Europeans and Americans had accepted as the normative code of behavior in relations both between individuals and between citizens and their governments. And this personalization and sentimentalization of affairs of state became naturally intensified as the democratization of local political systems progressed during the nineteenth and early twentieth centuries.

All of these developments within the Occidental political systems coincided with—and were, of course, organically linked to—the spectacular intellectual and political ascendancy of the West in world affairs. As time went on, this success, steadily reenforced by a growing egalitarian faith in the essential oneness and sameness of human nature all over the earth, had the effect of blinding Western minds to the realities of non-Western political systems, and of fortifying them in the conviction that the modern European states system was also the proper world system of political reference. Warnings about the relevancy of these assumptions had been signaled by many observers of the scene as early as the end of the eighteenth century, when Robert P. Ward, for example, wrote the following in his preface to *An Enquiry into the Foundation and History of the Law of Nations in Europe from the Time of the Greeks and Romans to the Age of Grotius*:[6]

. . . it appeared to me that we expected too much when

6 2 vols., London, 1795, pp. xiii-xv.

we contended for the *universality* of the duties laid down by the Codes of the Law of Nations; that, however desirable such an universality might be, the whole world was not susceptible of that intimacy and closeness of union, which many philosophers of high name are willing to suppose; that it falls into different divisions or *sets* of nations, connected together under particular religions, moral systems, and local institutions, to the exclusion of other divisions or *sets* of nations; that these various divisions may indeed present an intimacy among one another, and obey the same law; but that they may be contradistinguished from others who may have different religions and moral systems, operated upon by very different local circumstances: in fine, that what is commonly called the Law of Nations, falls very far short of *universality*. . . . and thus there may be a *different* Law of Nations for *different* parts of the globe. Not only this, but even, in the same part of the globe, there may have been very different sorts of Law of Nations, according as revolutions have taken place in the religion, system of morality, and local institutions of the nations which compose it.

The doubts here expressed were reiterated by representatives of scholarly and political circles in the ensuing centuries, when contacts between the West on the one hand and Africa and Asia on the other were intensified. Yet this type of political awareness was not allowed to affect materially the processes of decision-making that were entered upon after 1919. The knowledge of non-Western forms of political organization, carefully accumulated by Western scholars working in anthropology, philosophy, religion, mythology, science, art, and history, was scarcely tapped in those crucial decades between 1919 and 1945 when the destinies of all nations, but most notably those of Europe and America, would have benefited immeasurably from a comparative approach to the search for a transculturally valid international system. As it was, a uniform, ethnocentric approach came to prevail. Appalled by the experience of strife and war and deeply conscious of the new interdependence of continents and nations, the Western statesmen simply fell back upon their own most favored normative references, and proceeded to organize the peoples of the earth in international democracies, subjecting the entire arena of world politics to the rule of an Occidental ideal of international law. The worldspanning systems thus installed, first in 1919 and then in 1945, were far more ambitious and extensive in their scope and aims than the modern European states system and the Grotian law of nations. In fact, many of the principles projected by the Covenant of the League of Nations and the Charter of the United Nations were deeply held ideals of peace, unity, and law in international relations that had eluded realization even within the culturally unified realm of the West itself.

2.

THE ISLAMIC

Middle East

WHEN the Concert of Europe set about restoring peace after the Napoleonic wars, it was faced with the decision whether or not to include the Ottoman Empire officially in the Occidental system of public international law. The decision was negative in 1814, largely because of Russia's objections; however, jurists, reflecting on the state of actual relations with the Eastern Empire, had also expressed doubts about Turkey's ability to meet her obligations in accordance with European standards. In 1801, Sir William Scott had argued in *The Hurtige Hane* that the law of nations should not be applied to nations outside Europe "in its full rigour"; for

> It would be extremely hard on persons residing in the kingdom of Morocco, if they should be held bound by all the rules of the law of nations, as it is practiced among European states. On many accounts undoubtedly they are not to be strictly considered on the same footing as European merchants; they may, on some points of the law of nations, be entitled to a very relaxed application of the principles, established by long usage, between the states of Europe, holding an intimate and constant intercourse with each other.[7]

[7] J. B. Scott and W.H.E. Jaeger, *Cases on International Law* (St. Paul,

And this view was reiterated in 1845 by Henry Wheaton in his *History of the Modern Law of Nations*:[8]

> In respect to the mutual intercourse between the Christian and Mohammedan Powers, the former have been sometimes content to take the law from the Mohammedan, and in others to modify the International Law of Christianity in its relation to them. Instances of the first may be found in the ransom of prisoners, the rights of ambassadors, and many others where the milder usages established among Christian

---

Minn., 1937), pp. 62-64 (High Court of Admiralty, 1801, 3 C. Rob. 324). For an earlier case involving "The Hurtige Hane" in respect of a breach of blockade see 2 Robinson's Admiralty Reports (determined in High Court of Admiralty, July 19, 1799).

For other decisions bearing on the relations between European states and Mohammedan states see Scott and Jaeger, *op.cit.*, pp. 59ff, "The Kinders Kinder" (High Court of Admiralty, 1799, 2 C. Rob. 88); also "The Fortune" (2 C. Rob. 92) as cited on pp. 61f, n. 20, where Sir William Scott said that he does not "mean to apply to such claimants the exact rigour of the law of Nations as understood and practised amongst the civilised states of Europe; [since] it would be to try them by a law not familiar to any law or practice of theirs," and "The Helena" (4 C. Rob. 3), mentioned in Scott and Jaeger, *op.cit.*, p. 64, n. 23; in this case Sir William Scott held that the African Barbary states have to be held responsible for their piratical seizures even though "their notions of justice, to be observed between nations, differ from those which we entertain."

One of the most interesting cases in this collection of Admiralty decisions is "The Madonna Del Burso" (High Court of Admiralty, 1802, 4 C. Rob. 169); here Sir William Scott maintained that "the inhabitants of those countries [i.e. under the protection of the Ottoman Porte] are not professors of exactly the same law of nations with ourselves; In consideration of the peculiarities of their situation and character, the Court has repeatedly expressed a disposition, not to hold them bound to the utmost rigour of that system of public laws, on which *European* States have so long acted, in their intercourse with one another." This decision is briefly noted in Scott and Jaeger, *op.cit.*, pp. 65ff; for a full report see 4 Robinson's Admiralty Reports (James Humphreys, Philadelphia, Reprints of Cases Determined in the High Court of Admiralty, pp. 138-151. Pagination here is different from listing in Scott and Jaeger.)

[8] New York, 1845, pp. 555ff.

nations have not yet been adopted by the Mohammedan Powers. On some others they are considered as entitled to a very relaxed application of the peculiar principle established by long usage among the states of Europe in constant intercourse with one another.

Similar reasoning was employed by legal authorities even after the Treaty of Paris of 1856 when the European governments—convinced of Turkey's importance in their scheme of a durable balance of power—had explicitly included the Porte in the European Concert of States.[9] This association between Europe and the Near East set in motion certain political and intellectual movements that have continued to affect the cause of law and political organization on the local Asian and African, as well as on the international levels. Pressured both by the West and by the modernizing elites in his own administration, the Sultan was willing, in the last decades of the nineteenth century, to adopt Western military skills and weapons as well as to conduct foreign relations in accordance with Western models, so as to rehabilitate the status of his realm in foreign affairs. He was not as yet prepared to compromise Muslim law and institutions by accepting Occidental concepts of political organization.[10] However, these reservations were washed away with the defeat and breakup of the Empire after 1919, when spectacular legal and political reforms were allowed to transform the Turkish heartland of the Muslim commonwealth into a secular sovereign national state.

Constitutions, legal codes, and legislative enactments of all kinds were promulgated also in the Arab and

[9] See Majid Khadduri, *War and Peace in the Law of Islam* (Baltimore, 1955), pp. 279-90, for a discussion of these authorities.
[10] Cp. *supra*, pp. 7ff, with similar selective borrowings.

North African successor states. But the ruling elites of these realms maintained the ambivalent positions of their predecessors who in the nineteenth century had sparked the "Arab awakening." Aiming at the establishment of nation states that should be capable of holding their own in an international system postulating this type of political organization, they identified their goals more or less exclusively with the merely external attributes of Western institutions, and thus ignored the challenge to come to terms with the intellectual and political presuppositions of the formulas they borrowed. The fundamental internal order of Islam was thus not significantly disturbed by the pronouncements and activities that purported to set in motion revolutionary change. In fact, in most of the Western-type documents that have declared the establishment of new states and governments even in the last decades, the traditional indigenous value system implicit in Arabism and Islam has been explicitly validated as the mainspring of political life.

Recognition of the *sharī'a* as the primary source of legislation[11] is thus a major principle not only in the constitutions but also in the civil codes that were enacted during the fifties for Syria, Egypt, and Iraq, for example, where it usually appears in alliance with the reminder that each new nation state is simultaneously part of the greater Arab nation. For example, the Pro-

[11] The de facto administration of law by different local authorities and the courts of the *qāḍī* (judge), together with the acknowledgment of customary law, had had the effect, in pre-modern times, of limiting the theoretical supremacy of the *sharī'a* in many separate fields of law. It cannot be said, however, that these processes of amalgamation had materially altered the classical religious doctrine that passed for "public" or "constitutional" law in this culture zone. For a discussion of these interactions and developments see N. J. Coulson, *A History of Islamic Law* (Edinburgh, 1964), chaps. 9 and 10 in particular.

visional Constitution of April 28, 1964, describes Yemen as "a sovereign, independent, Arab, Islamic state," "part of the Arab nation," and "a democratic republic" in which "Islamic jurisprudence shall be the source of all legislations"; while the Iraqi Republic emerges from the same kind of document as "a democratic socialist state deriving the rudiments of its democracy and socialism from the Arab heritage and the spirit of Islam."[12]

[12] See Hisham B. Sharabi, *Nationalism and Revolution in the Arab World* (Princeton, N.J., 1966), pp. 107-73 for these and other excerpts from relevant documents.

For other documentary records see Muhammad Khalil, *The Arab States and the Arab League*, 2 vols. (Beirut, 1962), Jacob C. Hurewitz, ed., *Diplomacy in the Near and Middle East: A Documentary Record*, 2 vols. (Princeton, 1956), esp. vol. II, and Helen M. Davis, *Constitutions, Electoral Laws, Treaties of States in the Near and Middle East* (Durham, N.C., 1947).

See Erwin I. J. Rosenthal, *Islam in the Modern National State* (Cambridge, 1965), pp. 162ff for comments on Moroccan movements favoring restoration of the *shari'a*; W. C. Smith, *Modern Islam in India* (London, 1946), and *Islam in Modern History* (New York, 1957), pp. 208ff, for accounts of the Islamic Republic of Pakistan; and see F. Rahman, "Internal Religious Developments in the Present Century Islam," *Journal of World History*, II, no. 4 (1955), 862, for one of the most suggestive analyses of the entire problem; pp. 864 and 870ff, on Sir Muhammad Iqbal's idea for a Muslim state and Muslim League of Nations; p. 876 to the effect that many responsible persons in Muslim governments may themselves be secularists at heart, but that the popular movements—necessary if government is to exist in an Islamic country—are usually best carried by religious or quasi-religious forces.

On the reception of European laws by different Islamic societies during the nineteenth and twentieth centuries and the effect of this reception upon the administration of *shari'a* law see Coulson, *op.cit.*, Part II, pp. 149ff. *Ibid.*, p. 222 for the following conclusion: "In combination, therefore, with the opportunistic character of modern jurisprudential method, the nature of the substantive reforms themselves lends a general air of transience and instability to current Islamic law. The fortress of the traditional law has been breached beyond repair, but the complex structure that has taken its place does not as yet rest upon the same solid foundations, and its substance is almost volatile by comparison."

See also J.N.D. Anderson, *Islamic Law in the Modern World* (New York, 1959), for valuable brief surveys, and Sobhi Mahassani, "Muslims:

Furthermore, these dominant traditional motifs have become the stock-in-trade of policy statements by local rulers desirous of rallying their peoples, by contenders for power rationalizing their dissatisfaction with the status quo, and by ideologues and theoreticians commenting on the local scene or outlining visions of a better future order. On the regional level, meanwhile, all elites continue to meet on a common ground, at least rhetorically, when they remind each other and their followers, firstly, that pan-Arabism must transcend all local Arabisms, such as the Arab League of Nations, and secondly, that Arab and non-Arab Muslims alike are

---

Decadence and Renaissance, Adaptation of Islamic Jurisprudence to Modern Social Needs," *Muslim World* (1954), 44, 186.

For informative essays on family law, penal law, the law of *waqf*, etc., see Majid Khadduri and Herbert J. Liebesny, eds., *Law in the Middle East*, 2 vols. (Washington, D.C., 1955); Joseph Schacht, *An Introduction to Islamic Law* (Oxford, 1964), pp. 100ff on "Modernist Legislation," especially pp. 106f to the effect that the method used by the modernist jurists and legislators in the Near East savors of an unrestrained eclecticism: any opinion held at some time in the past is apt to be adopted, without regard to its historical and systematic context. The ideas and arguments of the Modernists come from the West, Professor Schacht writes, but the reformers nonetheless postulate that law, as well as other human relationships, must be ruled by religion.

On the westernization of Persian law see a brief review in Richard N. Frye, "The United States and Iran," in *The United States and Turkey and Iran*, by Lewis V. Thomas and Richard N. Frye (Cambridge, Mass., 1951), p. 206f; and Ann K. S. Lambton, "The Spiritual Influence of Islam in Persia," in *Islam Today*, ed. A. J. Arberry and Rom Landau (London, 1943), p. 170 to the effect that modern Persian law, for the most part, has followed French examples, but that the collection of common law follows both Shi'ite and French law. However, the Supreme Court, which is the final authority in the hierarchy of courts, has long been dominated by religious leaders.

For discussions of the entire framework of "modernization" see Manfred Halpern, *The Politics of Social Change in the Middle East and North Africa* (Princeton, N.J., 1963); Daniel Lerner, *The Passing of Traditional Society: Modernizing the Middle East* (New York, 1958); and Bernard Lewis, *The Middle East and the West* (Bloomington, 1964).

55

charter members of an eternal Islamic community of nations.

But the precise relationship between national, Arab, and Islamic unity has been and continues to be a matter of controversy as well as concern. It naturally evokes special interest in the Arab realm, notably in Egypt where it has been formulated programmatically by the Muslim Brotherhood as well as by President Nasser. According to pronouncements made at the end of the Second World War by the founder of the Brotherhood, "It is the duty of every Muslim to work for the revival and support of Arab unity," since Arabism is the root of Islam. And yet, although all Muslims are said to form "one single nation," and the Islamic homeland is viewed as "one single territory, no matter how far flung or remote the countries, . . . the Muslim Brothers owe respect to their own particular nationalism, Egyptian nationalism, which constitutes the primary basis of the revival that they seek. After that they support Arab unity, which constitutes the second link in the movement of revival; and finally they strive for the Islamic League. . . . It is only left to say," the statement then concludes, "that the Brothers desire the good of the whole world and indeed call for world unity, which is the purpose and final goal of Islam. . . ."[13] Moreover, this same set of interlocking circles of loyalty and organization, enlarged however by the addition of Africa as a sphere of Egyptian commitments, has been recognized and proclaimed by President Nasser.[14]

Actual mergers of originally separate Arab states have been consummated, usually at the bidding of Egypt, with

[13] Sharabi, *op.cit.*, p. 110.
[14] See Gamal Abdel Nasser, *The Philosophy of the Revolution*, introd. John S. Badeau (Buffalo, 1959).

the aid of declarative federal devices: but what is significant about the United Arab Republic, as distinguished from Egypt proper, is its elusive, fluctuating identity; for Syria, Iraq, and Yemen have participated in the venture in different roles and at different times, only to drop out as casually as they joined. Yet neither this set of experiences nor the generally recorded fact that political relationships in the culturally unified region have been disturbed continuously from the days of independence onward by fierce competition for leadership, conspiracy, and open, often violent, intervention in the domestic affairs of brother states, appears to have detracted significantly from the ardor of the felt unity. The contrary seems true: the return to traditionally trusted cultural forces—a natural concomitant of nationalism everywhere—has been accelerated and intensified during the last two decades under the psychologically compelling realization—shared by rulers and ruled alike—that power and success, security and unity, had after all not come in the wake of imitating Western forms of political organization. This disenchantment, together with a deep longing for what Professor Von Grunebaum has called "the dependable situation,"[15] has conduced to an irrational craving—irrational from the Western point of view—for the restoration of the good old medieval days, which are generally associated in the Arab mind with unqualified glory on all levels of existence. Moreover, this pattern of emancipation through retreat into the past is being steadily solidified by a common antagonism to the West, which is generally viewed as a false prophet, and to contemporary American policies in support of Israel in particular. Postulating the moral bankruptcy of Occidental culture and

15 *Modern Islam*, p. 251.

politics, modernists and traditionalists can thus converge in blaming imported liberal institutions, rather than their utilization by Arab governments, for all that has gone wrong in their domains,[16] and agree thereby upon entrusting the future to ancient forms of political organization.

It is in this context that terms denoting democracy, constitutionalism, representative government, individual rights, etc., are today being made to carry contents for which they were not equipped originally. From the Western point of view, most Near Eastern regimes are one man dictatorships, initiated by military coups d'etat and ousters, often by summary execution, of previous office holders. Yet each successful contender for the exercise of power has justified his takeover as the beginning of genuine representative rule, decreeing or promising a "real" constitution for the "real" democracy to take effect as soon as the preceding spurious constitutional order has been dismantled utterly.[17] And the same rhetorical alignment with the democratic cause marks most theological discussions of the problem of government. What emerges from the accumulation of intellectual and

[16] One of the most respected Islamic thinkers, the Pakistani Abul A'lā Maudūdi, describes Western democratic forms of government as satanic devices through which men satisfy their whims and evil desires. For a discussion of his views and his work, *The Islamic Law and Constitution*, reformulated in a second edition in 1960, see E.I.J. Rosenthal in *International Affairs* (July 1962), and *Islam in the Modern National State*, pp. 148ff. On the same subject, see Rahman, *loc.cit.*, pp. 878ff.

[17] Cp. documents in Khalil, *op.cit.* and Sharabi, *op.cit.* For President Nasser's philosophy of democracy, socialism and revolution, see *supra*, p. 56, n. 14, and other writings. For a résumé of "The National Charter of the United Arab Republic," which the Egyptian President meant to be an historic document in the Arab world as a whole, see Alan W. Horton, "The Charter for National Action of the UAR," American Universities Field Staff Reports Service, North Africa Series, vol. IX, no. 5 (New York, 1962); also Horton's discussion of "The Search for Popular Support," *ibid.*, vol. IX, no. 4 (1962).

political activities in the ranks particularly of the traditionalists is the common conviction that the true meaning of democracy may be discovered only in Islam,[18] where the community, conceived comprehensively as unbounded in space and in time, is destined to guard communal traditions and propagate unitarianism, provided that it is organized in accordance with the irrevocable principles of Koranic law.[19]

Missing in this set of conceptions are the ideas of the state and constitutional government, a fact acknowledged forthrightly by a Pakistani thinker in the following passage:

Having regard to the accepted notion of what constitutional law is, it is not possible to derive from the

[18] The view has even been expressed that it was Islam which set up democracy in the first place and then proceeded to teach it to the Europeans. See Wilfred Cantwell Smith, *Islam in Modern History* (New York, 1957), p. 149. For one of the most extreme versions of the Islamic identification with democracy see Khalifa Abdul Hakim, *Islam and Communism* (Lahore, 1951), pp. 123, 153-60.

[19] For some of these formulations see Sir Muhammad Iqbal, *The Mysteries of Selflessness: A Philosophical Poem*, trans. A. J. Arberry (London, 1953), pp. 29, 33, 37, 52ff, and *The Restoration of Religious Thought* (Lahore, 1958). Although Sir Muhammad was a Pakistani, he is venerated throughout the Islamic world as the outstanding poet and thinker of the century, that is to say, his views are also representative of traditionalists in Arab countries. It should perhaps be remarked in this connection that Pakistan, where pan-Islamism is particularly strong, is also the scene of especially lively intellectual activities.

According to the Muslim Brothers, Islam is "at once religion and state, spirit and work, Holy Book and sword." See *supra*, p. 56, n. 13.

See H. Lammens, *Islam: Beliefs and Institutions*, trans. E. Denison Ross (London, 1929, 1968), pp. 179ff, on the pervasive wish of reformists and modernists in the 1920's to restore the golden age of Islam by creating a pan-Islamic organization, while strengthening the cause of nationalism; p. 200 on the inconclusive records of two pan-Islamic congresses.

See also Duncan B. Macdonald, *Development of Muslim Theology, Jurisprudence and Constitutional Theory* (reissue, New York, 1965), pp. 59ff on pan-Islamism and the "backward" reform movements of the Wahhabites and the Brotherhood of as-Sanūsī.

text of the Quran any clear statement as to the actual content of the constitution of any state.[20]

These gaps—disconcerting to minds conditioned by Occidental political thought—are not felt as gaps and seem to have few if any adverse effects in e.g., Pakistan and Saudi Arabia where compensatory affirmative propositions, inherent in Islam, provide a secure sense of collective identity. But the situation is altogether different in Iraq, Syria, Jordan, and the Islamic arabized North African states.[21] Here modernists appear to want to break with the past at all cost while being determined at the same time to defend this past against all critical inquiry as the abode of historical success and wisdom. Unwilling to reexamine their historical resources soberly and engage in a realistic self-appraisal, unsupported by an indigenous tradition of secularist philosophy and disdainful of the Western philosophical heritage from which they had borrowed the momentum as well as the objectives of their modernizing movements, they have long been caught in a welter of ambivalent positions that paralyze the intellect and impede the recovery of direction and self-confidence.[22] These aspects of the general

20 For this quotation from A. K. Brohie see Rosenthal, *Islam in the Modern National State*, pp. 229f.

21 It was suggested earlier that Turkey is in a class by itself. Anchored in non-Arab, non-Islamic traditions of political organization, it had not only brought forth effective administrative designs, but more importantly, had had the courage to renew itself and adjust to changed circumstances. Much the same can be said of Iran, the other great non-Arab Mohammedan nation in the Middle East, which has existed for two-and-a-half thousand years as a political entity, albeit in different incarnations. For analyses of this set of problems in North Africa, see Jacques Berque, *Le Maghreb entre les deux guerres* (Paris, 1962), and I. William Zartman, *Government and Politics in North Africa* (New York, 1963).

22 For the keenest and most sympathetic discussions of this intellectual crisis, see H.A.R. Gibb's works, esp. *Modern Trends in Islam: A Critique of Islamic Modernism* (Chicago, 1947); G. E. Von Grunebaum,

Arab state of mind, evident throughout the century, have become more prominent in the last decades as the "revolutionary" regimes, programmatically committed to social, economic, and diplomatic success, have registered major economic setbacks and failures in the domain of foreign policy. And among the latter nothing in memory has equaled the humiliating defeat at the hands of Israel.

This event, commonly associated in the Arab mind with Occidental, notably American, complicity, has had the effect of further discrediting Western ideas of political organization even though it could, of course, be maintained that the Jewish victory represents the victory of common Semitic and Biblical principles of theocratic communalism and military aggression rather than that of the European complex of norms. At any rate, it is clearer today than it was in 1925 or 1945 that Western and Arab patterns of government are not easily reconcilable. It appears, furthermore, that the different elites —so-called progressives as well as so-called traditionalists—will not be in a mood in the foreseeable future to model the public order of their realms upon that of the West. In fact, the latter may well have outlived its usefulness as midwife to the birth of a new Near Eastern order; for not only are indigenous ideas and institutions being reinstated, spontaneously here, deliberately there, but competitive organizational schemes, released by Marxism-Leninism in either of its several formulations,

---

Modern Islam: The Search for Cultural Identity (Berkeley and Los Angeles, 1962); and Wilfred Cantwell Smith, *Islam in Modern History* (New York, 1957), esp. pp. 119ff; also Bernard Lewis, *The Middle East and the West* (Bloomington, 1964). For expositions of the prelude to this series of developments, see in particular Albert Hourani, *Arabic Thought in the Liberal Age, 1798-1939* (London, 1962), and George Antonius, *The Arab Awakening* (London, 1939).

project alternate promises of redemption and security to deeply troubled people. These options cannot be understood and the likely future configuration of the Arab scene cannot be anticipated realistically unless one ascertains the pivotal legal and organizational references to which Arabs attach enduring validity if only because their essence has survived metamorphosis and change.[23]

The Mohammedan commonwealth is at one with the West in acknowledging the supreme importance of law in human affairs. But the fundamental meaning attached to law is so different from that developed in Europe as to render comparisons misleading.[24] Formed neither under the impetus of practical needs, nor under that of juridical technique, but under that of religious and ethical ideas, Islamic law has been variously defined as "knowledge of the practical rules of religion"; "the knowledge of the rules of God which concern the actions of persons"; and "the knowledge of the rights and duties whereby man is enabled to observe right conduct in the world, and prepare himself for the future life." These are not merely dogmatic statements produced in an earlier age; they are living convictions that continue to suggest policy statements, as earlier references have illustrated.[25] Authoritatively formulated by learned theo-

[23] See *supra*, p. xv, n. 8 (Introduction) for Professor Gibb's reminder that revolutions rarely change the essential character of basic institutions, but only emphasize the tendencies which are already shaping them in a given direction.

[24] See Schacht, *Introduction to Islamic Law*, p. 199, for a succinct and brief presentation of the major principles of Islamic law; also the same author's "Islamic Law," *Encyclopedia of the Social Sciences* (New York, 1932), VIII, 344ff.

[25] *Supra*, pp. 55ff. See M. K. Nawaz, "A Re-examination of Some Basic Concepts of Islamic Law and Jurisprudence," World Rule of Law Booklet Series, no. 23, reprinted from *The Indian Year Book of International Affairs* (1963), pp. 10ff for other interesting examples: the Delegation of the Muslim States of the Far East stated in a note to

logians, they actually appear to emanate from certain fundamental ways of thought peculiar to the Arab mind, Gibbs suggests.[26]

Given to religious intuition rather than rational thought, responsive to the impact of artistic, inspired speech rather than to that of logical exposition, the Arabs venerate the Koran not only as divine revelation but also as a masterpiece of the spoken word and the fulfillment of their cultural genius. Any change, loosening, or disestablishment of Koranic law as an integral scheme covering all aspects of secular and religious life would thus strike at the very roots of Arabism. And other

---

the U.N. Committee of Jurists that "legal rules" (in Islam) stem from the divine command, expressed directly in the Koran or indirectly in the tradition of the Prophet "Al Sunnah." See *Documents of the U.N. Conference on International Organization*, XIV, 375-79 for text. And the Report of the Committee of Inquiry appointed by the Government of Punjab (Pakistan) to inquire into the disturbances in Pakistan in 1953, dealt with the meaning of Islamic law in similar terms.

[26] Cf. *supra*, pp. 11ff; the foundations of Arab thought became clear during the encounter with the thought of classical Greece: "The struggle between rationalism and intuitive thought for control of the Muslim mind was fought out, for the first time, over the postulates of Greek speculative philosophy in the early centuries of Islam. The intellectual consequences of that conflict were decisive. They not only conditioned the formulation of the traditional Muslim theology but set a permanent stamp upon Islamic culture; and they still lie behind the conflicts arising in more recent years out of direct contact with modern thought." *Modern Trends in Islam*, p. 7. *Ibid.*, p. 116 on the atomism of the Muslim mind which, by its rejection of abstract "law," hindered Muslim thinkers from evolving a systematic and practical doctrine. See the pioneering study by D. B. Macdonald, *The Religious Attitude and Life in Islam*, Haskell Lectures of Comparative Religion delivered before the University of Chicago, 1906 (Chicago, 1909), in which MacDonald suggests that "the lack of a sense of law" is a characteristic of the Oriental mind. Also Schacht, *Introduction to Islamic Law*, p. 205, to the effect that the mode of thinking revealed by Islamic jurisprudence is quite distinct culturally. For two of the most perceptive renditions of the Arab bent of mind see Charles M. Doughty's classic work, *Travels in Arabia Deserta*, introd. T. E. Lawrence, with a new Preface by the author, and all original maps, plans, and cuts, 2 vols. (New York, 1923); and T. E. Lawrence, *Seven Pillars of Wisdom* (New York, 1935), esp. pp. 38ff.

speech communities encompassed by Islam came to share these basic dispositions. Despite divisions in the interpretation of canonical traditions, notably that between Sunni orthodox law and Shi'ite law (the latter, dominant in Iran, for example, insists that the traditions as collected by the Sunnis are spurious),[27] all converged in the belief that God alone has the knowledge of the perfect law, and that Islamic law, being designed for all time, is the ideal, inalterable, and only rational system of law in the world. The actual validity of these axioms has certainly been put in question by contrary customs, considerations of expediency, and knowledge of nonreligious legal systems, but none of these influences has been allowed to detract from the absolute official supremacy of the *shari'a*. That is to say, in contrast to contemporary societies in the Christian commonwealth of the West where Roman secular jurisprudence was recognized early as the framework for a legal restatement of Christian principles of ethics, Islamic societies have been kept captive by religious law. In these intellectual conditions, then, law in the Western sense simply could never have arisen. And the same holds true of political theory, notably as it relates to government and political organization.

The model community presented by Arab-Islamic ideas of public order is the ideologically unified, transnational and transterritorial *umma* in which all believers are brothers, living together by obeying the ethical precepts of a congregational theocracy. Each individual is valued in this spiritual democracy regardless of race or status, but his destiny in this and the other world depends in the final analysis upon membership in the *dār*

---

[27] It has been suggested that Shi'ite judges in Persia, being essentially unconstrained by a body of canonical law, had greater freedom to develop, and therefore modernize, existing law than their counterparts in Sunni jurisdictions. See Frye, in Thomas and Frye, *op.cit.*, p. 206 and *infra* p. 68.

64

al-Islām. However, the union of all believers is not defined in canonical law. It bears no analogy either to a church or to a state as these associational forms are known in the West. Nor does it find expression in synods or other parliamentary assemblies representative of the whole or of parts of the vast constituency. Symbolized in the mosque and the pilgrimage, the *dār al-Islām* may be said to project the idea of agreement in its broadest sense. Indeed consensus or *ijmā'* is here accepted as the supreme normative principle; discord and segregation, by contrast, are viewed on the authority of the Prophet as sources of error. What needs to be stressed in particular in this connection is the fact that this floating Islamic "constitution" supplies no method by which a consensus or accord can be ascertained beyond sanctioning the doctrinal pronouncements of the learned theologians (ulema), generally accepted as the Prophet's heirs. Yet even in this limited context one looks in vain for reliable definitions or procedural rules. Since general consultations are neither required nor feasible in view of the existence of numerous separate schools of ulema, the *ijmā'* of the learned has traditionally merely meant that a certain group of theologians has agreed on a particular proposition for the duration of a particular period. Theoretically defective as this arrangement may appear to be, it has had the inestimable practical advantage, as Lammens points out,[28] of leaving the door open to the entry of new opinions and formulations.

Classical law and theory, then, do not give any advice as to the form and institutions by which the unity of the *umma* as a political organization might be expressed and maintained. In fact, it is never the nature or concept

[28] *Op.cit.*, pp. 94ff; on consensus and disagreement as interpreted by different Islamic schools of law, see Schacht, *Origins of Muhammadan Jurisprudence* (Oxford [1950], 1959), pp. 82ff.

of an *umma* as such that is discussed, but only the conditions of membership. Furthermore, theory does not provide political society with auxiliary concepts such as that of the "corporation"[29] or "the juristic person" that could support the building of a reliable secular order. Most importantly for a comparison with Western ideas of government, it does not exploit the institution of "contract"—fully developed in Near Eastern commercial law—for purposes of constitutionalism, or officially allow for the idea of legislation since God is presumed to have legislated once and for all.[30] The absence of these and related concepts and human dispositions explains why Mohammedan society, rich in cosmopolitan industrious cities, could not bring forth the polis, the commune, the

[29] See *supra* pp. 35ff for comparisons with Western usage; see *infra* pp. 71, 73ff, on the profusion of nonpolitical corporations in the Islamic world, and on the corporate structure of the Ottoman Empire.

[30] See Schacht, *Introduction to Islamic Law*, pp. 22, 76, 144, 151, 155; and Khadduri, *War and Peace in the Law of Islam*, p. 9, on the limitations of the idea of contract in Islamic law. These are also discussed by S. S. Onar in connection with his analysis of "The Majalla." (This digest of legal rules was the product of the Ottoman reform movement, published 1870-1877, and eventually superseded when the Swiss code was introduced.) "The Majalla embodies principles of contract quite different from those generally accepted by continental European and Anglo-American law. The fact that the rules of the Majalla are founded mainly on moral principles rather than on economic necessities is clearly shown in the rules on contracts. The Majalla does not accept the Western principle of freedom of contract. In the West, freedom of contract is limited by public order and general rules of behavior, but individuals are free to make any contract within these limits. The Majalla, by contrast, defines the types of contracts which may be concluded." Majid Khadduri and Herbert J. Liebesny, eds., *Law in the Middle East*, vol. I, *Origin and Development of Islamic Law* (Washington, D.C., 1955), 299. It is noteworthy also in this connection that there is no term for "obligation" in Islamic law. See Coulson, *op.cit.*, pp. 82ff, and Gibb, "Constitutional Organization," in Khadduri and Liebesny, eds., *op.cit.*, on "Constitutional Law." Also David de Santillana, "Law and Society," in *The Legacy of Islam*, ed. Thomas Arnold (Oxford, 1947), esp. p. 309f. On the *ijmā'* or consensus of the community on the one hand and of the learned on the other, see H.A.R. Gibb, *Mohammedanism* (New York, 1962), esp. pp. 95ff.

66

chartered town, or leagues of self-governing cities,[31] social organisms that favored the intellectual and political emancipation of the individual in Europe; and why it was fundamentally incompatible—at least before Ibn Khaldûn's restatement of the problem in the fourteenth century—with the idea of the state as this has been understood in the West from early times onward.[32]

Muslim law recognizes only one principle of political organization: the imam. But just as it fails to circumscribe the *umma* and the *ijmā'*, so is it silent on the precise jurisdiction allotted to this office. Vaguely identified as the leader of the community in his function as the defender of the *sharī'a*, the imam was soon subsumed by the reality of the caliphate (itself unknown to religious law as an institution), more particularly by the precedents set by the first caliphs, whose rule, greatly idealized by posterity, is acknowledged to this day as having at least approximated the standards set by the Prophet himself. Apart from aligning itself with these particular records of history, Sunni political theory as developed before Ibn Khaldûn (d. 1406) cannot be said to illumine the task of government as it devolves from sacred law.[33] The greatly various, and in many respects mutually antagonistic, doctrines it has spawned agree only on giving government the broad mandate to safeguard the Muslim community in relations with the non-

[31] Cp. J. J. Saunders, "The Problem of Islamic Decadence," *Journal of World History*, VII, no. 3 (1963), 715; Bernard Lewis, *Istanbul and the Civilization of the Ottoman Empire* (Norman, Okla., 1963), p. 127, on the government of cities in the Ottoman Empire.

[32] Cp. *supra* pp. 26ff. See also Von Grunebaum, *Medieval Islam*, p. 137; Schacht, *Introduction to Islamic Law*, pp. 76f that "the state" as envisaged by the theory of Islamic law, is a fiction which has never existed in reality.

[33] Cp. Gibb, *Studies on the Civilization of Islam*, p. 162, to the effect that classical Sunni theory was in fact only the rationalization of the history of the community.

67

Muslim world, to keep the *umma* from falling prey to schisms and heresies, and to enforce compliance with the ideal of the good life as prescribed by religious law.[34] No allowance is made for the exercise of secular power, the territoriality of jurisdiction, the fixing of a seat of ultimate sovereignty, or the division of administrative functions in terms of separate legislative, executive, and judicial branches.

The acting Arab caliph, then, was in the final analysis a creature of necessity. For the anguished question posed already by Omar in the seventh century AD: "Am I a king now or a Caliph?—and if I am a king, it is a fearful thing,"[35] was never to receive a principled answer. Challenged by unattainable ideals, deprived of legal sanction and normative direction,[36] unsure of his pre-

[34] It should be remarked in this connection that Shi'a Islam opposes the vacillating concept of the *ijmā'*, holding instead to the principle that the judgment of the imam, here identified exclusively with descendants of Ali, is infallible. See *supra* p. 64, n. 27 on the implications of this doctrine for the development of law.

[35] Eric Schroeder, *Muhammad's People: A Tale by Analogy* (Portland, Maine, 1955), p. 178-79.

[36] In addition to authorities listed earlier in regard to the nature of the state, the caliphate, and government, see in particular Sir Thomas Arnold, *The Caliphate* (Oxford, 1924), p. 182 and Santillana, *loc.cit.*, p. 302 to the effect that the caliphate, as some of the jurists had imagined it, never existed in fact. See also Khadduri, *op.cit.*, p. 152 for the view that few institutions in Islam have deviated so radically from theory as has the caliphate. After the sack of Baghdad by the Mongols in 1258, history mentions mostly sultans, save in Egypt where the Mamluks found it convenient to keep an empty puppet as caliph. For another interesting discussion see Albert Hourani, *A Vision of History* (Beirut, 1961), pp. 149ff. Lammens, *op.cit.*, p. 104, comments on the fact that the Friday noon sermon which precedes the prayer, contains certain allusions to the caliphate and the man representing this institution which may be viewed as a religious affirmation of the caliphate and the identity of the sovereign, since the caliph's name is mentioned in the *Khutba*. See to the same effect MacDonald, *op.cit.*, p. 56. Secular power in Iran is from the religious standpoint not only transitional and defective but also a usurpation. See William S. Haas, *Iran* (New York, 1946), p. 113. For certain comparisons with political theory and organization as developed in classical Rome, Christian Western Europe

rogatives and obligations, each ruler was constrained
to fashion his statecraft pragmatically in terms of his
particular talents, dispositions, and modes of perceiving
the multiple ranges of an ever-fluid reality. Given these
premises, the caliphate was bound to become a precarious and unstable form of political organization. Contrary to theory, it was from the very beginning at the
mercy of civil strife, rebellion, and secession, the object
often of forcible seizure, and the prey of rival thrusts for
power usually marked by regicide and assassination.
Furthermore, contrary to the democratic traditions of
the pre-Islamic Arab Bedouin communities and the
egalitarian nature of the spiritual *umma* of believers, the
caliphate had to evolve into a despotic system of government. And this innate tendency was of course confirmed
as the frontiers of the *dār al-Islām* were extended to
include the non-Arab, previously non-Mohammedan
empires of the Near East.

Indeed, the type of imperial scheme represented
through the ages by the Persians, traditionally recognized as "the prestige nation" in Western Asia, and the
Byzantines, strongly orientalized at the time of their contact with Islam, became the model for the upstart dynasties of the Umayyads and the Abbasids, which, while
thoroughly victorious in foreign affairs by dint of conquest and ideology, were yet severely constricted in the
management of government by the uncompromising
demands of the *sharī'a* as rendered authoritatively by the
ulema. For both neighboring civilizations were universal
empires, composed of multiple ethnic groups and religious sects, thus validating the fundamental commitment to cosmopolitanism implicit in Mohammedanism;

and the Eastern Orthodox Empire of Byzantium, see Bozeman, *Politics
and Culture in International History*, pp. 380, 428, 439.

and both acknowledged openly the principle of abso-
lutist personal rule inherent also in the notions of the
imamate and the caliphate even as it has been absent in
the communal institutions of the Arabs of the desert.[37]

The new and vital theme encountered in the superior
yet defeated international societies of the Orient, however, was the comprehensive and effective organizational
structure by which they had been held together despite
continuously trying political circumstances. This framework, Islamic statesmen discovered, was marked by an
elaborate bureaucratic establishment, a highly efficient
military system, and an intricate network of diplomacy
and espionage that had assured the political and psychological control of satellite peoples as well as of the native
populace. In Sassanian Persia[38] and the Eastern Christian
Empire,[39] then, where religion and the state were inex-
tricably intertwined, where government was conceived
as a matter of art rather than of principle, and where
society was allowed to consist of rigid yet essentially self-
contained sectors, the forces of personalism and despotism were buttressed, as far as the actual conduct of
government was concerned, by the continuous functioning of religious, bureaucratic, and military officials.

These principles of statecraft, summarized authoritatively in political manuals and "Mirrors for Princes,"

[37] See Doughty, op.cit., I, Justice in the Desert, 249ff, for eloquent
testimony to the fact that "the Arabs of the wilderness are the justest
of mortals," that the sheikh of a nomad tribe is no tyrant, and that the
Bedouin majlis functioned effectively each day as a congregation, a
parliament, and a tribunal dispensing justice impartially.

[38] See Richard N. Frye, The Heritage of Persia (New York, 1966),
pp. 265-273, for a brief evaluation of the system of public order.

[39] See the pioneering work by Georg Ostrogorsky, Geschichte des
byzantinischen Staates (Munich, 1940), notably pp. 16ff (English version, History of the Byzantine State, trans. Joan Hussey [New Brunswick, N.J., 1957], pp. 1-20), and other authorities listed in Bozeman,
op.cit., "The Byzantine Realm," pp. 298-356.

70

became the ruling references for all Islamic regimes, nowhere more emphatically so than in those set up by the Turks and the Mongols. These Central Asian peoples, originally as primitive and nomadic as the Arabs whom they eventually displaced as the ruling elements, established themselves in time as immensely talented carriers not only of the Asian idea of empire but also of the Islamic concept of the brotherhood of all believers. The *dār al-Islām* was thus early set in the mould of the Perso-Byzantine-Turkish synthesis of "the Power State,"[40] a form of organization carefully circumscribed by Niẓām al-Mulk (d. 1092) and Ibn Khaldûn.[41]

As elaborated in the Middle East first by the Seljuq and then the Ottoman Turks, this model was fashioned into an impressive international system of public order in which multiple peoples, affiliated with different cul-

[40] Albert Howe Lybyer, *The Government of the Ottoman Empire in the Time of Suleiman the Magnificent* (Cambridge, Mass., 1913), p. 227, expresses the view that Turkish ruling institutions were solidly rooted also in Chinese traditions of government.

[41] The actual base of Ibn Khaldûn's observations and analyses was the record of the Almoravids and the Almohads in North Africa.

Any estimate of Ibn Khaldûn's work on the actual secular manifestations of government must be viewed in light of the fact that this great Tunisian thinker never allowed his findings to detract from the absolute and inalterable validity of the theological order of things as originally laid down by the Prophet. See *The Muqaddimah: An Introduction to History*, trans. F. Rosenthal, Bollingen Series XLIII, 2nd ed., 3 vols. (Princeton, 1967), III, 154: "The intellect has nothing to do with the religious law and its views. . . . The perceptions which the Master of the religious law (Muhammad) had are wider (than those of the philosophers), because they go beyond rational views. They are above them and include them, because they draw their support from the divine light. . . . When the Lawgiver (Muhammad) guides us towards some perception, we must prefer that (perception) to our own perceptions. We must have more confidence in it than in them. . . ." Also p. 246 for "A Refutation of Philosophy." This orientation continued to control intellectual life in the Ottoman Empire. It explains why successive generations in the Middle East could not come to terms with Greek thought, and why the Renaissance in the nearby European world passed them by. See *supra*, chap. 1.

tures and religions, were held together for several
centuries by reliance on two major establishments: "the
Ruling Institution," essentially secular in nature and
composed of bureaucratic departments and the armed
forces, in both of which slaves or ex-slaves played dominant roles, and "the Muslim Institution," administered
by various categories of *sharīʻa* jurists.[42] Each of these was
theoretically independent, but both establishments were
joined as it were in a representative council, the *dīwān*.
Neither of these agencies was supposed to obstruct the
principle of centralized despotism as embodied in individual caliphs or sultans and their principal delegates,
the *wazīrs*, especially not after the recognition gained
ground that military power could constitute a valid
imamate.[43] These circumstances explain why a division
of governmental functions into legislative, executive,
and judicial branches was not fathomable in reality, just
as it had not been foreseen in theory, and why a unifying
system based on constitutional or public law and the
concept of citizenship (as these ideas are understood in
the West) could not arise. However, absolutism was
nonetheless curbed and the cause of the cosmopolitan

[42] See Lybyer, *op.cit.*, for an exhaustive analysis of the Empire's early
administrative system; also Appendixes I and II for 16th-century accounts by Italian observers, and Appendix IV for a comparison of the
Ottoman and the Mogul Empires. For another perceptive report see
Franz Babinger, *Mehmed der Eroberer und Seine Zeit: Weltenstürmer
einer Zeitenwende* (Munich, 1959). For the evolution of Ottoman government and society in subsequent centuries, see H.A.R. Gibb and Harold
Bowen, *Islamic Society and the West: A Study of the Impact of Western
Civilization on Moslem Culture in the Near East*, vol. I, *Islamic Society in the Eighteenth Century* (Oxford, 1957). Other important discussions of the subject are found in W. S. Vucinich, *The Ottoman
Empire: Its Record and Legacy* (Princeton, 1964); John J. Saunders,
ed., *The Muslim World on the Eve of Europe's Expansion* (Englewood
Cliffs, N.J., 1966); and Bernard Lewis, *Istanbul and the Civilization of
the Ottoman Empire* (Oklahoma, 1963).

[43] Gibb and Bowen, *op.cit.*, vol. I, part I, 32ff.

society furthered because this dynastic world state was also a "layered society," making full allowance for autonomy not only in respect of tributary vassal kingdoms but also of provinces, ethnic groups, and other associations gathering like-minded folk. Indeed this type of decentralization steadily gained ground as the central powers degenerated under the impact of personal caprice, intrigue, and corruption.

Under the umbrella of a nominal or defused centralism, then, organizational impulses had been channelled early into a variety of separate corporate structures, each representative of a special set of interests, callings, or commitments. In fact it was only through belonging to such a corporation that the individual, unrecognized either as a citizen or as a member of a nationality, acquired status in the Ottoman Empire. This was particularly true of his religious association with the millet, a nonterritorial communal formation encompassing the members of each officially recognized belief system; for since religion was the paramount rallying point for all Near Eastern peoples, it could be used effectively also by the imperial administration as a structuring principle in its governance of subject populations and as a control mechanism through which loyalty to the dynastic state could be assured.[44] However, it needs to be remembered in this context that each millet was an entity in itself, having scant, if any, relations with other organized sects. In retrospect no feature of the entire order seems therefore more odd, Thomas observes,[45] than the degree

[44] See Gibb and Bowen, *op.cit.*, p. 283 to the effect that religious guilds had existed in Islam long before the foundation of the Ottoman Empire; and Frye, *The Heritage of Persia*, p. 265, that Christians and followers of other religions were distributed in Persia into groupings greatly similar to the later millet system of the Ottoman Empire.

[45] Thomas and Frye, *op.cit.*, p. 46.

73

to which these millets, spread thin as each one was over practically the whole empire, still remained virtually so many closed corporations, "closed socially and closed intellectually as well."

And much the same remained true, throughout the centuries, of the numerous religious brotherhoods and secular guilds, whose varied members organized their private worlds in accordance with their own laws and customs and in conditions of aloofness from each other. In contrast to guilds in Europe which were "public persons," representing authorities delegated to them by the state, these Near Eastern societies were unsanctioned by a general public law[46] and usually quite hostile to the idea of government control. It is true that many were capable of resisting the exorbitant demands often made by state authorities, but not even those set up by liberal professions conceived of themselves as nuclei for constructive political reform. Indeed most corporations in this culture realm (outside of brotherhoods dedicated to the pursuit of transcendental mystical truths and therefore unconcerned with mundane phenomena) were so antagonistic to the governmental superstructure that they were apt to become hotbeds of political intrigue and rebellion. In such a climate of dispositions, dissimulation hardened into a state of mind,[47] flights into subversive

[46] See Haas, *op.cit.*, pp. 104ff for Persia; Gibb and Bowen, *op.cit.*, p. 290 for the Arab regions. Cp. Schacht, *Introduction to Islamic Law*, p. 125, that Islamic law does not recognize juristic persons: not even the public treasury is here construed as an institution, for its owner is the Muslim community, i.e., the sum total of individual Muslims. Also *supra*, pp. 66ff.

[47] In Persia, dissimulation was in some respects a doctrine, Haas explains, for a Shi'ite was allowed to pretend that he was a Sunni, or even a Christian or a Jew, whenever he felt he was in danger because of the fact that he actually was a Shi'ite. *Op.cit.*, p. 109. Furthermore, in the context of statecraft as this had developed before the twentieth-century reforms, there grew a technique of cunning, simulation, and

associations were commonplace, and "the secret society" became the normative organizational model for political activism, especially in Persia and the Arab lands.

These traditional moulds have carried and contained the great awakening of Arab nationalism in the nineteenth century and the Arab revolt against Turkish rule in the first part of the twentieth century.[48] And developments since then are persuasive testimony to the fact that they continue to shape political thought and conduct in each of the Middle Eastern states, not excluding Israel and the antecedent organizations, both overt and covert, that helped to establish this new state. Furthermore, modern Islamic thought has not really departed from the traditional view that government, being a necessary evil designed to stem the ever-latent trend to anarchy and civil strife, is bound to be the object of fear, distrust, or at best indifference,[49] and that its worth should be measured therefore not so much by standards of law as by the quality on the one hand of the leading personality and on the other of the administrative bureaucracy that

---

ruse that Persians in many walks of life learnt to master with rare perfection, nowhere more effectively than in diplomacy and in governmental circles in which "inferiors" evolved a strategy of self-defence against their superiors that allowed them to slip through the meshes of any net thrown around them. *Ibid.*, p. 113.

[48] See Antonius, *op.cit.*, pp. 8off, pp. 110ff on the role of e.g., the Bairut Secret Society at the end of the nineteenth century, and Lawrence, *op.cit.*, pp. 46ff on that of the *Fetah*, a Syrian freedom society, linking landowners, writers, doctors, and public servants, in a system of common oaths, passwords, a clandestine press, and a central treasury. See also Macdonald, *op.cit.*, for several chapters dealing with the *Ikhwān*, the Order of the Assassins, and the Wahhabites.

[49] In addition to authorities cited previously in support of this conclusion, see Henry Habib Ayrout, *The Egyptian Peasant*, trans. John Alden Williams (Boston, 1963), on the Egyptian fellah's "waking passivity," secretiveness, fear, and profound distrust of all governmental authority. Also Sania Hamady, *Temperament and Character of the Arabs* (New York, 1960); for attitudes to authority, the state, and law see esp. pp. 95, 103, 117-127.

hold the realm together. Illegitimate and coercive almost by definition, state as well as government thus continue to be prizes for which ambitious, often intensely patriotic, men contend in circumstances that are generally marked by a truly prodigious incidence of violence, factionalism, and caprice.

As the brief and superficial identification with Western political processes and systems draws to a close, it is clear that nationalism as understood in the Occident has failed to supplant the ancient ideology in public consciousness, and that the so-called democracies are scarcely distinguishable in practice from the old sultanates: like the latter they are passively accepted by the public in virtue of their power rather than their moral and legal authority.[50] What modernization has effected is the weakening of the moral and social order that used to compensate for, and at times mitigate, the harshness of political rule. For as governing elites, often acting through parliaments, have succeeded in dissolving brotherhoods and other traditional keepers of the public trust, power has become subject to fewer restraints than it used to be,[51] while the cause of social harmony goes begging.

[50] H.A.R. Gibb, "Social Reform: Factor x; The Search for an Islamic Democracy," in *Perspective of the Arab World: An Atlantic Supplement* (New York, 1956), remarks that violence is not less violence because clothed in incomprehensible legal forms.

[51] On this point see Schacht, *Introduction to Islamic Law*, p. 101: "Whereas a traditional Muslim ruler must, by definition, remain the servant of the sacred Law of Islam, a modern government, and particularly a parliament, with the modern idea of sovereignty behind it, can consolidate itself master." Also Richard Nolte, "The Rule of Law in the Arab Middle East," *Muslim World*, XLVIII, no. 4 (October 1958), 307: "By thrusting the Shari'ah into the background, the influence of secular conceptions from the West has mostly dissolved the qualified rule of law imposed during the centuries of classical Islam. Never fully controlled, the ruler now appears to be fully uncontrolled from a Shari'ah point of view. It remains to ask whether the modern Islamic

The multiple ambiguities in the relations between claim and reality, dream and fact, tradition and innovation, history and contemporaneity, that mark the records of Islamic law and politics from their very inception to the present day would no doubt be unnerving to Western minds which are tutored by their civilization to aim at objectivity, clarity, and precision in the definition and organization of their social and political environment. In the Middle East, by contrast, these dichotomies have traditionally been sources of an inner mental strength even as they have conduced to the erosion of such political structures as the caliphate and the modern constitutional state. What they manifest in the field of jurisprudence and political organization is a remarkable capacity to live pragmatically, accept that which is and accommodate "the new" under the mantle of an outward inflexibility. A kind of practical *ijmā'*, quite contrary to official law, has thus been allowed to arise in many periods, not excluding our own; for "where at first sight there appears to be nothing but unregulated confusion, and even, to the Western eye, a total disregard of law and justice, we shall find custom and tradition setting recognized limits to conflicting jurisdictions and dictating what may not be done and what may be done, even

---

states of the Middle East by establishing constitutions and bills of rights based on Western models have been able to establish in fact the substitute rule of law thus implied."

For an interesting case study of abortive reformist efforts on the part of Egypt's westernized lawyers, see Farhat J. Ziadeh, *Lawyers, the Rule of Law and Liberalism in Modern Egypt* (Stanford, 1968), esp. pp. 18ff, 77, 88ff; pp. 146f on the insistent clamoring for a return to the *sharī'a*; and p. 159 for the conclusion that "the Egyptian legal profession, the leaders of society, the upholders of constitutionality and the rule of law, and the supporters of liberal causes, were reduced to the status of legal technicians" as the regime of Naguib was replaced by that of Nasser.

though technically against the written law."[52] And the same kind of eclecticism is evident in the area of government. Here, Coulson points out, history appears to have turned full cycle and to have confronted Islam with a situation remarkably parallel to the one she faced during the Umayyad period: modern reformers, just like the Umayyad administrators, have managed to control the sudden surge of events by ad hoc measures adopted under a policy of pragmatism and expediency.[53]

Anyone attempting a comparative study of Western and Near Eastern approaches to law and organization must thus lay aside Western norms and models if he is to understand "the other." Instead he must face the fact that he is confronted here with totally different conceptions of the roles of law and government in society.

Future patterns of law and organization in the region are likely to reproduce the fundamental principles that have moved Islamic society up to the present, among them also that opposition of law and government which appears so paradoxical to denizens of the West, always seeking to merge the two. But what is necessary today if later generations, more particularly those in the Arab domain, are to be psychologically at ease in their own and the wider world environment, is a bold reexamination and reformulation of the major guiding norms; and only Arabs who are respectful of the past while yet closely attuned to the problems of the present, can undertake the task.[54]

The system of thought, moral persuasion, and political

[52] Gibb and Bowen, *op.cit.*, vol. I, part I, 214-215, commenting on life in the Arab provinces under Ottoman rule.

[53] *Op.cit.*, p. 223.

[54] On the preliminary, albeit inchoate, groping toward such a restatement see Gibb, "Social Reform: Factor X," *loc. cit.*; on the need for a critical revaluation of the data of thought through the cultivation of historical thinking, see Gibb, *Modern Trends in Islam*, pp. 122-129.

cohesion that informs law and organization on the local level is operative also on regional and international levels. In fact the most successful forms of rendering the collective destiny, namely, the transterritorial brotherhood of the *dār al-Islām* and the ethnically multifarious bureaucratic empire, are by definition universalist systems—in many respects, it is here submitted, greatly suggestive today for a restructuring of the modern multicultural world society. But here, as in the local context, "law" while aiming at the greatest possible ideological unity and stoutly adhering to the image of the *dār al-Islām* as the exclusive abode of peace, is quite tolerant of war and discord even among believers. Militancy was, after all, a dominant aspect of Bedouin desert life, which is the core of Arabism, of the Prophet's biography, which is the heart of Arab history, and of the life styles also of the Persians and the Turks. Recognized in the entire region as a manly virtue and as a fundamental article of the religious faith, it thus naturally became a permanent feature of relations between politically distinct entities. Indeed military activism carried by well-organized armies or ad hoc guerrilla bands had to become the mainstay of all ruling establishments, since Islamic theory did not allow officially for the recognition of separate, territorially bounded sovereignties. In this context of law and history, then, regional relations between actually functioning states have been left to fluctuate between war and peace, often in response to the qualities inherent in particular personal relationships between individual dignitaries or aspirants to power. Here intrigue dwells with mutual aid, betrayal alternates with keeping faith, and strife may give rise to accord—all part of a code of honor between ambitious, adventurous, but like-minded men.

Modern developments in regional relations repeat the pattern left by history. A League of Arab States, inspired by British statesmanship came into being in March 1945, but a Western observer doubted already in 1946 that it would be strong enough to overcome Arab divisions and provide the foundation for a single Arab state.[55] This estimate was to prove correct as power struggles and other variants of factionalism rent the newly closed ranks of Arab governments in circumstances that another Occidental authority, writing about events in the period 1958-1967, aptly defined as "The Arab Cold War."[56] Viewed as a regional organization in the strict context foreseen by the Charter of the United Nations, the Arab League is indeed a failure and likely to remain just that. However, the U.N. blueprint, vague as it is in respect of regionalism, is, after all, rigorously a-cultural in tone and content, having been composed at a time when constitutionalism was trusted to neutralize conflicting modes of thought and to override the facts of cultural diversity. These expectations have proved erroneous in the last decades, and it is only fair, therefore, to evaluate the Arab League and other Near Eastern unions in the older and trusted regional framework to which its peoples are accustomed, especially since Arab representatives had in fact held out for the recognition of a "new" type of regional organization more congenial to their own traditions. Thus it is significant, as Macdonald points out,

[55] Vernon McKay, "The Arab League in World Politics," *Foreign Policy Reports*, vol. XXII, no. 17 (November 15, 1946).

[56] Malcolm Kerr, *The Arab Cold War 1958-1967: A Study of Ideology in Politics*, Chatham House Essays, 2nd ed. (London and New York, 1967), pp. 52, on the impotence of the League; pp. 140ff on factionalism as the normal condition in modern inter-Arab relations. For the documentary record of the Arab League, see Khalil, *op.cit.*, vol. II; Robert W. Macdonald, *The League of Arab States: A Study in the Dynamics of Regional Organization* (Princeton, 1965), Appendixes.

80

that the founders of the League made a definite if reluctant decision against a political union of their states,[57] favoring instead a loose confederation with a stress on cultural unity, and that the first regional treaty sponsored by the League was a cultural agreement, requiring the signatories to disseminate the Arab heritage in a great variety of ways.[58] In the wider Islamic commonwealth, meanwhile, greatly similar traditions are being renewed, as previous references have suggested.[59] Here as in the narrower orbit of Arabism, conflict is being accommodated as the search for culturally reliable political structures continues.

Middle Eastern approaches to law and organization on the level of global politics are naturally informed by the theories and experiences that have combined to shape the life style of successive generations. Today as in the past they are marked, in particular, by that dichotomy between ideal and reality that contemporaries in the West have a hard time understanding. The major, and in the Islamic world view irrebuttable, assumption is the idea that the *dār al-Islām*, while rent by endemic internecine war, is nonetheless the exclusive abode of peace, held together by a supreme law of peace. This international law, which is inseparable from the divine law regulating the conduct of all believers, officially enjoins Mohammedans to maintain a state of permanent belligerence with all nonbelievers, collectively encompassed in the *dār al-harb*, the domain of war. War, then, is here an integral part of the legal system; for in accordance with the doctrine of the *jihād*, which is recognized as "the peak of religion," the Islamic commonwealth must be expand-

[57] Robert W. Macdonald, *op.cit.*, pp. 53, 282, 303. For another discussion of the subject matter, see M. F. Anabtawi, *Arab Unity in Terms of Law* (The Hague, 1963), and cp. *supra*, pp. 56ff.
[58] *Ibid.*, p. 173.   [59] *Supra*, pp. 21ff; 62ff.

ing relentlessly, like a caravan continuously on the move, until it become coterminous with humanity, at which time war will have been transposed into universal peace.

Rigorously uncompromising in their dogmatic stance, Mohammedan governments and statesmen have always been flexible in their actual international relations. Apart from acknowledging gradations of hostility depending upon whether the non-Muslims were scriptural peoples or not, they subjected warfare itself to elaborate rules which included, in certain situations, the application of the doctrine of "unnecessary destruction" (not incompatible, at times, with poisoning the waters if such a stratagem was likely to induce surrender). Furthermore, and beginning with the tradition of statecraft initiated by the Prophet himself, allowance has always been made for peace with the proviso, however, that it be viewed as a temporary cessation of hostilities.[60] That is to say, in the context of reality as it was shaped by later imperial governments, the *jihād* was often muted into a state of "dormant" or "protracted" war during which amicable relations with non-Islamic peoples could be cultivated more or less at will.[61] Indeed no aspect of

[60] One school of law limited the interval of peace, if established by treaty, to a maximum period of ten years; another held that suspension of the *jihād* was only possible when an urgent necessity had to be faced as e.g. internal conflict or the overwhelming power of the enemy. See Majid Khadduri "International Law," in Khadduri and Liebesny, eds., *Law in the Middle East*, vol. I, *Origin and Development of Islamic Law*, p. 354.

[61] The classical Muslim idea of a permanent holy war is in certain respects analogous to the medieval Christian notion of the "just war," (e.g. the crusade), but the latter was neither scripturally ordained nor was it conceived as a permanent state of political, psychological, and military belligerence. Modern communist doctrines of permanent war, permanent revolution, and protracted conflict are conceptually equivalent to the *jihād*, but nothing in actual Islamic history approximates the relentless totalitarian thrust that is implicit in Communist ideology and statecraft.

For a detailed analysis of the *jihād* and the Muslim law of war, see

international history in this region is quite as impressive as the flexibility of the Islamic diplomatic style. True to the pattern set by Mohammed in his dealings with Jewish and Christian communities, the stress has been on negotiation and compromise with all manner of "enemies" and on a great variety of subject matters.

These dispositions were no doubt usually corollaries of shrewd calculations—as when it seemed opportune to avoid or terminate military engagements—but they were also derivatives on the one hand of pragmatic experience as registered in centuries of coexistence with non-Arab, non-Islamic nations, and on the other of that native code of ethics with its curious mixture of humanitarianism and caprice which recognizes the individual infidel as a human being in need, at times, of guest-friendship, safe conduct, and asylum, and capable of binding himself honorably in such mutual arrangements. In short, personalism and pragmatism rather than principle and system provide the norms for the conduct of foreign affairs in this civilization. And this is true even of the treaty, a basic Arab institution, hallowed by precedents set by the Prophet and utilized by successive caliphs, sultans, and other potentates—ancient and modern—so as to secure allies, prevent attacks, arrange for the ransom of prisoners, guarantee safe passage to travellers and vessels, regulate the status of minorities, or conclude a special peace.[62] The practice of treaty making thus had

---

M. Khadduri, *The Law of War and Peace in Islam: A Study in Muslim International Law* (London, 1940), pp. 19ff, 32ff, 75, to the effect that this "dormant war" is analogous to what is known in Western international law as "nonrecognition"; and the same author's work, *War and Peace in the Law of Islam* (Baltimore, 1955), pp. 55, 144 that the *jihād* is comparable to what we call "a state of insurgency."

[62] See the works of Khadduri, Hurewitz, and other historians and lawyers, as well as documentary records cited earlier, for the nature of these diplomatic transactions and for occasions when resort was made to arbitration.

the effect of greatly tempering the officially rigid view of bipolarity, leading even some early jurists to acknowledge the existence of a third world, i.e. "the world of covenant."[63]

Most of the bilateral treaties linking Christians and Muslims in Mediterranean trade and politics between the eleventh and fourteenth centuries seem to have been initiated and drafted by Christians who, being heirs of the Latin legal tradition, excelled already in the art of finding proper legal forms for a precise expression of mutual accords, and of inferring general principles from a maze of particular transactions.[64] Muslim governments and merchant elites, by contrast, were not concerned with structuring such conceptual schemes. Nor were they inclined to compromise officially with the theory that treaties with non-Muslims were not treaties between equals, or that a peace treaty was properly viewed as merely a truce. Yet the idea of the treaty did emerge as a major rallying point between the two different law cultures, for both held to the principle that such a mutual pledge ought to be kept if at all possible. One of the reasons for this convergence was no doubt a shared code of chivalry. But another, perhaps of greater importance, was the continuous opportunity to develop a spirit of reciprocity and a common appreciation of pragmatic advantage. And this, again, was due in large measure to the absence of a formal rigid system of international law. Contrary to the post-Grotian modern period, the Occidental vision of the multinational reality had not yet become encumbered by formal legal presuppositions developed for use within the Christian realm. It

[63] Khadduri, *The Law of War and Peace in Islam*, p. 75.

[64] For a discussion of these aspects of intercultural relations see Bozeman, *op.cit.*, pp. 404-22.

too could thus proceed pragmatically, allowing its exponents in trade and politics to work out interculturally valid and useful arrangements while retaining the sense of security that goes with belonging to an authentic integral civilization.

3.

Africa

SOUTH OF SAHARA

NEGRO Africa presents the Occidental observer with altogether different ranges of meanings in the areas of law and organization. It had been subjected to Islamic influences for at least a millenium before it began experiencing the full impact of Western ideas and institutions in the last hundred years, but the diffusion of Muslim beliefs, the imposition of a ruling Muslim class as, for example, in the Western Sudan, and the establishment of the Koranic code of law which followed the military conquests and commercial penetrations of vast parts of the continent, did not effect radical changes in the structure of the indigenous societies or displace native norms and customs as controlling frames of organizational reference.[65] The first point to be made,

[65] Kenneth Little, "African Culture and the Western Intrusion,"

then, is that we are dealing here with an ancient, remarkably resilient culture world, capable of coping with foreign intrusions, however determined the thrust, without easy loss of authenticity.

The relatively recent Occidental intervention in African politics and culture may prove to have more lasting and far reaching consequences, if only because it occurred in an age marked by inescapable, relentlessly intense communications between societies in all parts of the world. And yet it is unmistakably clear already now, in the first decade of political independence from Europe, that traditional beliefs and institutions are being reinstated and revitalized everywhere, consciously

---

Journal of World History, III, no. 4 (1957), 951ff, suggests that this was probably so because, in a broader sense, the Muslim conquerors did not differ culturally very much from the peoples whom they took under control. Leo Frobenius, *Und Afrika Sprach*, Volkstümliche Ausgabe, (Berlin-Charlottenburg, 1912), p. 356, writes in this connection that Islam entered the Sudan as a primitive religion, i.e., without the Persian and Hellenic elements which it absorbed in the Near East, and that it actually encountered higher culture forms in Africa. These circumstances may contribute to an explanation why Islamic law is regarded as a very minor problem outside the sphere of family relations and succession, and why traces of the customary indigenous law survive even in the most rigidly Muslim areas, with the possible exception of Northern Nigeria. See to this effect J.N.D. Anderson, "The Future of Islamic Law in British Commonwealth Territories in Africa," in Hans W. Baade and Robinson O. Everett, eds., *African Law: New Law for New Nations* (New York, 1963), pp. 89, 94f. See also the works of I. S. Trimingham on Islam in Africa. See D. Westermann, *The African Today and Tomorrow* (London, 1949), p. 131, to the effect that neither the migrations of the Hamites and the political upheavals caused by them, nor the settlements of the Arabs and their devastating slave raids; neither the Indian and Persian immigrants on the East coast, nor even the slave and alcohol trade of Europe, have been able fundamentally to change the face of Africa. Foreign elements have always been completely absorbed so that today they appear as indigenous. R. Montagne, "The Teaching of Democracy in Islamic Countries," *Journal of African Administration* (April 1952), p. 62, expresses regret that the Islamic countries of the Maghreb did not have at their disposal the old African traditions which have proved so useful in e.g., the Hausa emirates and the sultanates of the Tchad.

and unconsciously, in response precisely to the challenge of political freedom, and that imported Western forms are inadequate to contain this newly released African spirit. The common theme that is being sounded by writers and politicians in official texts, autobiographies, novels, and political essays, at meetings of African heads of state and congresses of African intellectuals, and that emerges from the records of actual development in each African state, is the proposition that there are certain essential Negro-African values which require rediscovery and development in every realm of life, including that of law, because they are believed to provide the only suitable foundation for African societies in the future.[66]

[66] Alioune Diop, "The Spirit of *Présence Africaine*," in Lalage Bown and Michael Crowder, eds., *Proceedings of the First International Congress of Africanists*, Accra, December 11-18, 1962 (Bungay, Suffolk, 1964), p. 48, summarizes this conviction as follows: "A certain language of culture, different from any the West has taught us, has emerged, and we are now discovering it and are devoting our activities to developing and harnessing the drive behind this personality" so that it may manifest itself in art, politics, science, literature, and law. See to similar effect the different contributions in the *Proceedings of the First International Congress of Africanists* held at Accra (notably those by K. O. Dike); and in the Proceedings of the "Rencontres internationales de Bouaké," as collected in *Les Religions Africaines Traditionelles* (Paris, 1965), and *Tradition et Modernisme en Afrique Noire* (Paris, 1965). See also the writings and pronouncements of Kenyatta, Kaunda, Senghor, Sékou-Touré, Nkrumah, and other present and past heads of state. The awareness of the shared African heritage as a culture different from that of the West was expressed by M. François Tombalbaye (Tchad) at the Summit Conference of Independent African states in Addis Ababa in 1963 in the following terms: "La grande majorité de nos masses est restée très africaine, très originale, sans aucun vernis de culture française ou anglaise ou autre. . . . l'unité Africaine, c'est également la restitution de toutes nos valeurs morales et culturelles."

Henry L. Bretton, *The Rise and Fall of Kwame Nkrumah: A Study of Personal Rule in Africa* (London, 1966), p. 172, points out that the traditional structure of society—not much of a force during Nkrumah's reign—revived within hours after the successful coup against Nkrumah and promptly rallied to the support of the new regime.

For suggestive comments on the resilience of tradition in modern

If outsiders are to understand this search for identity, they must follow the advice given by Professor K. A. Busia (who became Prime Minister of Ghana in 1966) in *Africa in Search of Democracy,* and review "contemporary African problems in the context of Africa's own cultural heritage."[67] And this is of course what the most enlightened and observant of Occidental scholars, explorers, and statesmen were doing in the course of their

---

Ghana see also David Apter, *Ghana in Transition* (New York, 1963), esp. the Preface; and S.K.B. Asante, "Law and Society in Ghana," in Thomas W. Hutchinson, ed., *Africa and Law: Developing Legal Systems in African Commonwealth Nations* (Madison, Wis. and London, 1968), esp. pp. 131f. For a critique of modern Ghanaian law and organization that is held, essentially, in the framework of Occidental legal and political thought, see William B. Harvey, *Law and Social Change in Ghana* (Princeton, 1966). On the disestablishment of European legal and political structures in French-speaking Africa, see Guy de Lusignan, *French-Speaking Africa Since Independence* (New York and London, 1969); and a stimulating essay by Gabriel d'Arboussier, "L'Evolution de la Législation dans Les Pays Africains d'Expression Française et à Madagascar," in H. and L. Kuper, eds., *African Law: Adaptation and Development* (Los Angeles, 1966), esp. p. 169, to the effect that Senegal's constitutional order as instituted by the French did not assimilate the masses of the population, despite the fact that Senegal was linked to France for a long time.

For one of the most interesting discussions of the interaction between European and African modes of thought and political organization and of the persistence of indigenous forms, see J. M. Lee, *African Armies and Civil Order*, Studies in International Security, 13 (London, 1969), particularly chaps. I and III.

Most of these authorities suggest what many African statesmen, including Nkrumah, have said outright: that law is being, or should be, africanized, as part of the general process toward the recovery of cultural identity.

[67] London, 1967, p. 1: "We cannot fully appreciate the import of these issues, or understand how they appear to Africans without reference to their past, in an effort to appreciate the sentiments and mental dispositions with which they approach their own problems. The viewpoints and attitudes which people adopt towards their political, economic, or social questions are influenced by their historical experiences and judgments based ultimately on their world outlook which, conscious or unconscious, derives from their cultural heritage. The contemporary problems of Africa must be seen in the context of Africa's own cultural heritage."

88

encounters with Africa even before refined ethnographic skills became generally available.

Soon after England had established its colonial administration in East Africa at the end of the last century, Captain (later Lord) Lugard noted in his dealings with East African chiefs that he could get nowhere with the European treaty forms that he had been provided with because "the nature of a written compact was wholly beyond the comprehension of these savage tribes." Instead he chose the medium of the blood brotherhood, finding that was "the best parallel to our idea of a sacred bond in black and white," especially when it was combined with the proper use of the spoken word and ceremonies assuring the right degree of publicity, and that this kind of extraordinary pledge was generally known among the different, often mutually hostile, tribes.[68] Similar insights marked the work of another pioneering colonial administrator, R. S. Rattray, who could leave posterity a masterful explanation of how the Ashanti in West Africa were governed because he knew how to "decipher" the complex nonverbal symbolism and intricate mythological lore that assured the functioning of all politically significant institutions.

The cultural map of Africa as completed by modern linguists and anthropologists now shows more than one

[68] F. D. Lugard, *The Rise of Our East African Empire*, 2 vols. (Edinburgh and London, 1893), II, 579ff. A journal kept two centuries earlier by a certain James Barbot during protracted trade negotiations with the native ruler of Bonny in Southern Nigeria contains the following comments on the implications of nonliteracy in treaty making: "Thus, with much patience, all our matters were adjusted indifferently, after their way, who are not very scrupulous to find excuses or objections, for not keeping literally to any verbal contract; for they have not the art of reading and writing, and therefore we are forced to stand to their arrangement, which often is no longer than they think fit to hold it themselves." Thomas Hodgkin, ed., *Nigerian Perspectives: An Historical Anthology* (London, 1960), p. 140.

thousand small communities, each different from the other, each a tribute to that peculiar plastic talent for creating politically significant forms that sets the Africans apart from e.g., the Arabs, yet all participating in a common heritage marked by the absence of writing and the perfection of compensatory nonliterate modes of thought and life. Here where human communication required until very recently the physical presence of "the other," language developed as a mode of action, not as an instrument of reflection or a mirror of reflected thought. So conceived it is closely dependent upon the moment in which the spoken word is being uttered. As Malinowski explains it: in nonliterate societies all the material lives only in winged words, passing from man to man, for each oral statement by a human being has the aim and function of expressing some thought or feeling actual at that moment and in that situation.[69] The conception of meaning, then, can never be detached from the situation in which the word is being uttered—a circumstance that sets definite limits upon the elaboration of theories, abstractions, generalizations, and the kind of concepts that underlie, for example, jurisprudence as understood in the literate Occident.[70]

[69] Bronislaw Malinowski, "The Problem of Meaning in Primitive Languages," supplementary essay in C. K. Ogden and I. A. Richards, *The Meaning of Meaning* (New York, 1959).

[70] For one of the most stimulating discussions of these aspects of literate and nonliterate cultures see Robert Redfield, *The Primitive World and Its Transformations* (New York, 1958), esp. p. 83.

The importance of "action" as an instrument of propaganda as opposed to that of words was stressed by Nkrumah in the CPP's first pamphlet, "What I mean by Positive Action": "We must remember," the former Ghanaian leader wrote in 1949, "that, because of the educational backwardness of the Colonial countries, the majority of the people in this country cannot read. There is only one thing they can understand and that is ACTION." See also in this respect, W.J.M. Mackenzie and Kenneth E. Robinson, eds., *Five Elections in Africa* (Oxford, 1960). The political campaigns conducted in 1957 in Senegal concen-

This emphasis upon speech, the moment, and personal encounter explains also why future-oriented thought, essential in the Occidental literate scheme of law and political organization, is not easily accommodated in Africa. As M. Amadou Hampaté Ba put it during the "Rencontres Internationales" at Bouaké in 1962:

The African is like a hunter; he foresees nothing; makes all dispositions in the last moment. He is quite bewildered when asked what tomorrow will bring. . . . The questions which we ask ourselves here don't interest him at all. For example, he would not waste a thought on the issue as to what Africa's language should or might be tomorrow.[71]

Furthermore, and most importantly for purposes of this discussion, orality sets definite limits upon the control of space. It explains why the viable homogeneous community had to be the small, linguistically and ethnically unified community, and why vaster political ensembles, usually created by conquest, tended to disintegrate after the death of the conqueror through segmentation, fission, migration, or other processes of fragmentation. References to precolonial African "states" and "empires"

---

trated on oral propaganda and meetings and relied only slightly on the press and printed party propaganda.

[71] *Les Religions Africaines Traditionnelles* (Paris, 1965), p. 52. Similarly, Richard Wright observes in *Black Power: A Record of Reactions in a Land of Pathos* (New York, 1954), p. 222, that "the African did not strain to feel that which was not yet in existence; he exerted his will to make what happened happen again. His was a circular kind of time: the present had to be made up like the past. Dissatisfaction was not the mainspring of his emotional life: enjoyment of that which he had once enjoyed was the compulsion."

See to a similar effect M. Gelfand in *Medicine and Custom in Africa* (London, 1964); D. Westermann, *The African Today and Tomorrow* (London, 1949), and Redfield, *op.cit.*, pp. 120, 125, that life arrangements in essentially nonliterate societies are permeated by the conviction that the present does and should repeat what was and will be.

are thus misleading in most instances, at least if these
terms are associated with such traditional Western connotations as the ideas of territorial sovereignty, the
nation, citizenship, and secularism. This is well explained in Trimingham's analysis of the state system in
the Western Sudan:

> To write of kingdoms and empires implies the exist-
> ence of centralized states, but it is necessary to take
> what Africans consider constitutes a political group.
> There were two levels of political relation: the local
> group and a ruling lineage. The real rulers of the
> Sudan were not kings and emperors but patriarchs of
> families, councils of elders, and chiefs of villages on
> the one hand, and the heads of superimposed clans on
> the other . . . [the second] type of political authority
> was superimposed without seriously impairing the
> authority of the other system. . . . The state of Mali
> was such a superimposed lineage, whether it consisted
> of the primitive community from which it originated
> and in which it ended or that amorphous political
> sphere called the Mali empire. The states had no
> names and were known to the Arab world by the
> ruler's title such as Gana or Mali.[72]

The concept of dominion that developed here did not
refer either to a political unity, or to a territorial sovereignty. Hundreds of political groups at all stages of
development coexisted within e.g., the sphere of Mali
which had neither well-defined boundaries, a capital
city, nor any ethnic or cultural homogeneity. This and
other "steppe empires" emerge from the records rather

[72] *A History of Islam in West Africa* (London, 1963), pp. 34f. For
classifications of Africa's political systems see the work of M. Herskovits,
E. E. Evans-Pritchard, P. Murdock, Lucy Mair, and I. Schapera, among
others.

92

as loose agglomerations of kinship groups having little in common except the mythical recognition of a far-off suzerain, Trimingham writes, and their rapid rise, premature expansion, and swift disintegration was often coterminous with the biographies of the personalities that called them into being. The Mossi states, by contrast, which did not accept Islam, remained remarkably stable under dynasties that still survive.[73] Here as well as there, however, the real government was carried on throughout the centuries by local kinship and tribal organizations, and these too—it is important to remark as one watches contemporary changes in the configuration of modern African states—could dispense with the notion of "territorial sovereignty." For the constant element in the traditional states of Africa was not land but villages, i.e., the residential groups which could change their location under a great variety of compelling circumstances like "ships preserving identity in motion."[74]

[73] For richly suggestive analyses of these societies see Leo Frobenius, *Und Afrika Sprach*, 4 vols. (Berlin, 1912), II, chap. 8, "Ein Geschlecht von Kaisern und Koenigen"; and Elliott P. Skinner, *The Mossi of the Upper Volta: The Political Development of a Sudanese People* (Stanford, Cal., 1964).

[74] This image is used by J. A. Barnes in describing the Ngoni communities in Rhodesia. See Elizabeth Colson and Max Gluckman, eds., *Seven Tribes of British Central Africa* (London, 1951), pp. 196ff. Cp. Charles Monteil, *Les Bambara du Segou et du Kaarta* (Paris, 1924), for the view that the concept of "boundary" as it is understood in the West is unknown or incomprehensible to the Black. Diedrich Westermann, *Geschichte Afrikas, Staatenbildungen suedlich der Sahara* (Cologne, 1952), p. 390, writes (in connection particularly with the Congo Empire): "As in all African states, the frontiers were undetermined and fluctuating." Speaking of the Mvata Jumvo, this scholar observes that his residence was actually a camp that changed its location at each enthronement (p. 388). Westermann, *The African Today and Tomorrow*, pp. 28f, 129ff, to the effect that the significance of the African's attachment to land must not be exaggerated; the exhaustion of the soil, fear of malevolent spirits, disease, threats by neighbors, and great upheavals such as the Arab slave trade were some of the factors causing

Most African languages have been reduced to writing in the course of the last decades—decades that have also witnessed the assembling of hundreds of folk societies within the boundaries of about forty modern Western-type states and the writing of multiple constitutions. But today, as in Rattray's days, a simple maxim recently announced by an Ibo writer appears to hold: "If you want to know what we believe in, watch how we live";[75] for the fundamental informing principles shared by all Africans are neither these written instruments—most already either suspended or so critically amended and modified as to have become rather meaningless[76]—nor attachment to land, but rather the ancient trusted references of kinship and religion, the one inseparable from the other and both incomprehensible outside the context of nonliteracy. As Busia explains it, the primary loyalties have always been centered on family, lineage, and tribe, and this type of solidarity, universal through-

migration. Quarrels within the community, resulting in fission and fragmentation, supplied others.

[75] Stephen U. O. Anyaibe, "The Wisdom of My People," MS read by this author in 1967. Further advice designed to compensate for the absence of writing as a source of meaningful knowledge about things African is contained in the invitation to listen to proverbs, nocturnal tales, folklore, and jokes, i.e., "the dynamic encyclopaedia of my people" with which the mind of each child is saturated through repeated telling; to watch the naming system in terms of which a human being should grow into the name he carries, and to observe the idols that are being worshipped.

[76] See Amos J. Peaslee, ed., *Constitutions of Nations*, 3rd ed. (The Hague, 1965), vol. I, *Africa*, and a review of this work by John H. Spencer in *AJIL*, vol. 61 (Oct. 1967), in which the latter remarks, rightly, that African constitutional traditions are too frail and the internal struggles too acute to warrant confidence that a published text can long retain its relevancy. On the pervasive presence of traditional political motifs see among many other authorities, Jean Buchmann, *Le Problème des Structures Politiques en Afrique Noire*, Université Lovanium, Institut de Recherches Economiques et Sociales, Notes et Documents, no. 20/SP-I (Leopoldville, Republic of the Congo, 1961), esp. pp. 35ff.

out the continent, pervades the present, releasing grave tensions in the form of civil war, murder, and massacre, while at the same time providing as "the most persistent legacy of the traditional political system" a kind of tribal cohesion "which the various forms of the one-party organization and other political experiments seek to preserve and express within the larger unity of the state," and without which "no president or prime minister in Africa today can keep his place for long."[77] This state of affairs has led one of the most perceptive and erudite African scholars to conclude that "a kind of trusteeship is being exercised today by the traditional and customary

[77] This author counsels against repressing the tribal spirit and favors emancipation from Western models of political organization. After expressing great pride for having evolved the "one-party system"—"now the accepted pattern of government in a large part of independent Africa"—Nkrumah explains how he had had to combat not only tribalism but the African tradition that a man's first duty is to his family. Kwame Nkrumah, *Dark Days in Ghana* (New York, 1968), pp. 66ff. See also Ibrahim Abu-Lughod and Herbert Spiro in *Patterns of African Development: Five Comparisons,* ed. Herbert Spiro (Englewood Cliffs, N.J., 1967). Abu-Lughod points out that "the state" is losing its mystique in Africa, at least as far as its connection with territorial boundaries is concerned, and that African states look upon sovereignty as a device, or as a preliminary means toward the achievement of higher objectives (pp. 58ff). Spiro stresses the role of nomadism and other traditional attitudes to land as principal factors in this orientation. Busia, too, insists that the concept of citizenship is more closely associated with kinship than with territory.

For another representative African view of the living all-African heritage, see Kenneth Kaunda, *Zambia Shall Be Free: An Autobiography,* African Writers Series 4 (London and Ibadan, 1962); and p. 163, Appendix 1, by Stewart Gore-Browne. After commenting on the Bemba, Barotse, Lunda, and Ngoni—the principal component tribes of the new nation—and on their differences which caused incessant intertribal wars, the affinities are identified as: 1) the same approach to land problems; 2) the same kind of religious belief, i.e., a form of ancestor worship; 3) nonliteracy; 4) a firm belief in magic and witchcraft; 5) tribalism; 6) the same negative attitude to continuous labor.

See also Gabriel A. Almond and James S. Coleman, *Politics of the Developing Areas* (Princeton, 1960), p. 301, on the need to locate new forms of political organization by utilizing the principle of pluralism as a counterforce to dictatorship.

cadres over the modern State" in many African societies. Even great westernized cities are thus apt to revert to the security of ancient time-tested ethnic groupings—this observer remarks—when the effectiveness of modern municipal and national institutions is being put in issue by a crisis such as that which plunged the Congo into chaos.[78]

In Africa's systems of political and social organization in which the stress is put on the group and its solidarity and in which all human relations are dominated by tribal and kinship considerations, the individual counts for very little. Not only could he not become the carrier of civic rights and responsibilities,[79] but he could not

[78] Christian Vieyra, "Structures Politiques Traditionelles et Structures Politiques Modernes," in *Tradition et Modernisme en Afrique Noire* (Paris, 1965), pp. 203, 207. Julian Huxley, *Africa View* (London and New York, 1931), pp. 135ff, has some interesting ideas on the shaping of Africa's future: "Do not let us forget that the African in contact with modern ideas and economic forces is in a very different plight from any member of a Western civilization, even the humblest and most downtrodden. We have our ponderous system of ideas, rooted in centuries of tradition, actualized in powerful institutions. There are new ideas and forces that threaten the stability of our world, but for one thing they have sprung out of the tradition of that same world, and for another they are not organized; our world is not in contact with another and more powerful world of existence. Whereas the world of the African native is in contact with a world whose forces are immeasurably more powerful, whose science is a greater magic, whose ideas are on an altogether different plane of coherence and continuity." Having the chaos of African towns especially in mind, Huxley wonders whether something analogous to the medieval guild system would not prove to be the best way out: "It is certain that the African needs some organization which will appeal to his strong social solidarity and group loyalty; and that, in the present stage of his development at least, he is very susceptible to the influence of symbolism and ceremonial, both of which can be made to play a considerable part in a guild system. He already possesses something analogous in his widespread dance organizations, and it should not be impossible to extend the idea to industry."
[79] *Supra*, pp. 40ff; p. 107. See also S.K.B. Asante, "Law and the Society in Ghana," in *Africa and Law: Developing Legal Systems in African Commonwealth Nations*, ed. Thomas W. Hutchison et al. (Madison, Wis. and London, 1968), pp. 130ff, that in the traditional order the accent was on the group as the basic juridical unit, and that modern

emancipate himself mentally or physically from family and lineage ties. Thus he has always been first and foremost several people's relative and several people's contemporary, as Yomo Kenyatta writes about the Kikuyu in *Facing Mount Kenya*.[80] And Noni Jabavu relays the same truth as she describes life among her "umbilicals" in South Africa. "You are not left to be merely your private self: you represent others or others represent you so that you are ever conscious of relative status, classification, interdependent relationships in terms of which your conduct is being judged."[81]

Ghanaian developments do not substantially detract from this commitment to social collectivism. Although the individual person is officially recognized today as the carrier of rights and responsibilities, he continues to stress his basic traditional obligation, namely, to support and assist members of his extended family or his village. Constitutional bills of right, assuring the individual of his powers and duties as either an autonomous human being or a citizen, have therefore no organic connection with traditional African modes of political organization. Cp. the record of the discussions at the Eighth International African Seminar at the Haile Selassie I University, Addis Ababa, January 1966, as summarized and amplified by Allott, Epstein, and Gluckman in the Introduction to Gluckman, ed., *Ideas and Procedures in African Customary Law*, pp. 47ff in particular. On this occasion it was considered questionable whether the Occidental idea of "the person" has an equivalent in African law, and whether the term "corporation" carries the technical connotations attributed to it in European law.

The absence in African law of distinctions between crimes, torts, and breaches of agreement as these are recognized in English law is in many respects a function of the nonrecognition of the individual as a distinct legal entity. And the same explanation would seem to hold in regard to contract law; for although Africans have a highly developed sense of social obligation in the context of kinship relations and property rights, they have not been encouraged by their mode of thought and social system to develop such concepts as intention, consensus, adequacy of consideration, negligence, duress, etc. For comments on some of these issues see Y. P. Ghai, "Customary Contracts and Transactions in Kenya," *ibid.*, pp. 333ff.

In the absence of an understanding of "contract" as developed by the civil law and the common law, constitutionalism is bound to be an alien uncongenial reference. Cp. *supra*, pp. 36ff and *infra*, pp. 103ff.

[80] London, 1938 (1959), p. 309.

[81] *Drawn In Colour: African Contrasts* (London, 1961), p. 51. To the

97

No social or political arrangement and no order of thoughts and assumptions can be understood outside the context of Africa's shared religious heritage. As Busia reminds us, it is impossible to separate the sacred from the profane in this life style, and no intruding Asian or European faith has materially modified the all-pervasive sense of total dependence upon supernatural powers, magic, witchcraft and above all the ever-present and omnipotent ancestors.[82]

Law and organization derive their inner African meanings from this constellation of felt truths. Their major determinants—each incompatible with conceptual schemes prevalent in the Occident—have been tribalism, a view of time as undifferentiated in terms of past, present, and future, and a nonliterate mode of thinking complete with its own systems of logic, causality, and rationality. Furthermore, the records of social customs and government reflect the strength of the conviction that the experience of being human is tantamount to a continuous, intricately regulated participation in the plant and animal world; for each of the

---

same effect see Léopold Senghor, *On African Socialism* (New York, 1964), pp. 93ff. Cp. J. Faublée, "Madagascar au XIXe siècle: Esquisse d'histoire economique et sociale," in *Journal of World History*, V, no. 2 (1959), p. 466: "Dans cette société . . . l'individu n'existe pas. Il n'y a que des personnages. Le rôle de chacun est determiné par sa famille, et par sa place dans celle-ci."

Christian Vieyra, "Structures Politiques Traditionnelles et Structures Politiques Modernes," *loc.cit.*, pp. 201, 202: "Dans cette société l'individu était noyé dans le tout comme cette société elle même baignait dans le religieux et l'autorité y revêtait très souvent la forme du type religieux ou mixte. . . . cette conception de l'interêt de la société a conduit ici à la *subordination de l'individu au groupe* par des liens assez rigides." (Italics added.)

See Kenneth S. Carlston, *Social Theory and African Tribal Organization: The Development of Socio-Legal Theory* (Urbana, Ill. and London, 1968), for stimulating analyses of the relevance of African organizational forms for the construction of general theory.

[82] *Op.cit.*, esp. chap. 1.

myriad of social arrangements which the African genius has brought forth receives its actual and symbolic validation from the need to propitiate the dread and boon dispensing forces that emanate relentlessly from spiritual and natural forces beyond human control. The tribe, the chiefdom, or the state thus emerges in this culture world as a metaphysical entity, endowed with a mythical charter; or, as Leo Frobenius once described it, as a continuous rite, unifying the living and the dead, the occult and the mundane. In such circumstances, chiefs and kings actually had limited powers, even though in Western eyes many appeared to conduct themselves as "divine-right monarchs": the real power and responsibility for the performance of their duties, which included in many instances ritual murders on a mass scale, rested everywhere with nonempirical sources commonly located in the world of spirits and ancestors. And the same assumptions presided over the administration of so-called stateless societies and anarchies, of age sets, age villages, clans, secret societies, mythical unions between different societies, and boundary-transcendent spirit realms. In all African collectivisms the rulers as well as the ruled acknowledged the absolute superiority of impersonal, magical, essentially malevolent, powers. Caught up in a syndrome in which neither life nor death were individualized, they were capable of absorbing violence as, for example, in the form of regicide, succession wars, or human sacrifices, without in any way forfeiting the sense of belonging to a harmonious society.[83]

[83] These aspects have received great attention by early explorers, modern scholars, and native informants. Among numerous accounts see H. Ling Roth, *Great Benin* (Halifax, 1903); Réné Caillié, *Travels Through Central Africa to Timbuctoo*, 2 vols. (London [1830], 1968), I, 153; Richard F. Burton, *A Mission to Gelele, King of Dahome*, 2 vols. (London, 1893); the works of Captain R. S. Rattray on Ashanti; Jacob U. Egharevba, *A Short History of Benin*, 4th ed. (Ibadan, 1968); Mar-

99

The modern public order continues to rest on many traditionally significant myths, symbols, and beliefs, and individual lives in all sectors of society, by no means exclusive of the ruling elites, are still being fashioned not by self-determination but rather by a deep consciousness of dependence upon the workings of magic, ju-ju, witchcraft, and sorcery not easily compatible with any form of political organization known to the West. Indeed reliance upon occult forces and the modes of causality and reasoning implicit in such trust, as well as fear of becoming prey to witchcraft or sorcery, is said to be increasing as the area of human freedom (with its possibilities of human error and misfortune) is expanding, and as men become uncertain of their real roles in life.[84] For example, the official disestablishment of tribal

---

gery Perham, ed., *Ten Africans* (London, 1936; Evanston, Ill., 1963); Audrey I. Richards, ed., *East African Chiefs: A Study of Political Development in Some Uganda and Tanganyika Tribes* (London, 1959); *Les Religions Africaines Traditionnelles, loc.cit.*, pp. 75ff in particular.

On the Poro and other secret societies, see Frederick William Hugh Migeod, *A View of Sierra Leone* (New York, 1927), pp. 234ff; Kenneth Little, "The Political Function of the Poro," *Africa*, October 1965, pp. 349ff, and January 1966, pp. 62ff; F. W. Butt-Thompson, *Secret Societies in West Africa* (London 1929); P. E. Joset, *Les Sociétés Secrètes des Hommes, Léopards en Afrique Noire* (Paris, 1955); Kenneth L. Little, *The Mende of Sierra Leone* (London, 1951), pp. 240, 274; C. K. Meek, *Law and Authority in a Nigerian Tribe: A Study in Indirect Rule* (London, 1950), chaps. 1, 2; on the powers of the all-pervading Egbo society in southern Nigeria see K. O. Dike, *Trade and Politics in the Niger Delta, 1830-1855* (Oxford, 1956), pp. 37ff. On the organization of "spirit realms" in the Zambezi region see G. Kingsley Garbett, "Spirit Mediums as Mediators in Korekore Society," in *Spirit Mediumship and Society in Africa*, ed. John Beattie and John Middleton (New York, 1969).

[84] John Middleton and E. H. Winter, eds., *Witchcraft and Sorcery in East Africa* (London, 1963), p. 25: "Most Africans see the situation as having deteriorated: their defenses against witches have been weakened and the practice of sorcery is on the rise." For West Africa, see P. C. Lloyd, *Africa in Social Change* (London, 1967), pp. 244, 250, 262. The psychological and social problems implicit in this orientation have received persuasive treatment in the works of many modern African

war and other institutionalized forms of conflict, together with the demise of the masculine ideal of the
warrior, have left a vacuum favorable not only to fetish-
ism and sorcery but also to manipulation by forces inim-
ical to the cause of the modern independent state.[85]

Reflections on the present and future role of law in
Africa south of Sahara should issue from an understand-

---

novelists and dramatists, e.g., Achebe and Soyinka. See also the cover-
age of witchcraft and sorcery cases in the daily African press. It should
be remarked that the practice of killing people because of alleged
witchcraft or sorcery offenses has been outlawed by modern African
governments.

[85] Emanuel John Hevi, a former African student in Communist
China, reports on subversion schools for Africans in Communist
China and on Peking-supported camps for guerrillas where Congolese
freedom fighters, trained in China since 1961, acted as instructors. Commenting on methods of manipulating African beliefs in witchcraft as
they were being taught in these centers to Africans, he writes: "The
teacher's introduction to one lesson was: 'you know that in certain
underdeveloped countries of Africa, the people are highly superstitious,
and one can gain political objectives only by playing on these super-
stitions.' After pointing out the need to spread those same methods
which helped to kindle the Mau Mau revolt in Kenya, and stressing
that one single witch doctor operating among primitive peoples can
achieve more than a dozen lecturers, the teacher continued: 'You see
how far we can get if he is a Communist.' The teacher explained how
superstitious tribal men could be swayed by making a skeleton speak
through a microphone hidden inside it. A sample of what the skeleton
could say was: 'I am your ancestral spirit. I command you to go and
kill the British governor tonight and bring me his head. If you fail,
your family will always live under the evil eye.'" *The Dragon's Embrace: The Chinese Communists and Africa* (New York, 1967), pp. 100ff.

See J. M. Lee, *African Armies and Civil Order* (London, 1969), pp.
49ff, 66ff on Communist efforts to foment rebellion and unrest within
African states by activating some of these traditional beliefs; and for
numerous references to flights into violence and destruction on the
part of disoriented or frustrated elements of the population; p. 184 for
the view that many of the recent coups are properly viewed as "gestures
of frustration." Also Fulbert Youlou, ex-President of Congo-Brazzaville,
J'Accuse La Chine (Paris, 1966), for an interesting, albeit partisan,
account of Chinese, Cuban, and Algerian activities in behalf of "the
revolution," and of Nkrumah's role as "Mao's African Accomplice."

On the revival of secret societies and the emergence of "assassination
industries" (*industries de tueurs*) see P. E. Joset, *Les Sociétés Secrètes
des Hommes Léopards en Afrique Noire* (Paris, 1955).

101

ing of the life style and mode of thought with which recent generations have identified. If we were to apply the measure of the Western thought system, we would have to conclude that law as we know it was unknown in this culture world.[86] Similarly, it would be a mistake

[86] See Bohannan's essay, with its stimulating definitions, in Paul Bohannan, ed., *Law and Warfare: Studies in the Anthropology of Conflict* (New York, 1967); J. Keuning, "The Study of Law in African Countries," *Higher Education and Research in the Netherlands*, VII, no. 1 (1963), 3ff; Robert Redfield, *op.cit.*; A. St. J. Hannigan, "The Imposition of Western Law Forms upon Primitive Societies," *Comparative Studies in Society and History*, IV, 1961-62, 1ff; Gabriel d'Arboussier, "L'Evolution de la Législation dans Les Pays Africains d'Expression Française et à Madagascar," in H. and L. Kuper, eds., *African Law: Adaptation and Development* (Los Angeles, 1966), p. 165ff for a persuasive explanation of why African customary law should be viewed as totally different from "customary law" as this is understood in Europe, and for the general conclusion that concepts developed in one culture ought not to be assumed or utilized in another culture and in different contexts. To the same effect, see Jan Vansina, "A Traditional Legal System: The Kuba" in the same volume, p. 117: since Kuba law is very different from any European system of law, it is illusory to try to define it in terms of European legal concepts. Also Antony Allott, *Essays in African Law, with Special Reference to the Law of Ghana* (London, 1960), p. 67, who points out that one cannot find in Africa the kind of juristic thinking about law in the abstract that one finds in Europe.

See Paul Bohannan, *Justice and Judgment among the Tiv* (London, 1957), for a forceful statement of the view that Tiv law can be understood only if it is presented in the context of the ideas and processes in terms of which the Tiv think, and that attempts to translate the Tiv folk system into categories and concepts of another system are deplorable. To the same general effect see this author's *Social Anthropology* (New York, 1963), p. 283, where he states that no a priori theoretical model can be assumed. See also André Leroy-Gourhan and Jean Poirier, *Ethnologie de L'Union Française*, vol. I, *Afrique* (Paris, 1953), p. 340 to the effect that it is illusory to see parallelisms between forms of political organization in Africa and the West.

For the most persuasive refutation of the view that law carries the same meanings in Africa as it does in Europe if one adheres to the definition of law given by H.L.A. Hart in *The Concept of Law* (Oxford, 1961), see Lee, *op.cit.*, pp. 11ff, 17, 88.

For opposite views see Max Gluckman, ed., *Ideas and Procedures in African Customary Law* (London, 1969), especially the introduction on problems of research by A. N. Allott, A. L. Epstein, and M. Gluckman; also Max Gluckman, *The Judicial Process Among the Barotse of Northern Rhodesia* (Manchester, 1955). Other treatments are found in

to assume that the mere enactment of laws and establishment of constitutions in the nineteenth and twentieth
centuries has had, or will have, the same effects as in
England or France, for example.[87] Syncretisms between
imported legal systems and customary indigenous orders
have certainly made their appearance from early colonial
times onward, often under most careful supervision, as
for example under the direction of Sir Samuel Lewis, a
barrister from Sierra Leone who puzzled over the destiny
of the jury system in a society ruled by kinship principles, and who realized, in his dual concern for the
integrity of the English common law on the one hand
and of the native order on the other, that one might
have to recognize bona fide cannibalism.[88] All areas of
African life are today encompassed in legal categories,
some suggested by English law, civil law, Roman Dutch
Law, Hindu law and Islamic law,[89] others newly fashioned in response to social, economic, and political factors peculiar to African conditions. After surveying the
present state of the law in formerly British territories, a
sympathetic British observer has concluded, however,
that the rule of law "has not fared well" in the face of
preventive detention acts and suspensions of bills of
rights.[90] Challenged everywhere by the executive power
as expressed in the army, the police, and above all the

Julius Levin, *Studies in African Native Law* (Capetown and Philadelphia, 1947); A. R. Radcliffe-Brown, "Primitive Law," in *Encyclopedia of the Social Sciences* (New York, 1933), vol. IX.

[87] Cp. Jay Gordon, "African Law and the Historian," in *Journal of
African History*, VIII, no. 2 (1967), 335-46.

[88] See John D. Hargreaves, *A Life of Sir Samuel Lewis* (London,
1958). In Kenya the right to trial by jury has been eliminated on the
ground that there are not enough jurors to hear all capital cases (*New
York Times*, October 2, 1966).

[89] *Supra*, sections on the West, the Middle East; *infra*, India.

[90] L.C.B. Gower, *Independent Africa: The Challenge to the Legal
Profession* (Cambridge, Mass., 1967), p. 78.

ruling personality in the state, viewed in many circles either as a legacy of colonialism or as an ineffective device, law appears fundamentally uncongenial where a traditional respect for individual liberties is lacking, or where it is not understood as the uncompromising anti-force to violence.[91]

Here as in related fields of political organization it is likely that certain indigenous pre-European approaches to conflict resolution will reassert themselves in times to come; and this is indeed what seems to be happening already in many parts of the continent. Keuning's experience in Nigeria in 1961 taught him that the judges of the customary courts are never or hardly ever conversant with the decisions of the "English courts" (as the courts of English origin are still called there). It also led him to conclude that some ninety percent of all disputes according to customary law are dealt with by the customary courts, and that customary unwritten law will therefore continue to play a major role, especially because it is flexible almost by definition and has proved capable of absorbing changing conditions. But this body

[91] *Ibid.*, pp. 73ff, 80ff on Nkrumah's neurotic suspicion of law, lawyers, and judges.

Native dispositions in combination with Communist approaches to the role of law in society may explain why Sékou Touré subscribes to the view that "people" acting through their "party" are superior to the law, and why the law of Guinea today is characterized more by its repressive functions than by its restorative qualities. In presenting this conclusion, Charles F. Andrain points out that during 1959 and 1960 Sékou Touré condemned to death many Guineans who committed minor thefts; see "The Political Thought of Sékou Touré," in *African Political Thought: Lumumba, Nkrumah, and Touré*, ed. W.A.E. Skurnik, Monograph Series in World Affairs, vol. 5, no. 2 (Denver, Colo., 1968), pp. 125ff.

For an important discussion of the roles, respectively, of conflict and law in the integration of African social and political systems see Michael Barkun, *Law Without Sanctions: Order in Primitive Societies and the World Community* (New Haven and London, 1968), esp. pp. 36-58. This issue receives further consideration *infra*, pp. 110ff.

of law, he insists, can only be understood against the background of "how it used to be."[92] Greatly similar observations are presented by Lloyd Fallers, as when he writes: "What we see in operation today is a system of courts and body of law which has deep roots in traditional society and culture." These native traditions of litigation form, in his view, one of Africa's greatest cultural achievements, and he believes it would be a pity not to make use of them wherever possible.[93]

Despite the diversity of ethnic units and customary legal arrangements it is possible to speak of "African law," especially when one sees it in juxtaposition to Occidental legal systems. As the Nigerian legalist T. O. Elias explains it, "there are surprising similarities, at least in important essentials, in bodies of African customary law as divergent as those of the Yorubas, the Bantus, the Sudanese, the Ashantis, and the Congolese."[94] Everywhere it is the product of nonliterate ways

[92] *Loc.cit.* Cp. also Thierry Verheist, *Safeguarding African Customary Law: Judicial and Legislative Processes for its Adaptation and Integration,* Occasional Paper no. 7, African Studies Center, Univ. of California (Los Angeles, 1968), pp. 8-12 on the interaction between customary law and modern written law in Congo-Kinshasa where 9/10ths of the population still cling to their customary status, and where customary courts remain numerous and active, rendering 300,000 to 400,000 judgments per year.

[93] "Customary Law in the New African States," in *African Law: New Law for New Nations,* ed. Hans W. Baade and Robinson O. Everett (New York, 1963), pp. 8off, also pp. 71ff.

[94] *The Nature of African Customary Law* (Manchester, England, 1956), p. 3. A. N. Allott, *Essays in African Law, with Special Reference to the Law of Ghana* (London, 1960), chap. 3, "The Unity of African Law," pp. 64ff, for a discussion of differences; also A. N. Allott, ed., *The Future of Law in Africa* (London, 1960). The argument that one cannot generalize about things African, often heard in anthropological circles, is best answered by reference to Paul Vinogradoff's treatment of Greek law: the city states had greatly varied constitutions and legal systems, but the fundamental informing principles were nonetheless essentially the same. *Outlines of Historical Jurisprudence,* vol. II, *The Jurisprudence of the Greek City* (Oxford, 1922), pp. 3-6.

of thinking, emanating not from abstract juristic or philosophical cerebrations but from social practice,[95] and nowhere can it be separated from the kinship system and belief in supernatural agencies.[96] That is to say, the African himself is not consciously aware of what is law, what religion, what taboo, and what government, since he does not "departmentalize" his thoughts and activities. And those who set out to write about a particular community's law end up writing about all aspects of its life and culture; for one and the same set of laws has customarily assured the workings of government, regu-

[95] Fallers found in his study of the customary law of Busoga District in the Eastern province of Uganda (which he regards as illustrative of indigenous law in other areas formerly under British administration) that judges were unwilling or unable to discuss abstract rules of law, preferring instead to speak of the facts of a particular case. *Loc.cit.*, p. 82.

[96] Rupert East, ed. and trans., *Akiga's Story: The Tiv Tribe as Seen by One of Its Members* (London, 1939), p. 376, on the pervasive role of witchcraft in judicial trials and discussions; see also Stephen U.O. Anyaibe, *op.cit.*, pp. 173ff, on the use of "the drink and confess drug," the "touch and confess shrine," and different forms of hypnosis, as common techniques of discovering a culprit who refuses to turn himself in. For the use of "dream evidence," see Robert G. Armstrong, "A West African Inquest," *American Anthropologist*, vol. 56 (December 1954), pp. 1,051; also "The Idoma Court-of-Lineages in Law and Political Structure," in Arthur Wallace, ed., *Selected Papers of the Fifth International Congress of Anthropological and Ethnological Sciences* (Philadelphia, 1960), pp. 390ff. Cp. C. K. Meek, *Law and Authority in a Nigerian Tribe* (London, 1950), pp. 20ff; "The Sacred Sanction," pp. 238ff, for a description of a trial and interesting comments on the interpenetration of judges, priests, and diviners—the latter often also dealers in poison. Meek, *A Sudanese Kingdom* (London, 1931), p. 346, on the diviner who gives expression to the legal conceptions of the people since he is recognized as the agent of supernatural powers. Gluckman ed., *Ideas and Procedures in African Customary Law*, pp. 35ff that dependence on occult support will continue in modern times, particularly in cases where the offense complained of is itself "occult," as in charges of witchcraft and sorcery, or where the contending parties before the judges are too strong for the judges to give a decision against one of them—in short judicial "reason" is bound to be helpless whenever fear exists that occult forces are at work.

106

lated crops, kept locusts away, prevented epidemics, and above all appeased the ancestors.[97]

The primary function of this all-encompassing law is the conservation of the community and the maintenance of public order, not the development and protection of individual rights. This explains why the identity of the disputants or the accused, the particular episode in question, and the precise sequence of events are often not regarded as strictly relevant for the resolution of a conflict (the exception being cases involving witchcraft), and why situations are frequently judged in terms of what in the West would be "appearance" rather than "reality."[98] What is important is that someone be iden-

---

[97] Meek, *A Sudanese Kingdom*, p. 347; G.W.B. Huntingford, *The Nandi of Kenya: Tribal Control in a Pastoral Society* (London, 1953), pp. 25ff, on a special type of ritual tribal expert who mediates between man and the spirit world by virtue of his magical powers, is consulted on the state of crops, and on when or whether, to wage war. G. S. Snell, *Nandi Customary Law* (London, 1954), p. 1: "It would, of course, be both impossible and misleading to abstract into explicit categories the cosmological, religious and ethical notions of the Nandi as though they were expressly thought out dogmas; as with primitive tribes in general, their "philosophy" and religion were an indistinct combination of attitudes, ideas and beliefs and they drew no sharp distinction between the moral law and the law of the tribe such as has long been familiar in Western societies." Also, pp. 15ff on manifestations of magico-political authority. See R. S. Rattray, *Ashanti* (Oxford, 1923); *Religion and Art in Ashanti* (Oxford, 1927); and *Ashanti Law and Constitution* (London, 1956), for numerous illustrations of this proposition.

[98] J. F. Holleman, *Shona Customary Law* (London and New York, 1952), p. 282, for illustrations. For a particularly sensitive and artistic account of the workings of law and justice, see Isak Dinesen, *Out of Africa* (New York, 1938), p. 100: "The ideas of justice of Europe and Africa are not the same and those of the one world are unbearable to the other. To the African there is but one way of counterbalancing the catastrophes of existence, it shall be done by replacement; he does not look for the motive of an action. Whether you lie in wait for your enemy and cut his throat in the dark; or you fell a tree, and a thoughtless stranger passes by and is killed: so far as punishment goes, to the Native mind, it is the same thing. A loss has been brought upon the

tified as the disturber of peace and harmony within the group, for it is presumed that somebody must have erred if something has gone wrong, since accidents or other untoward events are not accommodated in traditional African approaches to causality. Furthermore, authorities seem to agree that the African cares less for the outcome of the decision than for the proceedings themselves; not so much for what is being said than for how it is being said and who is saying it.

Litigation and law enforcement are identified with a profusion of assemblies, councils, courts, arbitration boards, oracles, moots, age-group agencies, chiefs, elders, and a bewildering variety of special intermediaries functioning outside established institutions[99]—all a living tribute to that African talent for shaping organizations and maintaining peace in small communities to which

---

community and must be made up for, somewhere, by somebody. The Native will not give time or thought to the weighing up of guilt or desert. . . . But he will devote himself, in endless speculations, to the method by which the crime or disaster shall be weighed up in sheep and goats—time does not count to him." And see toward the end of this chapter how authoritatively a chief resolved a threatening dispute to everyone's satisfaction.

[99] The illustrations here are too numerous to mention. See *supra*, p. p. 99, n. 83 for some examples, esp. Huntingford, *op.cit.*, pp. 31ff; Fallers, *loc.cit.*; Meek, Little, Rattray, and Richards. For a particularly vivid account of a "palaver," held in Lunda territory, composed of about one hundred people and presided over by a woman chief, see D. Livingstone, *Missionary Travels and Researches in South Africa* (New York, 1858), p. 296: "The talker was then called, and I was asked who was my spokesman. Having pointed to Kolimbota, who knew their dialect best, the palaver began in due form. I explained the real objects I had in view, without any attempt to mystify or appear in any other character than my own. . . . Kolimbota repeated to Nyamoana's talker what I had said to him. He delivered it all verbatim to her husband, who repeated it again to her. It was thus all rehearsed four times over, in a tone loud enough to be heard by the whole party of auditors. The response came back by the same roundabout route, beginning at the lady to her husband, etc."

allusion has already been made. The ultimate source of law-abidingness, judgment, and sacred sanction is the will and wisdom of the ancestors, commonly circulating among the generations through the medium of proverbs, parables, ritualized speech, and other formulas of capsuled knowledge.

These and other African approaches to law and government matured during millennia of exclusive reliance upon the spoken word,[100] for in the absence of written codes, collections of rules and precedents, and a body of jurisprudential theorems, all stages in the various processes of judicial or political decision-making had to be conveyed orally if they were to be communicated at all. As a Kikuyu saying has it, "We have no code apart from hearing the words of person and person";[101] and this commitment to listening is matched by a proverb from Botswana (formerly Bechuanaland) that "roosters must crow face to face," which means that both parties to a dispute must be present and given the chance to express themselves (a legal party here includes, of course, the kith and kin of those immediately concerned). Furthermore, when ceremonious discussions of a judicial or quasi-judicial nature are taking place, interruptions are seldom allowed. Even when one discussant has stopped speaking, Father Tempels reports in *La Philosophie Bantoue*,[102] the chief or judge would ask: Have you finished speaking? And only then would he give the floor to the other side. Rules of procedure, then, are by

[100] *Supra*, pp. 89ff.

[101] H. E. Lambert, *Kikuyu Social and Political Institutions* (London, 1956), p. 118. See also I. Schapera, *A Handbook of Tswana Law and Custom* (London, 1955), and the same author's collection of Tswana legal proverbs.

[102] English translation: *Bantu Philosophy* (Paris, 1959), p. 30.

109

no means missing, but talk tends to be voluminous as well as roundabout, devious and imprecise from the Occidental point of view, all the more so as it frequently provides a safety valve for overstrained emotions and an alternative to physical violence.

The records of conflict resolution through regulated speech include certain other interesting customs. In cases in which vengeance, compensation, etc.,[103] are not allowed, ridicule and ritualized apologies may provide relief and sanction. Furthermore, no African society comes to mind that has not long depended upon the oath and the curse as part of its machinery of justice. Whole families or hierarchies of this type of spoken word, each one more potent than the other, have thus been developed in some tribes where they elicit more fear and respect than any "temporal" law; for the oath and the curse are of course functions of that trust in magic and witchery that is deeply imbedded in this intellectual tradition.[104] However, the major purpose of these, as well as of all other judicially important words, is conciliation. Indeed no aspect of African customary

[103] Punishments meted out by tribal courts naturally reflected the life style of societies that were not based on money economies and did not recognize e.g., murder as a particularly serious crime. Before the English introduced legal reforms, the courts of the elders in e.g., Kenya, could decree that thieves should have their hands chopped off in addition to restoring the stolen goods sevenfold; that witches be stoned to death or banished from tribal lands to perish among hostile neighbors, etc.

[104] See Middleton and Winter eds., *op.cit.*, for contemporary manifestations; also Lambert, *op.cit.*, on the use of oaths among the Kikuyu; George Bennett, *Journal of African History*, VIII, no. 3 (1967), 560ff for a review of the use of oaths in connection particularly with the Mau Mau disturbances. For West African practices see e.g. Rupert East, ed., *op.cit.*; Rattray, *Religion and Art in Ashanti*, pp. 148, 205f; *Ashanti*, pp. 151ff; also Lloyd, *op.cit.*, p. 36, for the role of Tiv experts in the art of manipulating rituals and the common belief that these men possess attributes of witchcraft; the works of Paul and Laura Bohannan on the Tiv; and authorities cited earlier.

law is as impressive—and as suggestive for a restatement of legal norms in modern times[105]—as the common understanding that disputes within the kinship-oriented community are resolved only when the feuding members are persauded in one way or another to return to their normal relationship. Charged with such a sweeping mandate, African judges are best viewed as arbitrators and conciliators who are allowed to draw upon all resources of society in order to execute their trust. And in this context the conclusion imposes itself that law and law enforcement are synonymous with society itself.[106]

The meanings carried by law and organization within the small, ethnically and linguistically unified community stipulate enmity and suspicion in intercommunity relations. Wars, feuds, raids, and other types of conflict have thus been endemic in this continent; in fact in the African world they are accepted as fixed institutions and organizing principles in their own right.[107] European ideas of unity and peace through law, or of federalism within a constitutional framework—all

[105] See to this effect N. A. Ollennu, "The Structure of African Judicial Authority and Problems of Evidence and Proof in Traditional Courts," in Gluckman, ed., *Ideas and Procedures in African Customary Law*, pp. 110ff. For a discussion of the task of traditional judges, see Gluckman, *The Judicial Process among the Barotse*, chap. 2.

[106] Cp. Jan Vansina, *loc.cit.*, in Kuper and Kuper, eds., *op.cit.*, p. 111, to the effect that there are no legal norms in Kuba society: the content of substantive law is no less than the totality of the institutions of the society.

[107] See specialized ethnographic studies for the place that war, the feud, the law of homicide, etc., occupied in each particular community. For a general discussion, see Bohannan, ed., *African Homicide and Suicide*. See P.E.H. Hair, "The Enslavement of Koelle's Informants," *Journal of African History*, VI, no. 2 (1965), pp. 193ff, for a documented study of intertribal wars, wars between sections of the same tribe, and inter-African enslavement through war, judicial process, sale by relatives, debt, razzia, and tribute in the context of the slave trade in the early nineteenth century. Peace and accord emerge from the records as exceptional conditions as in blood brotherhoods, joking relationships, and other ritualized forms, cf. *supra*.

the outgrowth of a long experience with the territorially conceived state and contractualism in international relations[108]—are thus fundamentally alien to Negro Africa. This incongruity between Occidental and African political systems, temporarily overcome in the brief period of colonial administration, has manifested itself since independence in the dissolution of all federal edifices erected by the English and the French in their respective territories.[109] The records of the various proceedings during which unions of one kind or another were negotiated into and out of existence permit the general conclusion that what the French ethnologist Jacques Richard-Molard has called "biological patriotism" has proved stronger than any desire either for peaceful political growth through expansion, or for economic advantage, progress, and reform. In formerly British East Africa where expatriate administrators and advisers tried to develop "common loyalties through common services" in communication, education, research, and economic and social welfare, the gap between technological unity and political unity proved to be too wide to be bridged. With independence attained, Kenya, Uganda, and Tanganyika extricated themselves promptly from the dense

[108] See Bozeman, *Politics and Culture in International History* (Princeton, 1960), pp. 162ff, 238ff, 438ff, for a treatment of this tradition.

[109] In regard to formerly British territories, see e.g. Record of Proceedings of a Seminar held at King's College, Lagos (August 8-15, 1960), Lionel Brett, ed., *Constitutional Problems of Federalism in Nigeria*, esp. Appendix II, "An Historical Account of the Evolution of Nigeria as a Political Unit," by S. O. Biobaku; Anthony H. Rwayemamu and Brack E.S. Brown, "Federation: An Unfinished Portrait," in *The Transformation of East Africa*, ed. Stanley Diamond and Frederick G. Burke (New York and London, 1966); Thomas M. Franck, *East African Unity Through Law* (New Haven and London, 1964). See also a particularly suggestive discussion of British colonial approaches to federalism in S. F. Nadel, *The Nuba* (London and New York, 1947), pp. 468ff.

112

network of complex legal enactments that had been
meant to provide "statutory uniformity," each deciding
to go its own way.[110]

Recent developments in all parts of Negro Africa,
especially in the local scenes of coups d'etat, mutinies,
revolutions, and civil wars, thus appear to suggest that
Western ideas of the state and government are culturally
uncomfortable to Africans, and that present generations
in that continent have not yet produced congenial, in-
ternally effective, and internationally reliable types of
political organization. "For all the recent judicial and
constitutional developments," T. O. Elias observes, "the
task of nation building is yet to be accomplished in
Africa."[111] The major obstacle everywhere[112] is the force
of ethnic particularism which continues to pit tribe
against tribe, or region against region, and which has

[110] Franck, *op.cit.*, esp. pp. 55ff and 121ff. See Albert Meister,
L'Afrique peut-elle partir? (Paris, 1966), for the view that Kenya,
Uganda, and Tanganyika should be left alone to work out their
separate and collective futures, and that all Negro Africa is perhaps to
be classified more properly as neolithic than as underdeveloped, a condition that might explain its intransigence in encounters with Occidental systems of ideas.

It is too early to speculate on the destiny of certain recent regional
unions, linking Congo-Kinshasa, Central African Republic, and Tchad
in a "United States of Central Africa"; Senegal, Mali, Guinea, and
Mauritania in "The Organization of States Bordering the Senegal
River" (*New York Times*, April 3, 1968); and Gambia, Guinea, Liberia,
Mali, Mauritania, Senegal, Upper Volta, Ghana, and Nigeria in the
"West African Regional Group," an effort to promote economic unifi-
cation (*ibid.*, April 25, 1968).

[111] "The Evolution of Law and Government in Modern Africa," in
Kuper and Kuper eds., *op.cit.*, p. 192.

[112] Notable exceptions are the old state of Ethiopia and the new
state of Somalia. The relative unity of the former may be due to early
contacts with literate thought worlds, the role of the Coptic faith, and
the place occupied by the ruling dynasty in interregional affairs. That
of Somalia should be ascribed to ethnic uniformity, the shared faith
in Islam, and a particular governmental arrangement in terms of which
all parties and governments are based upon coalitions of traditional
clans.

gained ground in recent years as the major structuring principle not only of political parties but also of the central government itself and its adjunct national services such as the army.[113]

It cannot be said that Western political organization has taken root, nor can modern African states be described as law states or legal systems. Customary law applies by definition to each of the small communities of which the nation is composed. That is to say, it supports particularism. Efforts to locate uniformities authoritatively so as to create a common legal foundation have so far not yielded substantial results, despite much rhetoric to the contrary. Furthermore, the public law that was to assure the constitutional order of the multi-ethnic nation state is grounded in European theories of law that have proved inapplicable to local conditions. In short, the central national government is a set of brittle institutions everywhere. Deprived of both legal sanction and national support and uncertain of the state's territorial contours, it is almost everywhere today a coercive, one-party administration, closely identified with the talents and interests of an individual ruler and with the sub rosa security organizations and para-military structures that this man requires if he is to stay in power.[114] It goes without saying that intrigue, conspiracy, civil war, and other forms of violence are concomitants of this type of rule, as they had also been in many traditional

[113] On ethnic ties in the army, the security forces, the police, etc., see Lee, *op.cit.*, pp. 65, 78.

[114] *Ibid.*, pp. 22, 47ff, 56ff, for analyses of the relationships between armies and governments, of different coups and revolutions, and of "private" intelligence systems and security organizations; p. 50 for the interesting view that the modern African state is primarily a job- and patronage-dispensing organization. Cp. Lusignan, *op.cit.*, pp. 75, 83, 366, 373, for discussions of regimes and revolts in French-speaking Africa.

systems. However, the difference between then and now is this: former regimes and their constituencies knew when violent disturbances could be expected and were in accord also on the rules of the game in the annual customs, slave raids, rebellions, or wars of succession. Modern states, by contrast, provide no normative references for the governance of political behavior. This vacuum invites capricious conduct on the part of the ambitious, makes for fear and quietism in the public, and is generally unfavorable to the initiation of long-range legal and political reforms.

The same factors that account for instability and unpredictability within the modern African state are operative on the level of bilateral, regional, and other kinds of international relations. An African states system, officially encompassed since 1963 in the Organization of African Unity, may be said to exist also in reality; however it is as resistant to clear definition as the state itself. And in this connection it bears remembering that the realm of foreign affairs is not everywhere commonly perceived as being different from that of domestic affairs: in some instances ethnically distinct groups within the state continue to view each other with the kind of enmity elsewhere reserved for a hostile state; in others one finds tribal components of the state strongly conscious of close affinities with groups outside its frontiers.[115] Since it is difficult in such conditions to fathom the concept of "the national interest" as an organizing axiom in inter-African affairs, foreign-policy making, like government, must perforce become the preserve of leading personalities and of the parties or other organiza-

---

[115] For a suggestive discussion see I. William Zartman, *International Relations in the New Africa* (Englewood Cliffs, N.J., 1966), pp. 105ff, "The Politics of Boundaries" (with reference mostly to West Africa).

tions they control.[116] As such it is bound to be determined by individual hopes, fears, and ambitions, to be communicated in the language of interpersonal discourse, and to culminate in essentially short-term commitments to either discord or cooperation. That is to say, the contemporary pattern of inter-African relations —marked as it is by frequent reversals of position, sudden formations and dissolutions of blocs and alliances, the absence of a steadying frame of shared legal or other philosophical principles,[117] and a pronounced stress on speech, often charged with invective—restates many of the characteristics noted earlier in respect of traditional nonliterate African societies. This type of eclecticism or pragmatism explains on the one hand why Africans can tolerate all manner of violence, subversion, and war in interstate affairs,[118] and why on the other hand they are often eminently successful in resolving even the most acrimonious disputes in their midst. In other words, and as the Charter of African Unity pro-

[116] Cp. Zartman, *International, Relations in the New Africa*, p. xi, on the importance of the political party in foreign relations. Also d'Arboussier, *loc.cit.*, p. 170.

[117] Cp. on these subjects the views expressed by Vernon McKay, I. William Zartman, and L. Gray Cowan in *African Diplomacy: Studies in the Determinants of Foreign Policy*, ed. Vernon McKay (New York, 1966); Doudou Thiam, *The Foreign Policy of African States* (New York, 1965), pp. 44, 65, 71ff; Thomas Hovet Jr., *Africa in the United Nations* (Evanston, Ill., 1963), pp. 63, 87, 153f.

[118] For an interesting case study of this issue see Kenneth W. Grundy, "Ideology and Insurrection: The Theory of Guerrilla Warfare in Africa" (prepared for presentation to the Annual Convention of the International Studies Association, San Francisco, Calif., March 1969), pp. 32, 40, 42, on the absence of interest in ideology or theory, the essentially pragmatic temperament of Africa's guerrilla leaders, the magico-religious conduct of the Congo rebels in battle, and the conclusion of one observer on the scene that "the worldview of the Congo rebels was fundamentally traditional and Bantu" (p. 30). On this point see also Lee, *op.cit.*, pp. 54, 86f.

116

claims it with admirable clarity, regional order in this culture is a function of persuasion rather than law.

Ambivalent as these dispositions toward local and regional organization may appear to be in Western eyes, they do not paralyze or weaken the African role in international relations. It is in this latter context that pan-Africanism has become a most persuasive force today even though precedents for such a conception of unity cannot be found in traditional African thought and practice. Two main reasons may explain its success. For one thing, pan-Africanism carries the general cultural and racial consciousness of being African, and thus different from other political presences on the world scene;[119] for another, it does not commit Africans to setting up an effectively functioning inter-African government, or to combatting the strong trend toward intrigue and political and military intervention across state boundaries that has marked relations between governments since the attainment of political independence. In other words, pan-Africanism is compatible both with the type of floating or nomadic nationalism that this culture has brought forth, and with that pronounced ethnic or biological sense of oneness which makes each small traditional group regard the other as different and therefore hostile.

The actual record of African diplomacy in the last years seems to justify the view developed by Abu-Lughod, that African nationalism is sufficiently different from European and Asian nationalism to warrant a separate treatment; that it is properly cast by African leaders in demands for *continental* rather than *national* independence; and that the Charter of the Organization of African Unity rightly affirms "the legitimacy of re-

[119] *Supra*, pp. 87ff.

117

grouping states to create more viable or perhaps more natural entities" even as it upholds officially the principle of the sovereign equality of states.[120]

The principal unifying cause, for the time being at least, is thus the negative phenomenon of joint hostility to the "white societies" of South Africa, Rhodesia, and Portuguese Africa, and to all governments outside Africa that do not accede openly to this enmity.[121] It is this shared emotion that is being administered successfully in the multiple contexts supplied, in particular, by the United Nations, the Specialized Agencies, and other international organizations so as to modify or deform the substantive concepts in behalf of which the international democracies had been set up by the Western powers. For example, the Seventeenth Session of the Regional Committee for Africa of the World Health Organization adopted a resolution in September 1967 that disapproved of any WHO assistance whatever to Portugal and Portuguese Territories, even though the Director General of the Organization, acting in behalf of the very purpose that his institution is constitutionally bound to serve, had stated in his Annual Report to the World Health Assembly "that the Organization might intervene in the event of an emergency where there was a serious threat to public health or where health relief was needed by victims of a calamity."[122]

120 See Herbert Spiro, ed., *Patterns of African Development: Five Comparisons* (Englewood Cliffs, N.J., 1967), pp. 37ff, 54ff. See also Ali A. Mazrui, "On the Concept: 'We are All Africans,'" in *American Political Science Review*, LVII, no. 1 (1963); "The U.N. and Some African Political Attitudes," in *International Organization*, XVIII, no. 3 (Summer 1964); and *Towards a Pax Africana, A Study of Ideology and Ambition* (Chicago, 1967).

121 Among the few African statesmen who have dissociated themselves from this position is Dr. H. Kamuzu Banda, President of Malawi.

122 AFRO Press Release 67/27, September 28, 1967. See also statements made by African delegates at the Regional Meeting of 1963 to the

What we are witnessing today, then, are multiple attempts, some quite deliberate, others involuntary, to transform the core concepts of the United Nations Charter and the general Occidental vocabulary of law and political organization so that these may come to stand for the preferred African form of identity. In a cogent analysis of pan-Africanism and its implication for the present international order, the Kenyan scholar Ali Mazrui remarks[123] that the Anglo-Saxon liberal idiom may well continue to play a part in African diplomatic discourse, but that affinities between words and the ideas covered by these words are becoming increasingly deceptive.[124] Terms like self-determination, sovereignty, and ministerial responsibility, are certainly still in use, he writes, but the constitutional language is being rapidly outdistanced by contrary political developments in accordance with which only pigmentational self-

---

effect that "there is simply no question of ever dissociating the political from the Health factor," and that the constitution of the WHO "was regarded by African nations, who were in a state of evolution, as a means to an end. . . . If necessary, it should be moulded accordingly, but if that were not possible it should be set aside." Afr/RC/13/-Min., November 15, 1963; and the Official Records of the WHO Assemblies of 1965 and 1966, as well as of meetings held under the auspices of UNESCO, ECOSOC, and the xxviind International Conference on Public Education.

The verbal belligerence often displayed during diplomatic sessions (see e.g., text of Statement on the Congo Question, U.S. Mission to the United Nations, Press Release no. 4479, December 14, 1964, which refers to abusive language used by African delegates in the United Nations Security Council in connection with the rescue of white hostages in the Congo—described as "a murderous operation" and "massive cannibalism") may well be the modern counterpart of the traditional curse, see *supra*, p. 110.

123 *Towards a Pax Africana: A Study of Ideology and Ambition* (Chicago, 1967). Apart from corroborating African diplomatic practice, this book is of unusual interest because it shows by implication the close connection between modern and traditional themes of political organization. See *supra*, p. 24, n. 17 for other references to this work.

124 Cp. *supra*, pp. 3ff on the relation between words and ideas.

determination and sovereignty make any sense. And this concept again, being directly related to the African view of colonialism as "permanent aggression," is an effective challenge to the meanings of war and peace as covered by the United Nations Charter. Indeed, in the African scheme peace and war rank much lower in the list of priorities than what Mazrui calls "human rights at large," meaning the rights of groups rather than of individuals. South Africa's domestic policy of apartheid is thus generally viewed in African circles as a much more serious assault on human liberty than, for example, China's genocide in Tibet. Movements to liberate Angola from Portugal by resort to force are in this perspective not violations of Charter provisions, but European or American interventions in the Congo are.

One of the most interesting developments to emerge from African practice and African comments on this practice is the appreciation that it would be best to recognize two quite different levels of law and organization in the international field: the traditional Occidental order today encompassed in the United Nations, and a special continental and racial order ruled by a pan-African law. The latter, inchoate as yet, would have its own categories and definitions of what is "aggression," for example, or what constitutes "treason" between African states. Similarly, whereas the test of "legitimacy" is being taken seriously when states and governments are evaluated in the context of Western thought as deposited in the United Nations, it carries little significance in Negro Africa where states and regimes should be judged by applying the criterion of racial representation.[125]

[125] Mazrui, *Toward a Pax Africana*, pp. 118ff and 135ff, and policy statements by African statesmen as reported in the daily press in Africa, Europe, and the U.S.

4.

$\mathcal{I}$ndia

AND INDIANIZED ASIA

INDIAN Asia, one of the oldest and most complex literate civilizations in the world, has experienced the same overwhelming influences of Islam and Christian Europe that have swept over nonliterate Africa, having first absorbed, moreover, those emanating from classical Iran. Here, as there, the extraneous authorities have proved most incisive in the field of political organization: the records of the ancient Persian Satraphy covering the Indus valley, the Sultanate of Delhi, the Moghul Empire, and contemporary Pakistan attest to a continuous impact from adjoining Oriental lands, as do those of the British raj to the more recent domination of European principles of rule. Yet there are many modern Indian scholars who have found in their research that the ancient Hindu system of political thought and practice has retained much of its validity, and that its presence should also be reckoned with in any estimation of India's future. Reflecting upon the fact that the Muslim occupation had not materially affected the nature of Hindu political theory, and that the meaning of the *dharmaśāstras* and *arthaśāstras* remained unspent throughout that epoch, K. V. Rangaswami Aiyangar concluded in 1916 that "at no period of our history has the

influence of our ancient polity been quite moribund."[126]
And in 1927, when English ideas of government seemed
firmly implanted, U. N. Ghoshal wrote:

> ... the truth is that there is such a gulf fixed between
> the whole habit of thinking of Bodin and Grotius and
> that of the Hindu writers or rajadharma that to expect
> in the latter the parallel of the precise and coherent
> political thought of the former is to expect the im-
> possible.[127]

Other doubts about the relevance of European thought
for India's political system were voiced by K. M. Panikkar:

> The textbooks which are taught in our universities
> and the doctrines which are expounded by our teach-
> ers and studied by our students are unrelated to our
> social order, and are generally speaking foreign to
> our experience, [so] that I have often wondered
> whether as at present constituted these studies serve
> any purpose at all. To study Aristotle, Bodin, Hobbes,
> Rousseau, Green and others may be an intellectual
> discipline; . . . to be concerned with such imprecise
> terms as democracy, dictatorship, will of the people
> and social contract, may not be less useful than being
> engaged in perpetual discussions on metaphysical
> problems, but no one could pretend that they touch
> the hard core of power in society.[128]

126 *Considerations on Some Aspects of Ancient Indian Polity* (Madras, 1916), p. 34, as quoted in D. Mackenzie Brown, *The White Umbrella: Indian Political Thought from Manu to Gandhi* (Berkeley
and Los Angeles, 1958), p. 8.

127 *A History of Hindu Political Theories: From the Earliest Times
to the End of the First Quarter of the Seventeenth Century* AD (London, 1927), p. 240.

128 "Indian Doctrines of Politics," lecture delivered at the Premabhai
Hall on July 22, 1955 (Ahmedabad, 1955), pp. 2-3.

The real core of power, this scholar and diplomat writes elsewhere,[129] is to be found in the doctrines and practices of Chanakya Kautilya, Mauryan prime minister in the fourth century BC, and author of the most famous *arthaśāstra*; and these will be found still in force if India's present administration is analyzed to its bases.

The pattern of law and organization whose permanence is so often and so eloquently affirmed in India has indeed few if any affinities with that of the West. Understood as the organic part of an immutable metaphysical order, it is authoritatively enshrined in sacred epics, traditions, and scriptural texts. Chief among these at least in the context of this discussion, are the *dharmaśāstras* and *arthaśāstras* which set out, in meticulous detail, the laws by which men must live and kings comport themselves.

Lest it be thought that we are dealing here with the Indian counterpart of what is constitutional law in the Occident, it should be noted that *dharma* means the duty of following the laws of one's birth; and that the latter, again, are determined by the caste system and other rigid socio-religious and cosmological concepts. In the Western juridical perspective, then, the Hindu "law books" are most inappropriately known under the name of "codes," as Sir Henry Maine remarked;[130] for they systematize and regulate all of life, the seen and the unseen worlds, in accordance with orthodox brahminic teaching. That is to say, Hindu law (not unlike Muslim

---

[129] *A Survey of Indian History* (Bombay, 1954), pp. 2, 16, 29, 80; see also the works of N. C. Chaudhuri, especially a recent essay "On Understanding the Hindu" in which he warns that imported ideas, institutions, and standards of achievement are no indication whatever of future potentialities, or even of the actual quality of the life as it is being lived. *Encounter*, XXIV (June 1965).

[130] *Dissertations on Early Law and Custom* (New York, 1883), p. 376, also pp. 7ff.

law in this regard) originates in myth and religion, not in human intelligence. Neither secular jurisprudence nor legislative enactments responsive to changing human needs are thus fathomable here. Furthermore, and for the same built-in reasons, Hindu law does not know the idea of the person either as a citizen possessing civil liberties and responsibilities, or as the bearer of what we call human rights.[131] Since it exists primarily as an emanation and protection of the caste system, this law makes different provisions for life in different castes, stressing in each case the duty of conforming with one's appointed *dharma* and thus making inequality a fundamental legal axiom.[132]

The conceptual and social premises upon which the comprehensive Hindu order rests explain two other fundamental aspects of law in India: firstly, the absence of distinctions between public and private law, civil and criminal law, and between the law of persons and that of things; and secondly, the presence of a severe accent

[131] Sir Henry Maine, *Lectures on the Early History of Institutions* (New York, 1888), pp. 329ff, for a classic comparison of Hindu and Roman law. B. L. Atreya, "Indian Culture, Its Spiritual, Moral and Social Aspects," in UNESCO, *Interrelations of Cultures: Their Contribution to International Understanding* (Paris, 1953), p. 146, that Indian thought includes no concept of "rights." See Joseph Campbell, "Human Rights in Oriental Beliefs," *Sarah Lawrence Alumnae Magazine,* vol. xxx (Spring 1965), for a lucid explanation of why the concept of human rights is absent. For a discussion of the philosophical framework in which the caste system originates and functions, see Heinrich Zimmer, *Philosophies of India,* ed. Joseph Campbell (New York, 1951); for the caste system see e.g., A. L. Basham, *The Wonder that was India* (London, 1954), chap. 5.

[132] Maine remarks in this connection: "I have myself heard an Indian Brahmin dispute it [equality] on the ground that, according to the clear teaching of his religion, a Brahmin was entitled to twenty times as much happiness as anybody else." *Op.cit.,* p. 399.

See E. J. Rapson, ed., *The Cambridge History of India* (Cambridge, 1955), vol. I, *Ancient India,* "The Growth of Law and Legal Institutions," p. 252, for e.g., the category of theft in which "concealed thieves" are subdivided a thousandfold.

on punishment. In fact the imagination is staggered by the myriad cases of possible wrongdoing that are listed, the dense catalogues of punishments, all increasing in severity as social status diminishes, and the dictionaries of lurid tortures, each described in meticulous detail, in the framework of which human nature is envisioned and held in check so that each earthly government may assure continuous compliance with unchanging cosmic and religious truths.[133]

This task of government is entrusted to the king who is by definition a representative of the *kshatriya* (warrior) class and must wield *danda*, the rod of punishment, if he is to exercise his primary mandate of keeping the people of his kingdom in their respective caste roles and of preventing one subject from interfering with the *dharma* of another; for only when men are thus made virtuous with the aid of *dandanīti* (the science of punishment) can they hope for release from life and its illusions and, eventually, for escape from the cycle of rebirths.[134]

As outlined in the *dharmaśāstras* and *arthaśāstras* and as recorded during the period from the Mauryas to the Muslim conquest, royal power emerged as absolute

[133] According to the sacred Laws of Manu, the whole race of man is kept in order by punishment. However, a *śūdra* could be deprived of his life for an action which would cost a *brāhman* only a small fine or reprimand. A *śūdra* showing contempt for a *brāhman* should have an iron spike, ten fingers long, thrust down his throat, but greater insults might cost him his tongue or having hot oil poured in mouth and ears. For excerpts from lists of punishments and tortures as set out in the Laws of Manu, the *Mahābhārata*, the *dharmaśāstras*, the *arthaśāstras*, and other Hindu sources of law, as well as from Buddhist texts, see John W. Spellman, *Political Theory of Ancient India: A Study of Kingship from the Earliest Times to ca.* AD *300* (Oxford, 1964, pp. 113ff, 117ff; also Charles Drekmeier, *Kingship and Community in Early India* (Stanford and Bombay, 1962), pp. 232ff. For comparable Chinese approaches to punishment see *infra*, pp. 145ff.

[134] Cp. *supra*, pp. 26f for an Arab definition of government.

power.[135] It was neither hallowed nor limited by considerations of divinely appointed rights and duties, as in the divine-right monarchies of Europe; nor was it supported or restrained by parliamentary or legal institutions. The *brāhmans* were the king's advisers and in theory also his critics, but they seem to have made use of this right only seldom.[136] Instructed by his *dharma* to practice the art of winning by means fair and foul, an Indian king was thus left to his own devices in the world of *artha* where success is all that counts. And among the devices at his disposal he relied chiefly on his own intelligence (which was supposed to function without legal or ethical inhibitions), his power to pass decrees (generally accepted as commentaries on existing laws), an elaborate bureaucracy, the police, and, above all, his espionage establishment. For as it was written already in the *Mahābharāta*, to be repeatedly confirmed in subsequent centuries, "A kingdom has its roots in spies and secret agents . . . as the wind moves everywhere and penetrates all created beings, just so should the king penetrate everywhere by sending spies through the land, to report on disloyalty among subjects, ministers, and heirs."

Political organization in India thus devolved from a

135 See U. N. Ghoshal, "Some Aspects of Ancient Indian Political Organization," in *JWH*, VI, no. 2 (1960), pp. 223ff, to the effect that the *dharmaśāstras* and the provisions of the *arthaśāstra* were not constitutional law: the former were sacred law enjoining the king to act in conformity with the general scheme of religious life, the latter claim to lay down the general "law" in accordance with which a king must conduct himself if he wants to be successful. See also Nilakanta Sastri, *Studies in Chola History and Administration* (Madras, 1932), pp. 97-98, where the author warns against importing the associations of democracy to the interpretation of Indian records and ignoring the whole complex of notions associated with caste, custom, and religion which dominated social life. See also Basham, *op.cit.*, chap. 4, "The State"; Zimmer, *op.cit.*, pp. 87ff, "The Philosophy of Success."

136 Ghoshal, *loc. cit.*

"science" of statecraft that is unique in the world,[137] and has been viewed by Indians ever since as a manifestation of their native genius at its best, even though it was directly responsible for unparalleled turbulence within each of the multiple monarchies of which India was composed before its conquest by the Muslims. The element of stability within the vast subcontinent as a whole and under each of the manifold royal umbrellas was supplied by towns, castes, guilds, and above all villages, small and large. Each of these was rigidly controlled by tax-gatherers and other agents of the kingly court for whose benefit the entire economy was maintained;[138] yet each was in great measure self-governing, having brought forth its own privileges and customary laws, its own councils and assemblies for the dispatch of local business and, in many instances, its own courts for the adjustments of disputes between members of a village, caste, or other autonomous entity.

The existence, through time, of this collectivity of separate villages—which was to sustain Ghandi's preferred image of India as an a-political rural folk society[139]—together with the essentially personal and dy-

[137] But cf. *infra*, pp. 146f, 153ff for China's system under the Legalists and the Communists.

[138] The theory that we are in the presence here of tax-taking rather than of legislating kingdoms and empires is well illustrated by Sir Henry Maine's references to the Punjab under Sikh rule: a most perfect order was kept in this region by the levying of exactions, and by the punishment and execution of a great many people. However, the ruling despot never made a law. The rules regulating the lives of his subjects were derived from their immemorial usages, as administered in families and village communities. See *Lectures on the Early History of Institutions*, p. 380.

[139] Ghoshal, *loc.cit.*, 228ff, insists that the progressive development of self-government during the period of the Guptas and their successors was by no means tantamount to a gradual transformation of the country into a vast rural democracy, as maintained by some Indian authors. He adds, furthermore, that there is not much information on how most of the councils actually functioned. See *ibid.*, on Buddhist

127

nastic interests inhabiting the institution of kingship, goes a long way toward explaining why the idea of the nation-state could not possibly be conceived in pre-British India. What we have instead on this subcontinent and in hinduized Indo-China and Indonesia are vast fields of interstate relations in which each king, guided by the principles of *artha*, was forever trying to "acquire and maintain the earth," i.e., to outwit and conquer his neighbors. This unabashed philosophical and actual commitment to power and victory, whether rendered through the symbolism of geometry or that of chess—pursuits in which Indians excelled—was obviously incompatible with anything resembling international law or international organization as these terms are understood in the Occident. The only kind of law governing this Oriental state system was the law of the fishes (*matsya nyāya*), in accordance with which the big fish eat the little fish, might is above right, and right is in the hands of the strong. Inequality was postulated as the everlasting condition of political existence, power as the only measure of political worth, war as the normal activity of the state, peace as a lamentable condition of inferiority, and espionage as the most reliable, indispensable shield of royal fortune. Indeed, as the following advice from the *arthaśāstra* shows, the skills of intrigue, tabulated and annotated under such titles as "Government based on Deceit" and "The Administration of Subversion," were more highly prized than material power:

---

republics in East India, wrongly called democracies. Cp. Drekmeier, *op.cit.*, p. 280, to the effect that India has not developed a systematic theory of republicanism. See also R. C. Majumdar, *Corporate Life in Ancient India* (Calcutta, 1918); R. S. Sharma, "L'économie dans l'Inde Ancienne," in *JWH*, IV, no. 2 (1960) pp. 256ff, on guilds and corporations.

He who has the eye of knowledge and is acquainted with the science of polity, can with little effort make use of his skill for intrigue and can succeed by means of conciliation, and other strategic means, by spies and chemical appliances in overreaching even those kings who are possessed of enthusiasm and power.[140]

These *artha* principles of international relations, absolutely logical in terms of Indian political science and philosophy and therefore of necessity unrelieved by contrary tenets informing the search for release from worldly chores, for instance, were followed, in their essentials, by all Hindu kings from the Maurya dynasty onward. Wars were thus endemic on the subcontinent, readying it for invasions from without.[141]

The same state of affairs marked relations between the indianized states in adjoining South and Southeast Asian areas, that is to say in the polities antecedent to those known today as Burma, Cambodia, Thailand, Laos, Vietnam, and Indonesia. The major additional determinant in this culturally unified, politically divided region is the presence, throughout millennia, of cosmo-magical principles of political organization. States and empires here were conceived as representations of the universe, their separate provinces or divisions mirroring celestial constellations, their capitals and palaces symbolic microcosms of the magical realm, their kings divinely appointed impresarios for the enactment of the cosmic drama on earth. Sovereignty and political identity in Burma, Siam, Cambodia, or Java were thus not functions either of recognized boundaries, concrete material

---

[140] R. Shamasastry, ed., *Kautilya's Arthaśāstra* (Bombay, 1951), p. 368; pp. 293ff, on the elements of the Mandala system of states; pp. 367-459 on subversion, espionage, ways of waging wars of nerves, and use of "fiery spies," i.e., guerrillas.

[141] Cp. Panikkar, *op.cit.*, p. 27f.

power,[142] or even of legitimate royal succession, but rather of the existence and occupancy of the palace, the actual possession of the sacred royal regalia, and the due performance of state rituals, such as the royal ploughing and the churning of the waters, that were commonly believed to assure the continuity of life. These modes of conceptualizing order on earth had been concretized in ancient times in the vast and intricate architectural harmonies of Angkor (Cambodia), Boro-budur (Java),[143] and other palatial sites and temple compounds, to be echoed as late as the mid-nineteenth century in the building design of Mandalay in Burma, where no kingdom was fathomable without a palace. However, they did not suggest or require equivalent systems of organization on the level of government and politics.[144] Indeed the contrary was true and may have been intended; for power could be, and frequently was, seized effectively by simply occupying the palace, as in Burma and Siam, for example, or by taking possession of the objects symbolic of government as in Indonesia. Furthermore, claimants to the throne could always pretend that they were incarnations of the divine principle, or that the necessary *karma* for the office had been acquired in former lives. Thus, as Heine-Geldern ex-

[142] Cp. *supra*, p. 128.

[143] See Bernard Croslier and Jacques Arthaud, *The Arts and Civiliza-tion of Angkor* (New York, 1957); Christopher Pym, *The Ancient Civilization of Angkor* (London, 1968); Heinrich Zimmer, *The Art of Indian Asia: Its Mythology and Transformations*, ed. Joseph Campbell, Bollingen Series XXXIX, 2nd ed., 2 vols. (New York, 1960).

[144] The dichotomy between the symmetry and harmony of these architectural orders on the one hand, and the confusion of the po-litical design on the other, that mark the Southeast Asian scene, has an analogy in the Middle East: here, too, it is the mosque rather than the caliphate or kingdom that represents the world view in an ordered comprehensive way.

plains, Buddhism,[145] Hinduism, and the concept of divine kingship could none of them be said to have been stabilizing factors in the area of political organization.[146] The crown might just fall to the prince who was the quickest to seize the palace and to execute his brothers, or it might be usurped by others. Rebellion, unrest, and anarchy, then, were common aspects of this *artha* theater not only in the third century AD, when Chinese observers commented on the situation in the kingdom of Funan, but also during the eighteenth and nineteenth centuries, AD, when European authorities noted their incidence as quasi-popular tradition. With different kingdoms locked in chronic combat and intrigue and ignorant of alternatives inherent in ideas of peace, unity, or law, conflict must be viewed as the norm in regional relations here, as it was in the traditional interstate system on the Indian sub-continent.

The Islamic administration of vast parts of India, which culminated in the persianized Moghul Empire, introduced principles of public order that have been discussed earlier.[147] Chief among these was of course the legal system, with its stress on egalitarianism, which was decidedly an advance over what had existed in India before. However, the actual operation of this legal prin-

[145] The view rather commonly held in the West today, namely that Buddhism denotes peace in local and international politics, has no foundation in the context either of religion or of history.

[146] See this scholar's seminal essay, "Conceptions of State and Kingship in South East Asia," *Far Eastern Quarterly*, vol. 2, no. 1 (November 1942). Also Georges Coèdes, *Les Etats Hindouisés d'Indochine et d'Indonésie* (Paris, 1948); H. G. Quaritch Wales, *The Making of Greater India* (London, 1951); John F. Cady, *Southeast Asia: Its Historical Development* (New York, 1964); Reginald Le May, *The Culture of South-East Asia: The Heritage of India* (London, 1954); Lawrence Palmer Briggs, *The Ancient Khmer Empire* (Philadelphia, 1951); Pym, *op.cit.*, esp. pp. 30ff, 36ff, 88ff.

[147] *Supra*, pp. 69ff.

ciple was frustrated by factors similar to those prevalent in the Middle East, as well as by the absence in India itself of any well-built framework for the dispensing of justice. Furthermore, it was seriously put in issue by India's stubborn adherence to the caste system and locally cherished privileges. Successive Muslim governments thus concluded by leaving village life and religion alone, respecting existing legal customs and traditions of self-government, and relying upon the bureaucratic establishments as the main conduits of central control—a proclivity in the art of government that accorded with preexisting Indian traditions and expectations of political authority. In foreign affairs, too, strong affinities must be noted: Muslims and Hindus proceeded from totally different assumptions about the nature and function of war and peace, yet their approaches converged upon a strongly militant style. In fact in this domain the conquering culture was captured by the *artha* world of the defeated, and India thus continued to be the desultory scene of wars, struggles for succession, and states of anarchy, only occasionally redeemed by the efforts of outstandingly gifted imperial autocrats.

The modern Indian world was structured by the British between the end of the eighteenth century and the middle of the twentieth century, particularly in the period 1790-1870 when the different branches of Indian law—excepting modern Indian and Pakistani constitutionalism—were developed and defined. This transformation of the traditional normative systems emerges as one of the most remarkable achievements from the records of intercultural relations, comparable in intent as well as in effect to some of the revolutionary legal structures invented by the Romans in the course of ordering the alien realms that they had conquered.

Initiated by such versatile, law-conscious imperial administrators as Sir William Jones (d. 1794), who studied Sanskrit in order to penetrate law-related Hindu thought and was determined to compile a digest of both Hindu and Mohammedan law, and by H. T. Colebrooke, also a Sanskrit scholar, who recorded the proceedings of hundreds of cases he heard in his capacity as judge and magistrate so as to clarify what he felt to be the disturbing uncertainty of Hindu law, the English endeavor was ruled by the conviction that Hindus should be subject to Hindu law, Mohammedans to *sharī'a* law, and Buddhists (mostly in Burma) to Buddhist law. However, when native law was either silent, or unclear, or obviously incompatible with English notions of public order, recourse was had to principles of "justice, equity, and good conscience." And this reference, again, made possible a *renvoi* not only to English law and equity, but also to Roman law and natural law as well as to French, Dutch, and German law.[148] The most powerful influence was of course exerted by the law of England, nowhere more so than in respect of contract and constitutional law—legal categories that Indian thought had not developed. (Other branches of law to become almost wholly anglicized were those of tort and evidence.)[149]

Greatly similar principles informed the English approach to *sharī'a* law. Here the interplay between two quite different legal traditions led eventually to the creation of a comprehensive hybrid system, aptly termed

[148] See J. Duncan M. Derrett, "Justice, Equity and Good Conscience," in J.N.D. Anderson, ed., *Changing Law in Developing Countries* (New York, 1963), pp. 139ff; and, by the same author, "The Administration of Hindu Law by the British," *Comp. Studies in Society and History*, vol. IV (1961-62), pp. 10ff.

[149] See Maine, *Village-Communities in the East and West* (New York, 1880), pp. 295ff, 298, for an interesting discussion of this process.

Anglo-Mohammedan law, and described by Coulson as an expression of Islamic law unique not only in form—for it was genuinely applied as a case-law system through a hierarchy of courts which observed the doctrine of binding precedent—but also in substance, inasmuch as it absorbed English influences, particularly those of equity.[150] It cannot be said that these modifications were actually intended. Their evolution, not unlike that of the anglicized Hindu law, is testimony rather to the positive role of *mis*understanding in intercultural borrowing,[151] rendered particularly felicitous in this case by resort to the European formula of equity, justice, and conscience. No doubt is left by the records that the courts tried conscientiously to apply what they understood as Islamic law.[152] However, in the very nature of things they did not possess total knowledge of strict *sharī'a* doctrine with the result that they did not always know how to ascertain or to interpret *sharī'a* principles. This attitude to existing intellectual and political challenges, together with the fact that English judges were simply not tutored by their tradition to adhere strictly to established authorities in the manner taken for granted by their Islamic counterparts, the *qāḍīs*, goes a long way toward explaining why equity could become the major structuring principle in the building of modern India's legal systems.

The political organization of India that was to culminate in the establishment of parliamentary government is in very large measure a function of these understandings of the rule of law. For in the crucial decades before the Mutiny, when the Indian legislature had not

---

[150] *A History of Islamic Law* (Edinburgh, 1964), p. 171. See also Ronald K. Wilson, *Anglo-Muhammadan Law*, 2nd ed. (London, 1903). [151] Cp. *supra*, pp. IXff. [152] Coulson, *op.cit.*, pp. 164ff.

yet become active, it was the court of justice which "legislated," often in revolutionary ways, through the instrumentality of judicial interpretations,[153] thus readying governments, both English and Indian, for democratic rule, and engendering that respect for law without which secular government cannot function in a unified society.[154]

The other major mainstay of the emergent Indian state was the Indian Civil Service. According to Panikkar, this "administrative machine," built after the Mutiny in the mid-nineteenth century, has no parallel in the history of the world:[155] neither the Byzantine nor the Chinese empires, both typically bureaucratic, had produced anything comparable to the responsible enlightened services that the British built up in India, both at the center and in the provinces. This Service, fathomable only in the general context of the rule of law, was instrumental, through its exemplary performance, in assuring the supremacy of the civil over the military organization that had held sway in previous centuries when most of India had been encompassed in the Moghul Empire.

The entire process of readying India for self-government and eventual independence through the agency of

[153] Cp. Maine, *Village-Communities in the East and West*, pp. 296, 300.

[154] For one of the most lucid and scholarly retrospective analyses of the British impact upon India see S. P. Sen, "Effects on India of British Law and Administration in the 19th Century," *JWH*, IV, no. 4 (1958), pp. 859, 866 to the following effect: "Perhaps in no other sphere has the impact of British rule been more evident to the common people and more fruitful for the orderly development of India into a modern State than in the sphere of law and justice." This was so, Sen explains, because British law and justice were secular and impartial, whereas both Hindu law and Mohammedan law were religious and in many respects discriminatory. See also Sir Percival Griffiths, *The British Impact on India* (Hamden, Conn., 1965).

[155] *Op.cit.*, p. 207.

law, and the peculiar service rendered in this process by a single nineteenth-century Englishman, have been evaluated in the following terms by the ardently nationalist Indian scholar and statesman mentioned above:

> Thomas Babington Macaulay is not a popular name with educated India and yet on a true appreciation of values, it will be seen that it is the genius of this man, narrow in his Europeanism, self-satisfied in his sense of English greatness, that gives life to modern India as we know it. He was India's new Manu, the spirit of modern law incarnate. The legal system under which India has lived for over a hundred years and within whose steel frame her social, political and economic development has taken place is the work of Macaulay. An examination of the *Minutes* . . . will show how even those elementary principles of law which we now take as axiomatic, e.g., that the accused is to be considered innocent unless proved guilty, had to be fought for and established by him against the opinion of his colleagues. The establishment of the great principle of equality of all before law, in a country where under the Hindu doctrines a Brahmin could not be punished on the evidence of shudras and even punishments varied according to caste and where according to Muslim law, an unbeliever's testimony could not be accepted against a Muslim, was itself a legal revolution of the first importance. . . . The imposing and truly magnificent legal structure under whose protection four hundred million people live is indeed a worthy monument to Macaulay's genius.[156]

It is difficult to estimate the long range chances for survival of institutions and mental dispositions called

[156] Panikkar, *op.cit.*, pp. 204-05.

forth by a revolution as recent as the one Panikkar tells about. Twenty-odd years of independence have brought a partition of the country into India and Pakistan, steadily mounting pressure for secession by disaffected ethnic and religious groups, the rise of communalism, a staggering incidence of violence in public life, and, with it all, the specter once again of disunity and fragmentation. These developments have had the effect of eroding the federal structure and of weakening the role of national parties in the democratic process.[157] However they have so far not invalidated the cause of constitutional organization. In fact on the plane of representative government one must note a steadfast adherence to the electoral principle and a strong commitment to protect fundamental liberties as these are incorporated in the constitution.[158]

As the ranks of the small anglicized elite thin and the Indian middle class comes into its own, the Civil Service will no doubt shed some of the "new" qualities it had acquired and revert to more traditional bureaucratic methods of administration. And the same trend may affect even the judiciary, the most europeanized of India's institutions, unless the legal elites are capable of preserving the admirable integrity of the court system

[157] More than a quarter of the total population is being ruled directly by the central government, since state governments could not ensure the functioning of local legislatures or the maintenance of order.

[158] See A. Gledhill's essay on "Fundamental Rights" in Anderson, ed., *op.cit.*, pp. 82-92, for an analysis of the positive as well as the negative aspects of the Indian approach. Cp. also Sir Orby Mootham, "Constitutional Writs in India," *ibid.*, pp. 97ff, 110f. For the impact of the British rule of law on Burma and its Buddhist laws and customs, and the dismantling of the constitution after independence, see Maung Maung, *Law and Custom in Burma and the Burmese Family* (The Hague, 1963), pp. 23ff, 115ff. Many representative Burmese believe, this author writes, that the introduction of the rule of law—being alien to Burmese traditions—has led to the disintegration of Burmese social life.

while simultaneously doing justice to revitalized traditional forces of social and political life. The most enduring sources of order are likely to be on the one hand the villages which have steadfastly resisted reformist policies,[159] and on the other, the military[160]—a reduction to Asian essentials that has already marked the process of nation-building in most of the neighboring, culturally closely related, societies of Southeast Asia.

The records of the present and the past do not suggest that law will be the basic principle of political organization in the region, or that peace and respect for the territorial integrity of states will be dominant ideals in the conduct of international relations. The convergence of these records upon princely rivalries, royalist rebellions, monk-led violence, plots to unseat rulers, subversions across state boundaries, and all manner of guerrilla operations[161]—particularly striking in the af-

[159] For an exhaustive analysis of this issue see Hugh Tinker, *The Foundations of Local Self-Government in India, Pakistan and Burma* (London, 1954). This scholar stresses the constant lack of harmony between social prejudice and custom, and alien administrative and technical methods, as well as the perennial shortage of funds, as the twin features of Indian and Burmese local government that made reform impossible. It is his view that "they still exist as the most implacable barrier to future success" (p. 342).

[160] It must be remembered, firstly, that the military has been a highly respected profession throughout the millennia in all of Asia with the exception of Confucian China, and secondly, that there is a traditional rapport between army and peasantry. These aspects of "the public order," amply corroborated in history, are discussed by Hugh Tinker, *Ballot Box and Bayonet: People and Government in Emergent Asian Countries* (London, 1964).

[161] See John F. Cady, *Thailand, Burma, Laos, and Cambodia* (Englewood Cliffs, N.J., 1966), for an analytical survey of these patterns, i.e., pp. 99, 103, 141f for accounts of interstate strife and of monastic violence in Burma. On the "royalist rebellions" (1933) in Siam—the most convincing of the modern "nation-states" in the region and not coincidentally also one in which the traditional symbols of divine kingship are still respected—see also H. G. Quaritch Wales, *Ancient Siamese Government and Administration* (London, 1934).

The ultimate source of politically significant behavior in all of

fairs of modern Burma, Cambodia, Laos, Vietnam, and Indonesia—indicates firstly that conflict is a way of life here, perhaps even a major principle of organization.[162]

Secondly, it shows that the viability of states will continue to depend upon the character of leading personalities, their capacities to administer conflict, and, above all, their sensitivities to indigenous cultural traditions.[163]

---

these states, including South Vietnam, where government is more democratic than elsewhere in the Indo-Chinese region, is not laws created by the government, but rather the customs of the particular locality in which a man was reared and the intricate codes of loyalty by which his membership in a family, class, or profession is being governed. Cp. Schecter, *The New Face of Buddha* (New York, 1967), pp. 151ff; see also Clifford Geertz, "The Social-Cultural Context of Policy in Southeast Asia," in *Southeast Asia: Problems of United States Policy*, ed. William Henderson (Cambridge, Mass., 1963), p. 47, for a discussion of the relation between government and society, and Heine-Geldern, *loc.cit.*, for the connection between cultural traditions and political organization.

[162] Bernard K. Gordon, *The Dimensions of Conflict in Southeast Asia* (Englewood Cliffs, N.J., 1966), suggests that the widespread incidence of conflict (along with some attempts at cooperation) is one of the major factors that justify reference to Southeast Asia as "a region," the others being the awareness by its different political leaders of shared problems, and the threatening presence of Communism as a major force.

See *ibid.*, pp. 6off, 120ff, 140f, for comments on the personalization of disputes and, conversely, the role of long-standing historical tensions in producing or aggravating these personalized recriminations. P. 169 for the conclusion that the "organizational style in diplomacy" is marked by a strong emphasis on privacy.

[163] After admitting that the common cosmo-magic conception of statehood has its dangers for the cause of peace and order, Heine-Geldern nonetheless suggests that it be taken seriously as a constructive principle of future political development, concluding that "it would be a grave mistake to disregard the importance of native culture and tradition for a future satisfactory reorganization of the region"; *loc.cit.*, p. 29.

5.
CHINA

THE waning of Occidental ideas of law and government and the waxing of indigenous Oriental motifs within contemporary Indian and South Asian societies are accentuated today by a massive orientalization of the external regional environment in which each of the new states is functioning. This movement, which emanates from Communist China in the form of overt military and covert political activities, both openly designed to frustrate the Western-inspired process of nation-building in the South, is in many respects the twentieth-century counterpart of traditional Chinese approaches to neighboring Asian societies, in much the same way as Maoist China's inner order subsumes some of the most significant features of preceding classical regimes.

Among the fundamental beliefs that have permeated the organizational scheme of the great North Asian realm, one must note these time-transcendent convictions: firstly, that China—to be exact, the Middle Kingdom—is the center of the world and therefore by definition superior to any other society; secondly, that China is a unity; and thirdly, that the governance of China, and therewith of the earth, proceeds from Heaven's Mandate as bestowed upon an imperial dynasty, to be made manifest by each emperor in strict correspondence with the ideal order of nature.

Most of these propositions are prima facie mythical, at

least from the European point of view, while others find scant if any support in history, as Homer H. Dubs points out in his careful refutation of the much-vaunted thesis,[164] restated at the beginning of this century by Sun Yat-sen, that China has been unified since millennia in race, economy, language, religion, and culture. What the records show instead are continuous efforts to expand or cope with invasions from without, and concomitant difficulties—exacerbated by a pronounced racial bias against non-Chinese on the part of "the real Chinese"[165] —in the assimilation of greatly various and ever-changing populations. The concept of unity was contradicted by reality also in the sense that China's territorial limits were usually uncertain.[166] Furthermore, within the area that seemed to constitute China at a given moment, the imperial government was often quite unsure of the reach of its authority, since it was plagued by internecine wars and discords between contending provinces, lords, and armies as well as by popular revolts. In these circumstances it is not surprising that the dynasties themselves

[164] "The Concept of Unity in China," in Stanley Pargellis, ed., *The Quest for Political Unity in World History*, ed. Stanley Pargellis for the American History Association (Washington, D.C., 1944), pp. 3-7.

[165] See H. R. Isaacs, "Group Identity and Political Change: The Role of Color and Physical Characteristics," in *Daedalus* (Spring 1967). All non-Chinese were regarded as "devil slaves," "ghosts," "inhabitants of the nether world," "animals," or "issue of union with animals"— epithets, Isaacs adds, which are heaped today by the Communist Chinese upon Americans.

Maoist China continues to be plagued by the minority problem. According to a dispatch by Charles Taylor of the *Toronto Globe and Mail* (*New York Times*, April 11, 1965), there are more than 50 minorities totalling about 40 million people, or 6% of the population in China occupying 50-60% of China's vast border areas. In Tibet and Sinkiang minority groups have risen in revolts that continue to smolder. Yunnan has 20 million people, more than 6 million of whom belong to 22 national minorities.

[166] See Albert Herrmann, *An Historical Atlas of China*, new ed. (Chicago, 1966).

usually acquired their Heavenly Mandates by force of arms, and that they relied heavily and without compunctions on military means as the ultimate shield of the celestial empire and the perfect natural order.

In brief, China's territorial and political identity, being in large measure a function of cyclical movements of contraction and expansion, was shifting, rather than uniform and stable as the classical ideology had it.[167] And, as one reflects upon the first two decades of Communist China's actuality, a greatly similar analysis would appear to hold today. These orientations toward political organization make it doubtful whether the vocabulary of Western political science as it bears on the twin ideas of "the state" and "the nation" is applicable in this civilization without many prior adjustments and qualifications.

What we have instead by way of basic design is the conception of China as a cultural order, coextensive with the civilized world, into which barbarians are assimilated once they have been tutored successfully through the application of force and persuasion. This conception of an ordained unity with all its attendant myths and make-believe remained intact even in those century-spanning epochs during which even the sem-

[167] See to this effect Shih-Hsiang Chen, "The Cultural Essence of Chinese Literature," in UNESCO, *Interrelations of Cultures*, p. 46f, who supports his thesis that China is not "properly speaking a nation or state" by reference also to the recent writings of the Chinese historian Lai Hai-tsung, in accordance with which true states comparable to those of modern Europe existed in China only in the period of the Warring States. The same view, Chen notes, is presented by a Japanese scholar, Hasegawa Myoze Kan, namely, that the Chinese realized 2,000 years ago that the state is an unnecessary evil.

See Richard L. Walker, *The Multi-State System in Ancient China* (Hamden, Conn., 1953), for an analysis of the early political order. See Charles O. Hucker, *The Traditional Chinese State in Ming Times (1368-1644)* (Tucson, Ariz., 1961), pp. 30ff on the intricacies of the social order and the absence of large-scale organization.

142

blance of actual unity had disappeared. In other words, the identity of the Middle Kingdom was traditionally independent of the actuality of unity, and independent also of success in what we call foreign relations. In fact it seems to have been felt most acutely in periods of internal instability and turbulence on the periphery of the nuclear Chinese realm, when it was necessary to invoke the doctrine of the Heavenly Mandate.[168] For the major structuring principle in this system of politics and culture has always been the *theory* or doctrine of unity, not its realization. Embodied in the mythical charters of *The Book of Odes, The Book of History* and other classics, propagated through the continuous cultivation of sinocentrism and use of sinocentric terminology,[169] the ideology has been administered effectively not through impersonal laws, legislatures, federal devices, and judicial systems, but through the mechanisms of family ethics, personalism, and social ritual, on the one hand, and of an elaborate administrative bureaucracy on the other. The first carries the full authority of the Confucian school, the second that of the Legalists, but both—it must be remarked[170]—had the same purpose, namely the maintenance of the social order. All meanings carried by law in China derive from the operation and interaction of these two sets of principles.

[168] Maoist China's present state of contending factions, tenuous territorial controls, and relentless activism in foreign affairs, thus appears to be true to classical type.
Cf. *supra* pp. 91ff, with broadly analogous trends in the African search for identity.

[169] On this particular point see John K. Fairbank, "China's World Order: The Tradition of Chinese Foreign Relations," *Encounter*, XXVII, (December 1966).

[170] See Jean Escarra, *Le Droit Chinois* (Peking and Paris, 1936), on the interpenetration and combined effect of these informing principles. Also Joseph Needham, *Science and Civilization in China*, 4 vols. (Cambridge, 1954-70), II, 519-582, where many of Escarra's interpretations are restated and elaborated.

The pivot of China's normative order as it functioned on all levels of society was the Confucian system, with its carefully graded social relationships, each requiring compliance with a special set of unalterable rights, responsibilities, and attitudes; its insistence upon maintenance of status; and its commitment therefore to proper education, rectification, and government by example. This was essentially the domain of *li*—a maze of social rules, moral principles, etiquette requirements, references to natural correspondences, and taboos that supplied directives for each person's life in strict accord with his birth, sex, family status, profession, guild membership and so forth.[171] Precise prescriptions thus regulated his behavior, his name, his decorations, the color of his dress, the kind of carriage he was allowed to ride in, and the type of material his mattress could be made of. That is to say, each subject had his proper *li*; if he did not, he really had no life. It followed that a society in which *li* was not properly observed was not deemed to be governed well. For the customs, usages, and ceremonies which *li* summed up were believed to exist because they corresponded with the Will of Heaven and the structure of the Universe. In the very logic of this scheme, then, feuds, disputes, and disorders were subject to the particular customs of the group in which they occurred; the authority interpreting *li* had to be the head of the family, the chief of the clan, the elders of the village, or the superiors of the guild; and ultimate adjustment proceeded through resort to conciliation, mediation, and ritual arrangements, for the primary purpose in this system of "law" was not to find out who

171 See T'ung-tsu Chu, *Law and Society in Traditional China* (Paris and The Hague, 1961), pp. 221ff, for definitions of *li* and discussions of the concept; p. 235, for *li* in connection with the five classical Confucian relationships. Also Needham, *op.cit.*, p. 526.

was right and who wrong, but rather to eliminate a threat to or violation of harmony and the status quo.[172]

The need for direct or positive "legal" intervention was recognized only on subsidiary levels—at least officially—and the reference here was to *fa*, a category of precepts usually invoked as the source of ultimate sanctions for wrongdoing. That is to say, *fa* stood for a system of force and punishment that was applicable to all who were incapable of observing *li*. However, this purpose did not invest *fa* with the properties of an objective impartial public law, since the penalties (and they remained fearfully severe throughout the centuries) were totally dependent upon *li*, whose categories they matched in every detail. For example: since the power of the parent over the child was virtually absolute, the father was entitled to punish the latter's filial disobedience—which might have consisted of scolding a parent or driving him to suicide—by beheading, strangling, or burying him alive. And similar destinies could be meted out to daughters-in-law if they falsely accused parents-in-law. In the same combined *li/fa* context juniors were forbidden to fight back when attacked by seniors. Inquiries into motivation, intent, and possibilities of accidental wrong doing were not required, since it was not the act per se that was in issue but the affront to the status occupied by the superior person in the case. The same reasoning, with its stress on the appearance of things, explains also why violations of the code of conduct associated with a man's particular place in society as defined in the sumptuary laws—i.e., provisions as to what dress to wear when, which carriage to use—carried such drastic penalties as, under T'ang and Sung law,

---

[172] Escarra, *op.cit.*, pp. 15ff, 451f; John Henry Wigmore, *A Panorama of the World's Legal Systems*, 3 vols. (Washington, D.C., 1936), I, 145ff.

from forty to a hundred strokes, and, in case of government officials, instant dismissal.

Since China's administration was understood as an extension of familism, it was in the final analysis controlled by *li* and *fa* as applied to each life and human relationship. However, the bureaucratic dimension of political organization received its main impetus from the Legalists who reinforced *fa* in a manner that has proved decisive to this day.[173]

Legalist ideas of statecraft emerged as early as the seventh and sixth centuries BC, to become fully discernible in the border state of Ch'in, then still regarded as a barbarian society, during later centuries when the foremost representatives of this school of realism, Lord Shang (4th BC)[174] and Han Fei Tzu (3rd BC),[175] set in motion sustained programs of political action that were responsible, eventually, for the termination of the period of the Warring States, the unification of China through a series of wars,[176] and the establishment of a new administrative order.

The revolutionary theory under which this momentous development occurred issued from the view that

173 See the works previously cited, especially T'ung-tsu Chu, *op.cit.*, p. 87, on familism and administration; pp. 128f on gradations in the class system: the role of regulations regarding "the mean people" (i.e., government and private slaves, prostitutes, entertainers, beggars), and "the good people," and on prohibitions attending the mutual relations between members of these categories. Needham, *op.cit.*, II, 531, that *fa* suited the bureaucratic irrigation administrators. See Escarra, *op.cit.*, pp. 97ff on the T'ang Code which originated actually in the remote period of the Warring States, and on its diffusion to Annam; also on the Ming Code which was carried to Japan and Korea.

174 Wei Yang, *The Book of Lord Shang: A Classic of the Chinese School of Law*, trans. J.J.L. Duyvendak (London, 1928).

175 Han Fei Tzu, *Basic Writings*, trans. Burton Watson (New York, 1963); see Arthur Waley, *Three Ways of Thought in Ancient China* (New York, 1940), pp. 239ff, for an analysis of Realist literature.

176 In 230 Ch'in annexed Han; in 228, Chao; in 225, Wei; in 223, Ch'u; in 222, Yen; and finally, in 221, Ch'i surrendered.

146

human nature, being intrinsically evil and not amenable to rule by virtuous example, must be held in check by ruthless controls applied from above in the form of legal decrees and force. In behalf of this cause the Legalists— whom Fairbank calls "the inventors of bureaucracy"— designed an administrative network in terms of which the Empire was divided into commanderies and districts and ruled by professionally qualified officials, who were paid fixed salaries and supervised by written correspondence. Furthermore, in lieu of the Confucian system of indirect, hierarchically staggered, controls,[177] the Legalists introduced an egalitarian, wholly public, law before which ministers and humble folk alike were equal, albeit usually in fear and trembling; for (as the penal codes of the centuries encompassed in the period show), the essence of law here as in Confucianism was derived from the conviction that one must punish severely so that one will not have to punish again.

The official prominence of the Realist School was as short-lived as the supremacy of the Ch'in Dynasty, but the basic concepts and institutions of law and organization with which it is identified survived in Han China and thereafter in symbiosis with those belonging to the classical Confucian order, ready to be rediscovered and reaffirmed in times of trouble when the theory of China's unity was questioned from within or from without. This long-range function of Legalism was to become evident in the critical first decades of the twentieth century, when China, in the throes of revolution, embarked on a vast modernization program in the course of which it was decided to borrow law from the West. Commissions were sent abroad and an ambitious program of codifica-

[177] The Legalists did not altogether deny *li*; see T'ung-tsu Ch'u, *op.cit.*, p. 241.

147

tion begun, but it was soon realized that the grafts would not take and that the new codes had no relation to China's thought world. The cure for China's ills—thus many thoughtful reformers argued—lay in a return to Han Fei Tzu.[178] That is to say, nothing had been accomplished by way of law reform when the Japanese and Civil Wars began.

The fundamental reasons for this turn of events, which acquires particular significance in the light of China's subsequent transformation under the guidance of Mao Tse-tung, have been closely analyzed by Escarra in his seminal study of Chinese law. This work begins with the statement that the difference between Orient and Occident is nowhere so clearly manifest as in the domain of law. In the West, he writes, the (Roman) jurisconsults had built, over the centuries, a structure of analysis and synthesis, a corpus of "doctrine," ceaselessly tending to perfect and purify the technical elements of the systems of positive law. But as one passes to the East this picture fades away, and nowhere in the Orient more completely than in China. Here, where the notion of order excludes that of law, where the concepts of the state and the nation are unknown, and where individual rights are inconceivable, one looks in vain for analytical jurisprudence, systematic treatments of law as distinct from morality, or differentiating views of what is public and what private. For the same reasons, Escarra explains, there is nothing remotely comparable to *ius gentium* or international law in this region of the world.

China's Asian orbit, then, was not a system of equal sovereign states. In the context of the doctrine of unity

[178] Escarra, *op.cit.*, pp. 31, 39, 59, 436, to the effect that the Legalists were returned to influence deliberately in the twentieth century, and that Chinese legislation of those decades strongly reflects their impact.

and the Heavenly Mandate it had to be viewed by Peking as merely the outer fringe of its administration of China proper.[179] As administered by the Bureau of Rites (which continued functioning even after 1861 when the Department of Foreign Affairs was established to deal with Western nations)[180] all neighboring societies were inferior members of a macrocosmic Confucian family, cast in the roles of sons or younger brothers, in need of rectification through sinification, obliged, as the Middle Kingdom's satellites, to do the imperial patriarch's bidding, yet proud to participate in an elaborate system of tribute, etiquette, and ritual that afforded each of the lesser rulers rank, prestige, and such tangible amenities as gifts.[181]

The incompatibility of East Asian and Occidental traditions of diplomacy was to become apparent to representatives of both culture worlds in several encounters during those momentous decades in the nineteenth century when classical China showed signs of breaking up, even as she was being drawn into the Western scheme of things. It found the following recognition in a letter addressed by the Chinese emperor to George III:

Our ceremonies and codes of law differ so completely

[179] Fairbank, *loc.cit.*; also by the same author "Tributary Trade and China's Relations with the West," *Far Eastern Quarterly*, 1 (February, 1942), 129-49; and *The United States and China* (Cambridge, 1948), pp. 305ff on China's tradition of using barbarians to control barbarians, followed by dynasty after dynasty in dealing with militarily stronger alien invaders and clearly manifest also in the records of the nineteenth and twentieth centuries.

[180] Melvin F. Nelson, *Korea and the Old Orders in Eastern Asia* (Baton Rouge, La., 1945), p. 93.

[181] *Ibid.*, where the relationship between China and Korea is developed step by step; also J. L. Cranmer-Byng, *An Embassy to China* (London, 1962); Alastair Lamb, *The China-India Border* (Oxford, 1964), for brief discussions of the status of Tibet, Sinkiang, and the Himalayan States, and of the Manchu tribute system, pp. 27ff.

149

from your own that even if your Envoy were able to acquire the rudiments of our civilization, you could not possibly transplant our manners and customs to your alien soil. Therefore, however adept the Envoy might become, nothing could be gained thereby.[182]

This position, Nelson remarks, was to be held adamantly whether the issue concerned Tibet, Annam, or Korea; for the Chinese have at no time been willing to assent either to the Occidental concept of a family of equal sovereign nations, or to those limited and neatly defined categories of political organization and international law in terms of which nonsovereign political entities had to be treated as protectorates, colonies, etc. These classifications simply did not cover realities in the Chinese regional system, as the U.S. Department of State was to find out toward the end of the last century when it was concerned with negotiating a treaty of amity with Korea. Treated before the seventeenth century on the analogy of a "son" in China's Asian family and thereafter more as "a younger brother," Korea viewed its dependency as a mark of civilization not as vassalage as the European legalists would have it. In refusing, at that time, to negotiate with Western powers, her spokesmen maintained, after explaining that Korea was "protector of the hedges" for China and that her king was a minister of the emperor, that "our respective dispositions are mutually dissimilar; our guiding principles are not alike."

Such a status was incomprehensible to Western representatives, all the more so since China disavowed control over the internal administration of the country, insisting

[182] Nelson, *op.cit.*, p. 98; the following account draws heavily on Nelson's study.

150

that Korea was not a vassal. And it was still ambiguous in 1883 when a Chinese statesman wondered whether the Western states could rightly assume that their international law was the only system to be recognized and applied, particularly in a part of the world whose divergent system antedated that of the West by thousands of years, and when an American diplomat echoed this doubt in a dispatch to his superiors in Washington:

> Vattel discusses . . . the status of dependent states with reference to foreign powers. This discussion furnishes little information applicable to the peculiar relations existing between China and her dependent states. The text has little application to countries which, in their history, antedate international law of which, also, they never had any knowledge. What unwritten law or tradition controls the relations of China with her dependencies remains unknown.[183]

Over half a century later even, when scholars had provided policy makers in the Occident with the missing answers, rigid adherence to the textual formulations of international law continued to control foreign-policy making. For example, the status of Tibet, a vast non-Chinese, nonsinified realm, was not viewed in the light of almost two thousand years of cultural and political independence under a variety of indigenous governments (neither, to be sure, easily encompassed in Western legal terms), but rather in that cast by Western-type treaties which had been concluded in more recent centuries, after China's administrators had recognized international law "as a useful defensive weapon" fit for integration in the *li/fa* arsenal of diplomacy.[184] And

183 *Ibid.*, p. 190.
184 Jerome Alan Cohen, "Chinese Attitudes Toward International

similar blind spots are on record in Occidental relations with the hinduized and sinified states in the culturally syncretic world of Indo-China.[185]

The *fa* dimension of the Chinese art of ruling was by no means absent in the Greater China zone of influence. Here it was made manifest by war, and war was presented consistently by the Confucians and even the Mohists as a necessary chastisement of undeveloped, uncouth peoples, or as punishment for states that were badly ruled.[186] However, unlike in the small community in the Middle Kingdom proper, *fa* was not mitigated in international relations by the operation of an interstate court or arbitral commission, for example, that would investigate grievances and charges against a government or try to compose differences impartially. The "righteous war" principle was thus openly understood as a moral cloak under which to cover acts of aggression, often after first preparing the ground through the spreading of atrocity stories about the society singled out for punishment. The overt avowal by the Legalists of the absolute need for rule by war was thus in point of fact no radical departure from so-called classical tenets. What deserves attention here is rather the sublimation of war as the dominant purpose of all political life and the denigration of peace as "the source of the six maggots of the state." If these parasites (among them filial piety, history, and sincerity) are at work, the ruler is unable to make people farm and fight, and then, Lord Shang concludes, the state will be so poor that it will invite disintegration. In deference to these views, all Realist

Law and Our Own," *Proceedings of the American Society of International Law* (April 1967), pp. 108ff.

[185] See *supra*, pp. 21ff, 128ff.

[186] Waley, *op.cit.*, pp. 123ff, 138ff, 152ff.

authorities agree that the state exists for the sole aim of conquest; that it is a misfortune for a prospering country not to be at war;[187] that government must be organized for the exclusive purpose of conducting military operations and assuring the food production requisite to support war efforts;[188] and that a ruler who can make people delight in war will become king of kings. In Lord Shang's view such a king should be a wicked man, for only when wicked people rule, can virtue be maintained in the state.[189]

The Chinese were vastly superior to contemporary Greeks, Persians, and Indians in military talent, weaponry, and offensive and defensive tactics when the "new" China was being created in 221 BC.[190] However, a science of political organization was needed if the monolithic state was to triumph lastingly over its foreign enemies, cope with domestic insurrection and instability, and coordinate farming, large-scale hydraulic works, wall-building, registration of the populace, tax-collecting functions of the bureaucracy, and other essential activities. This science, which was to become the "constitution" of the restructured China, had been promulgated by Sun Tzu between 400 and 320 BC, in the period of the Warring States when All-under-Heaven was in chaos, large states were eating up smaller ones as systematically as silkworms eat mulberry leaves, and generation after generation was being consumed by endemic warfare. Sun Tzu's *Art of War*, a martial classic for all times every-

187 *Ibid.*, pp. 220ff.

188 Cp., *supra*, pp. 137-38 for comments on the traditional Asian affiliation between army and peasantry, and *infra*, pp. 156ff. The agro-military commune upon which Mao Tse-tung relies in his administration of China appears deeply rooted in Realist traditions of government.

189 *Op.cit.*, p. 84.

190 See Preface by Samuel B. Griffith in Sun Tzu, *The Art of War*, trans. Samuel B. Griffith (Oxford, 1963).

where,[191] deserves special notice in any discussion of law and organization in Asia. Although it had shocked ardent Confucian contemporaries (whom the Realists, in their turn, belittled as intriguing moralizing ideologues), it had been accepted by successive dynasties as the authoritative guide for military operations. Today this work is a living source of Maoist thought and statecraft in domestic and foreign affairs, as a mere reading of Mao's works with their abundant paraphrasing of Sun Tzu convincingly shows. And this revival of Legalism[192] is by no means arbitrary or coincidental, at least not in the context of Chinese history; for the failure of unity in the twentieth century was not unlike that which had confronted Sun Tzu and his contemporaries (just as it bears analogy to the condition of disunity that invited the Mongol conquest in 1279). Then and now power and cunning had to be invested methodically, so the leadership argued, in order to rectify what rule by goodness had allowed to happen.

The further convergence between Chinese Realism, ancient and modern, on the one hand, and Leninism in its Stalinist and most orientalized version on the other, is equally logical: after all, Communism issued from the same view of the purposes of life, stood for the same type of organizing humanity, and aimed at the realization of a greatly similar theory of unity. In other words, Leninism could be sinified easily. Armed with this new science and guide to action and secure in the wisdom of

191 *Ibid.*, to the effect that China's and Russia's grand strategies cannot be understood without reading this work; see also *supra*, pp. 19ff, n. 7.

192 Not all Legalists have found official favor: Han Fei is classified as a reactionary representative of the newly arising landlord class. Mencius, by contrast, who was not a Legalist, comes off well with his strong accent on rightful war and the need for self-examination. See Wing-tsit Chan, *Chinese Philosophy, 1949-1963: An Annotated Bibliography of Mainland China Publications* (Honolulu, 1967).

154

his own tradition, Mao Tse-tung could say authoritatively:

> Apart from armed struggle, it is impossible to understand our political line and our party building.[193]

> Every Communist must grasp the truth: "Political power grows out of the barrel of a gun."[194]

> In China the main form of struggle is war and the main form of organisation is the army. Other forms, like mass organisations and mass struggles, are also extremely important, . . . but they are all for the sake of war.

> Experience in the class struggle of the era of imperialism teaches us that the working class and the toiling masses cannot defeat the armed bourgeois and landlords except by the power of the gun: in this sense we can even say that the whole world can be remoulded only with the gun.[195]

The military and militant language upon which the Maoist and Legalist vocabularies converge,[196] carries the unqualified conviction that all organization—whether of the village or of the world—is war organization,[197] to be pursued and maintained by the same rules of tactics and strategy that apply also (in Occidental habits of thinking exclusively) on the battlefield. Indeed war in the Asian syndrome is not an aberration, a misfortune, a singular interruption of peace, but the highest form of

---

[193] Stuart R. Schram, *The Political Thought of Mao Tse-tung: Anthology* (New York, 1963), p. 208.

[194] Mao Tse-tung, *Selected Works*, rev. ed., 4 vols. (London, 1958), II, 228.

[195] *Ibid.*, p. 224, 229.   [196] *Supra*, pp. 19ff, 140ff.

[197] See Samuel B. Griffith, *The Chinese People's Liberation Army* (New York, 1967) for an elucidation of this point; also by the same author, *Mao Tse-tung on Guerrilla Warfare* (New York, 1961).

struggle in behalf of which individuals and nations must commit themselves relentlessly in manners carefully prescribed by their guides and mentors.

For China this has meant the dismantling of the remnants of the Western structure and the establishment not only of "democratic dictatorship," "revolutionary class justice," "people's courts," and public mass trials, but also of conciliation/struggle sessions, mass mediation commissions, and other devices evocative of traditional Chinese practice—all designed exclusively for the purpose of guiding and controlling thought and of enforcing the monolithic program of the rulers.[198] And similarly concordant Leninist and Chinese precepts—both rooted in the recognition that the military Asian state is absolutely dependent on the peasants—have combined to supply the blueprint for "the organization of the countryside." To rely on the peasants—after these had been aroused and organized—and establish rural base areas was the Maoist motto in the early days of the civil war, and it continues to be echoed in pronouncement after pronouncement bearing on China's approaches to regional and international wars. This is borne out strongly in Lin Piao's famous speech, "Long Live the Victory of the People's War" (September 1965), where the theory and imagery of the land-based people's war are adapted to the world at large: just as Mao's revolutionary leadership had used the Chinese countryside to encircle the cities, the general explains, so is it now engaged in organizing the land masses or "rural base

[198] For the evolution of some aspects of this system see Shao-chuan Leng, "Pre-1949 Development of the Communist Chinese System of Justice," *China Quarterly*, no. 30 (April-June 1967), pp. 93ff. It should be remarked that "law" is hardly, if ever, mentioned in accounts of Chinese intellectual life today: see Wing-tsit Chan, *op.cit.*; also Shanti Swarup, *A Study of the Chinese Communist Movement* (Oxford, 1966).

areas" represented by Asia and Africa so as to encircle, throttle, and eventually capture "the city system" portrayed by Europe and the United States.

Chinese strategy and tactics, being "laws for conducting war, constitute the art of swimming in the ocean of war," Mao writes.[199] They are also comparable in his view to the basic processes of play and of command decision that mark *wei-ch'i*, the game of strategy favored by Chinese generals, statesmen, and literati from the early Han dynasty to modern times, for what counts in the Maoist game of "enclosing" or "forming" territory (and territory is here viewed in geographical as well as psychological connotations), is what counts in the *wei-ch'i* game:

> Thus there are two forms of encirclement by the enemy forces and two forms of encirclement by our own—rather like a game of *weichi*. Campaigns and battles fought by the two sides resemble the capturing of each other's pieces, and the establishment of strongholds by the enemy and of guerrilla base areas by us resembles moves to dominate spaces on the board. It is in the matter of "dominating the spaces" that the great strategic role of guerrilla base areas in the rear of the enemy is revealed.[200]

199 Mao Tse-tung, *Selected Works*, II, 158. For an analysis of Lin Piao's speech, see Samuel B. Griffith, *Peking and People's Wars* (New York, 1966).

200 See Scott A. Boorman, *The Protracted Game: A Wei-Ch'i Interpretation of Maoist Revolutionary Strategy* (New York, 1969), p. 6; p. 208 n. 8 for historical references to the pervasive influence of this game (known in Japan as "go"), and for the suggestion that Sun Tzu's theories bear a distinct similarity to *wei-ch'i* dicta.

Boorman's study develops the significant thesis that Chinese Communist policies and *wei-ch'i* are products of the same strategic tradition—one for which parallels cannot be found either in Occidental military tradition or in chess as played in the West. It presents the hypothesis that *wei-ch'i* is an important, if little recognized, model of

In the Maoist theory of insurgency, as in the *wei-ch'i* context, time is long, the grid is large, and warfare is protracted or continuous, shifting from one sub-board of the world arena to the next.

The commitment to war and military science as the major source of guidelines for the successful administration of international relations pending Communist China's ultimate victory, and the cancellation of the idea of peace in the thought systems of Chinese theoreticians and their disciples in modern China's hedgeguarding satellites, are carried by a whole family of interlocking tactical and strategical rules. And these too reflect the coalescence of Leninist, Legalist, and Maoist genius. Just as tunnelling operations—vividly described in Sun Tzu's as well as in Mao's manuals—are designed to undermine the physical foundation of the enemy's military position, so are psychological offensives, pursued relentlessly through all available media, meant to subvert the moral and intellectual ground upon which he stands. To attack his plans, isolate and confuse him, "if possible drive him insane" (Sun Tzu) in "peace" time so that costly battles would be unnecessary, were the instructions then as they are today. And among these techniques none has received as much careful elaboration as the art of dissimulation and simulation.[201] In Sun

---

the Maoist system of insurgency, and that it should be studied seriously in the West with a view to gaining a better understanding of Chinese Communist statecraft and psychology.

See pp. 6-7 for other Maoist references to the game; also *Selected Works*, II, 100-101; 150ff on another *wei-ch'i* image, the "Jig-Saw" pattern of structuring conflict.

See *ibid.*, "Strategic Problems in Guerrilla War," pp. 90-100 on the establishment of base areas, types of base areas, modes of converting guerrilla areas into base areas, and ways of arousing and organizing the people for purposes of psychological "encirclement."

201 See Griffith, *Peking and People's Wars* (New York, 1966), esp. pp. 33ff, on dissimulation. Cp. Fairbank, "China's World Order," where

Tzu's language this called for deceiving the enemy by "creating shapes" or concealing one's own shape from him; in Mao's, for "creating illusions," as for example propagating possibilities for peace when "peace" is in fact understood as "protracted warfare" in behalf of which the "peace-loving" peoples must never relax the guerrilla posture. The historical and actual significance of the war principle for the organization of a Chinese or sinified society (in this case North Vietnam and the Vietcong) has been circumscribed by Dennis J. Duncanson in the following terms:

Guerilla warfare, as perfected in China and Vietnam, is not just a special kind of battle tactics. It embraces, in a vaster field of activity, the entire revolutionary process by which government is worn away, superior forces are split up and neutralized, and political domination is established. The resourcefulness of Ho Chi-minh . . . has been to appreciate and to exploit, to a degree that was not called for in China, the affinity between Leninist organization and revolutionary method and the social attitudes found in a Confucian village, whether it be in China or in Vietnam. All

---

he comments on traditional Chinese diplomacy: in cases where Chinese power was not dominant abroad, efforts to save face and buy tribute by commercial or other means were made. But when both force and purchase failed, the Chinese tradition had a kitbag of diplomatic manoeuvres—how to put foreign envoys at their unease, how to lay rules so that the foreigner was half tied up even before he struggled. The most skill was applied to the analysis of the foreigner's situation and motivation. The correct appraisal of foreign intentions was half the game. The Maoist version of this commitment is well expressed in *Selected Works*, II, 172ff. In the same essay "On the Protracted War," p. 171, Mao quotes Sun Tzu's "law" approvingly, namely, "know your enemy and know yourself, and you can fight a hundred battles without disaster."

political groups in both countries are habitually organized on a conspiratorial basis.[202]

The convergence of Asian traditions of statecraft on the idea that politics is war and diplomacy the art of deliberate make-believe or deceit is amply documented in the records of Oriental philosophy, history, and contemporary policy-making; but it is rendered most poignantly perhaps by the shadow play—an ancient folk art as popular in Egypt and Indonesia as in India and China—which teaches that the real world behind all appearances and facades is being held together by conflict and conspiracy.

[202] "How–and Why–The Vietcong Holds Out," *Encounter*, XXVII (December 1966), p. 80. For a thorough analysis of the Communist Chinese view that international relations must be structured as a conflict system see Sir Robert Thompson, *No Exit from Vietnam* (New York, 1969).

CONCLUSION

TIME PRESENT AND TIME PAST

ARE BOTH PERHAPS PRESENT IN TIME FUTURE,

AND TIME FUTURE CONTAINED IN TIME PAST.

IF ALL TIME IS ETERNALLY PRESENT

ALL TIME IS UNREDEEMABLE.

T. S. Eliot, *Burnt Norton*

EACH of the separate sections in the foregoing discussion of several and diverse systems of law and organization contains a summary of locally and regionally prevalent theories that are likely to remain dominant in the future. These findings suggest that the world will continue to be multicultural under the surface of unifying technological and rhetorical arrangements.[1] Indeed existing patterns of thought and modes of relating to the needs of the present and the compelling impact of the past are so infinitely various that no one vision of "the

[1] Similar conclusions were reached by Harold D. Lasswell in 1935: "Indeed, the pursuit of unity is itself an unrealized phantom of the human imagination. . . . A united world would be something new under the sun." See "In Quest of a Myth: The Problem of World Unity," in *World Politics and Personal Insecurity* (New York, 1935), also pp. 239f; by Denis W. Brogan in 1956: "The adoption by one country of the political structure of another or the creation of world organization may disappoint hopes simply because the basic difficulties are unaffected. There is no common body politic, only common devices; there is no common memory, only a common set of problems and inherited difficulties." See "Conflicts Arising out of Differing Governmental and Political Institutions," in Brookings Institution, ed., *The Changing Environment of International Relations* (Washington, D.C., 1956), p. 39; and by C.A.W. Manning, *The Nature of International Society* (London, 1962), p. 174, where he describes the social cosmos as a multicultural world, a mosaic of belief systems, and a jungle of luxuriant myths.

future"—especially not one issuing from the time perspective of the West—can possibly comprehend them adequately in their authenticity, just as no summary description such as "the bi-polar world" or "the third world" can convey world politics in its reality.

The following attempt to synchronize the likely "futures" of multiple societies while also noting, first, certain broad affinities or parallelisms in African and Asian approaches to law and organization, and next, surveying developments in Europe and the United States, is thus in no way meant to invalidate the particularized conclusions presented in each of the preceding sections.

1

Asian and African traditions had been at one for millennia in stressing the primacy of the group, assigning essentially role-playing functions to the individual, and keeping thought subordinate to custom and authority. Impressive conceptual systems relating in particular to philosophy, religion, and mythology, were recorded in the Orient, but, as administered by elites claiming a monopoly of knowledge, they proved to be impediments rather than stimuli to secular, innovative thinking. This was so firstly because they instructed men to aim at the elimination rather than the development of the personality; and secondly, because—being comprehensive normative orders in every sense of the term—they did not allow for the evolution either of distinct categories of thought or of politically significant ways of perfecting society. No possibility thus existed either here or in Africa of disengaging "law" as a separate system of

162

norms, of fathoming "contract" as a structuring principle for human relationships, and of rendering rights and obligations in the language of legal abstractions.

Modern westernized elites had been able, in the nineteenth and early twentieth centuries, to loosen many traditional restraints, borrow Occidental forms of politically and socially relevant thought, and eventually establish states on models found in European and American realms. However, with the waning of Western influence and power, the advent of independence, and the restoration of cultural self-confidence, African and Asian leaders have ceased to be "marginal men" in Toynbee's sense of the phrase. Drawn inward by the demands of their respective societies and functioning in a psychic environment in which the major dispositions are traditional in nature, they are now representatives of their native orders rather than mediators shuttling between two different worlds. And in this connection it bears remembering that few of the personalities now dominant or ascendant on local planes of politics have had, or are likely to have, the kind of intellectual connections with the legal thought world of the West that had stimulated many of their predecessors to think of "national self-determination" in the context of law and constitutionalism.

The general transcultural accord upon the importance of codes, constitutions, and other legal documents, in which earlier generations of legally trained non-Western elites seem to have had a genuine stake or interest, will no doubt retain some measure of formal or rhetorical validity. However, there is scant evidence in any of the diverse systems of public order—with the possible exception of the Indian region—that law in general will become either a paramount value, a trusted carrier of

163

major socially controlling values, or a favored normative reference for the muting of critical tensions and
disputes and the assurance of communal harmony in
the group.

In the absence of a pronounced appreciation of law
and legal institutions, and in the presence of a clearly
discernible fear of the implications of individualism for
the maintenance of social order, the sense of individual
legal rights and obligations can hardly be expected to
develop. Bills of human or civil rights on the order of
those taken for granted in the West and registered explicitly in the Charter of the United Nations and related
international documents as mankind's common heritage,
will therefore continue to be as deceptive of the real state
of affairs as they have been in the last decades. And the
same prognosis naturally holds for constitutions: many
are on record and many more will no doubt be written,
but their normative effectiveness in the realm of public
life is bound to be limited indeed.

Although law is of minimal importance in all non-
Western societies, organization is everywhere of the
essence. However, in this context too one notes a dual
frame of reference; for under the surface of organizational structures that are analogous in outline, even if
not in inception and function, to those found also in the
West, a great variety of very different associational
forms exist and are likely to remain viable in response
to local needs. Thus it appears clear after an analysis of
modern Asian and African states that "the nation" is
not a widely meaningful composite concept, that the
territorial contours of the state—be it a mini-state or a
quasi-imperial orbit—can be indeterminate and shifting
without detracting from the identity of the political
organism, and that the cause of the central government

is not necessarily linked to principles denoting either internal stability or popular representation and respect.

Traditional Oriental regimes had similar characteristics but they could compensate for the shifting nature of popular and territorial supports by reliance, firstly, upon competent, centrally directed bureaucratic, military, and espionage services; secondly, on the efficacy of such indirect nonpolitical controls of the populace as religious, symbolic, and ritual systems; and thirdly, perhaps most importantly, on the continuous functioning of numerous "small" organizations such as extended families, clans, villages, tribes, guilds, crafts, castes, sects, brotherhoods, and secret corporations, in which people found security and satisfaction. Here, as in traditional Africa where the associational instinct was also strong, a central administration acted as an umbrella: society existed in its shadow as a composite of intricate, more or less autonomous yet interlocking groups, rather than as a community of men sharing political loyalties as citizens.

Confidence in the "small" organization and distrust of the apparatus of the state continue to mark life in modern non-Western states. Indeed the polarization in the relationship between the state and the functionally limited associations it accommodates is becoming increasingly pronounced in all societies excepting those effectively levelled and controlled by Communist force and ideology. For in the absence of firm guidance and restraint by law or other superior norms of legitimacy, such as religious or dynastic principles, and of reliable adjunct national institutions, such as representative councils, bureaucratic establishments, and security services, the cause of central government has become an intensely personal and thus precarious matter. Determined mainly by the ambitions, talents, and fortunes of a few leading individuals and the close supporters they can organize in one form or another, it is today pragmatic and unstable, veering everywhere to arbitrary, even despotic rule, and therefore stimulating counter-organizations in the diffuse ranks of the alienated and the disaffected who find themselves outside the realm of power.

The striking incidence of factionalism and intrigue, of coups d'etat, assassinations, revolutions, and liberation movements directed against "established" governments, upon which recent developments in Africa and Asia converge, may thus be viewed as a natural corollary of the interaction between these two parallel yet mutually antagonistic trends. However, it is also an expression of two other dispositions, both rooted in traditional life styles, and both crucially important for any estimate of emerging models of political organization: namely, a delight in secrecy, in underhand and clandestine operations on the one hand, and on the other, a predilection for viewing conflict positively, as an emotionally satisfying, politically structuring, principle, even in situations in which it proves virulent and violent. These dispositions, together with the time perspectives informing Asian and African societies, contribute to the mobile nature of most organizational units; for by favoring chronic activism, they stifle processes of thought and action that would aim first at the achievement, and next at the consolidation, of fundamental changes in society.

The peculiar dynamic inhabiting Afro-Asian political systems is kept going in its essentially circular motion by yet another set of interconnected principles: the paramountcy of the biographical factor in government and the automatically ensuing rivalry between leading contenders to power whose ambitions are naturally limited

166

(in the absence of transcendent national purposes) by their respective life spans. Furthermore, and most importantly perhaps, the power that is wanted and respected in the life of an individual as well as in society is nowhere primarily materialistic in nature; that is to say, it need not be invested in long-range programs assuring social and economic development to be convincing. What one observes on most non-Western local scenes today is rather that "power" continues to relate to the same essentially supernatural, intangible, or psychic forces that had ruled the minds of men in traditional societies. This may explain why political prestige is more closely associated with external symbols of power than with concrete achievements. The conclusion is not untenable, then, that power as understood in Africa and Asia relates to what in the West is usually regarded as appearance rather than reality, and that non-Western governments must be adept in the art of administering illusions if they are to be effective in the contexts of their cultures.

The supremacy of personalism and familism over system, and of psychological and political factors over considerations of social and economic well-being, combine with the absence of a pronounced sense of ethical and legal responsibility in the public domain to explain why nepotism and corruption are almost everywhere natural aspects of political life not likely to elicit public protest. And the same circumstances, in conjunction with the penchant for secrecy and indirect action to which allusion has already been made, make it easy to understand why rival aspirants to power and position, deprived of regular or "legal" avenues toward leadership or advancement, often resort to more or less artful manipulations of their human environment, thus contributing to the web of intrigue in which all organization, both covert or overt, is apt to be caught. In fact given this entire syndrome of human associations, intrigue may well be viewed as a reserve of freedom, at least for the strong-willed and the talented.

Post-independence developments in both continents also justify the following limited forecasts: firstly that both opposition and governmental power—commonly projected in executive rather than in legislative and judicial action—will continue to be harsh, arbitrary, and fraught with violence; and secondly that this type of authority will be accepted by the governed as long as they can relate it, however tenuously, to traditionally trusted forms and practices. That is to say, since the cause of independence and organizational stability in the non-Communist states of Africa and Asia, precarious as it is, is found today mainly to be a function of the tutelage that certain normative institutions of proven worth exercise indirectly over the conduct of modern government, it could probably be furthered appreciably in the future if policies aiming at national survival and development were to be related consciously to that which is resilient in the culture.[2]

The thesis that a given country's conduct and organization of its foreign relations is an organic aspect of the life style that informs its inner order, has been stated and developed in preceding sections dealing with the Mohammedan Near East, Negro Africa, Indianized Asia and the Chinese orbit. In this framework, as in that of domestic law and organization, greatly diverse patterns are on record. Yet here, as there, certain broad affinities

---

[2] Similar conclusions have been reached by H.A.R. Gibb and other authorities on the civilization of Islam, see *supra*, pp. 60, 75ff; by M. Christian Vieyra in respect of Africa south of Sahara, *supra*, p. 139, n. 163; and by Professor Heine-Geldern in his reflections on governments in Southeast Asia, *supra*, pp. 95-96.

are evident. It thus appears that interstate relations are in large measure extensions of relations between the personalities who symbolize the idea of the nation (India, Pakistan, Iran, and Turkey are in this respect among the exceptions to the rule); that foreign rather than domestic policy is viewed as the arena of action most favorable to the enhancement of personal power and prestige, and that a government's power and effectiveness in the management of foreign affairs are not contingent upon either the stability of the state and its government, or the strength and promise of the economy.

Furthermore, international relations within each culturally unified region are marked by suspicion toward "the other" and by an easy aggressiveness in deed and discourse. Here, as on domestic levels of politics, one observes great tolerance for conspiracy, verbal abuse, and all manner of belligerent and violent interventions in the domestic affairs of neighboring countries. In fact conflict seems to be accepted everywhere not only as the ruling norm but also as the major and sustaining source of politically significant normative thought and behavior. International peace, as this term has long been understood in the Occidental region, is by contrast an alien concept. Although it is being stressed today in the borrowed contexts of internationalist rhetoric and ideology and in such formulations as "nonalignment," it does not seem to be viewed as an attainable condition in the regional affairs of Negro Africa, the Middle East, and Southeast Asia. Nor can analogues be found in any non-Western tradition (excepting that of the Islamic Middle East) either for long-range moral or political commitments to collective security and mutual aid, or for consistent efforts to develop international organizations and international law.

The recent official affiliation with the public order

169

system of the West, especially as this is subsumed in the Charter and Organization of the United Nations, had stimulated some representatives of the westernized elites to think of the past of their own cultures in terms suggested by the past of the West, and thus to assume the existence of some kind of international law in ancient times. However, the dominant bent of mind today and the one most likely to prevail in the near future—if only because it is fully consonant with the resurrection of the native orders in all other politically relevant contexts—inclines rather to a refutation of international law and international constitutionalism (and thus also of the original purposes implicit in international organization), on the ground that these are Western inventions not meeting African and Asian needs.[3]

[3] These conclusions are supported by the records of a Conference on International Law that was held at the University of Hong Kong in January 1967 under the auspices of the Carnegie Endowment for International Peace, the Asia Foundation, and the Ford Foundation. At this occasion Asian lawyers are said to have presented ritual statements of their countries' enlightened views of "international law" in the remote past, without, however, producing tangible evidence in support of these references. In the discussion of "peaceful settlement of disputes," observers noted, furthermore, a total lack of interest in specifically regional views or solutions. Most participants, excepting those representing Japan, are said to have seen the problem in political rather than in legal terms.

In this connection it is interesting to note that the eighteenth-century Western jurist G. F. de Martens could find few records bearing on treaty relations between Asian states; the treaties he records were concluded between European and Asian governments. For valuable comments on this subject and conclusions that differ from those here presented, see Charles Henry Alexandrowicz, ed., "Studies in the History of the Law of Nations," in the *Indian Year Book of International Affairs*, vol. XIII (1964); also by the same author, *An Introduction to the History of the Law of Nations in the East Indies* (London, 1967), where diplomatic and treaty relations between European and South Asian governments are presented.

Few non-Western governments have gone as far as those representing modern Africa in disavowing the validity of constitutional provisions regulating the work of e.g. the World Health Organization and other Specialized Agencies.

170

The absence, in each of the regions here discussed, of a felt need for organized unity and collective security, and the unwillingness to make long-range commitments in bilateral and multilateral relations, have by no means precluded the emergence of regionally distinct arrangements for the conduct of international relations in general and the settlement of disputes in particular. Indeed, as the awareness of a common heritage deepens and norms borrowed or imposed from without fall into disuse, culturally congenial ways of stabilizing peaceful as well as belligerent interactions between neighboring societies are bound to become increasingly evident.[4] However, few if any of these slowly emergent "regional arrangements" are likely to conform to the models vaguely foreseen in the United Nations Charter as geographically delimited microcosms of the world organization. For in each regional realm the emphasis will continue to be on pragmatism rather than principle, on ad hoc diplomacy and mediation rather than on law and organization.

Whether these regionally or culturally distinct orders are properly viewed as "systems" is a matter of individual perception and definition. If by "system" is meant a set of identifiable regularities in behavior,[5] each of the

[4] For another approach to the relationship between international and regional law see José Sanson-Teran, *Universalismo y Regionalismo en la Sociedad Interstatai Contemporanea* (Barcelona, 1960), p. 32, as rendered by Robert W. Macdonald, *The League of Arab States* (Princeton, 1965), p. 28: "Universal internal law exists common to all civilized communities, but alongside this law is particular law applicable exclusively to certain regions of the world. Put otherwise, the historical, geographical, psychological, political, and economic individuality of a region determine a complex of juridical principles unique to the states of this region which derogates in part from the universal law regardless of the extent to which all implicitly recognize the existence and validity of it."

[5] Cp. Charles A. McClelland, "The Function of Theory in International Relations." *Journal of Conflict Resolution* (December 1960),

groupings here discussed may qualify. If, on the other hand, "system" connotes a deliberate organization and management of shared customs and affinities, then the term may not be applicable anywhere outside of the Western order of coordinate states and the Communist blocs in which satellite states are grouped securely around a major power center.

2

As Oriental and African societies are recovering their native styles of thought and organization, those in the West show signs of disorientation. This is particularly true of the United States where theory, ideology, tradition, and experience combined at an early time to foster the vision of a multinational, egalitarian, and open society in which members, however various their background, are yet in the final analysis subject to the same laws of social evolution. Conceived after the initial English settlement as a melting pot of diverse immigrant strands and dedicated to the principle of the active pragmatic individual who is ready to cast off tradition in order to develop freely in his own right, the United States had in fact stated its case as a nation by transcending ethnic, religious, and linguistic particularities before

---

pp. 303-306, and Barkun, *op.cit.*, pp. 28ff, 39ff, 57, 69, for comments directly relevant to this complex of issues; *ibid.*, p. 154 for the valuable reminder that activities apparently devoid of function or meaning may seem so only because they are viewed in the perspectives of our own culture.

See also Richard N. Rosecrance, *Action and Reaction in World Politics* (Boston, 1963), pp. 12ff on criteria by which one system may be distinguished from another, and chap. 11, p. 219 for a presentation of several "international systems" that existed in Europe between 1740 and 1960.

proposing similar models for the organization of the world. In other words, it stands almost by definition for overcoming culture and therewith also for overlooking the past[6]—orientations that diverge significantly from the parental European civilization where greatly similar intellectual dispositions had been held in check by a profound respect for the cultural legacies of the past.

These perspectives, marked as they are by the assumption that the world order and the American order rest on parallel if not identical evaluations of man's destiny, are being put in issue today by contrary developments not only in all non-Western regions but also within the American commonwealth itself where symptoms are not missing that a history and culture transcendent design cannot assure the kind of unity and stability that existence as a nation-state requires.

The moral and political crisis that has ensued as a matter of course from the erosion of the favored conceptual framework for political organization has its most serious corollary in the fact that contemporary generations, having been led to identify with the future fortunes of mankind at large, are today cut off from the regenerative roots of their own past. That is to say, unlike the Asians and the Africans, they cannot easily recompose themselves, restructure their society, and thus steady the faltering sense of nationhood by turning inward in time and space in search of promising directions for the future. In fact, since their civilization has been utilized almost mechanistically for the binding of different cultures and political systems, they are apt to view it

[6] This aspect is discussed in Adda B. Bozeman, "Do Educational and Cultural Exchanges have Political Relevance?" *International Educational and Cultural Exchange*, a publication of the U.S. Advisory Commission on International Educational and Cultural Affairs (Washington, D.C., 1969).

as a mere function of the desired international order rather than as the latter's motive force. And in the logic of this vision, of course, all discomfiting disorders in the world environment are being readily deflected so as to incriminate the nation's inner order.

The road back to authenticity is temporarily blocked in the United States for yet another reason. The impulsive leap in mid-twentieth century from a national self-view to a self-understanding derived from membership in a utopian world community—shortlived and abortive as it was bound to be—has been rationalized, ex post facto in most respects, by deliberate efforts either to reduce the meanings inherent in certain fundamental Occidental values so as to make them commensurate with those found elsewhere in the world, or to fashion value-neutral schemes for the integration of value-related phenomena all over the world. These approaches, academically convincing as many of them are, have made for a marked insensitivity to the intangible forces by which the political community is being held together, and for an undue extension of skepticism about the worth of American institutions.

Thus it appears that the principle of individuation, which distinguished the Occidental from other thought systems to become the primary reference in law and government, is being widely experienced either as an unbearable psychological burden or as an irrelevant antisocial guide to thought and action. Similarly strong evidence exists that the very idea of law, especially as it relates to power and authority, is at present either being misunderstood, questioned, or openly resented as dissident segments of the citizenry extol the virtues of militant lawlessness and coercive power. These states of moral confusion explain why "organization" is often

174

being made to serve ends that are either not compatible with, or clearly subversive of, the structure of government as understood in the context of constitutionalism. Furthermore, since the American version of the state is an outgrowth not of ethnic or religious unity but rather of an accord on the binding force of constitutionalism, the conclusion is not untenable that the very notion of the state is at present embattled as men deprived of access to an understanding of their own culture and society follow instinctual anarchic drives, seek attachment in the traditional worlds of Africa and Asia, or get engulfed by modern totalitarian ideologies that are antithetical to their native public order system.

Present trends, dim, confused, and limited as they may be, thus point to a reversal of direction in intercultural relations. For whereas the past century in international history was marked by a general convergence upon patterns of law and organization as well as on futuristic visions of society perfected in the West—a process commonly circumscribed as westernization—signs today point to a rather massive borrowing by Americans of Oriental, African, and Communist motifs. In the social strata of those susceptible to these influences from abroad one thus finds a strong stress on communalism, "now"-centered action and group organization that is openly hostile to the state. However, certain significant differences are suggested by a preliminary comparison of these two borrowing processes. Firstly, the present alignment of cultures upon common foci of concern proceeds without the kind of guidance exerted in the earlier epoch by African and Asian "marginal elites"— men who knew, by virtue both of a strongly felt commitment to their own indigenous societies and of considerable familiarity with Occidental institutions, just how

175

to effect the necessary grafts without undermining the existing moral order. Secondly, the official establishment in non-Western regions of the Western norm of the nation-state did not eliminate preexisting or substratal local forms of social organization. Here, then, the subsequent erosion or denaturing of the imported superstructure, critical as it is in many respects, has not conduced to anarchy in the inner social order. That is to say, the latter has remained intact, capable of absorbing, even of stemming, the tides of political turmoil. In modern American society, by contrast, rebellions against the established order are bound to raise the specter of anarchy on external as well as internal levels of existence; for not only do they proceed without the services of elites that know the respective margins of contending civilizations, but also, and most importantly, they occur in a society in which the nation-state, far from sitting lightly on strong state-defiant organizational schemes such as the self-sufficient city, village, caste system, corporation, tribe, or clan, is in fact the basic or primary reference. The future of democratic political institutions here is therefore absolutely dependent upon the resuscitation of a convincing national will and upon the reaffirmation of law. Both processes require a refinement of the historical sense and therewith a return to European origins.

In the past and culture-conscious European heartland of the Occidental thought world, meanwhile, where the classical model of the law state had disengaged itself slowly from other associational designs also held together by shared conceptions of the role of law,[7] the cause of the sovereign nation-state has been adversely affected in the last decades by totally different factors: namely, the

[7] *Supra*, pp. 35ff.

experience of two devastating inter-European wars, the rise to brief prominence of a law-defiant German imperialism, and the marked spatial contraction of the nuclear area of Western civilization that has attended the expansion of Soviet Russia's dictatorial hegemony in the long aftermath of the Second World War. These developments made for the realization that independence would have to be qualified deliberately if any of the remaining nations were to survive, and led, in time, to the creation, by wide-ranging accords between formerly antagonistic states, of boundary-transcendent economic communities, all evocative in structure and inception of the inter-European concerts, leagues, and corporations that had also functioned successfully in earlier ages.[8]

The new uses to which the West's intellectual and political traditions have been put have conduced to unprecedented well-being in the geographically truncated continent—thus discrediting the thesis that Europe's wealth in the first decades of the present century has been due to the exploitation of imperial possessions in Africa and Asia. However, coordination and integration in the area of economics are not matched today, and in view of the traditional and modern spirit of European diversity will not likely be matched in the future, by equivalent modes of structuring relations on the plane of political and military affairs as these are envisaged in several utopian designs for a United States of Europe. The contraction of the geographical domain, the withering of the traditional independent state, and the crumbling of military armor have thus left the base area of the culture weak, perhaps defenseless, in the presence of a vast adjoining Communist empire whose totalitarian

8 *Supra*, pp. 42ff.

administration is assured by the maintenance of military force. In short, whereas the future of a stable, morally unified, state in North America is made uncertain not by the absence of material power but by the erosion of respect for law, the only unifying institution in this realm, that of the separate Western European entities, is placed in jeopardy by the absence of credible power.

The joining of Europe and North America—disparate as these two societies are today—in an Atlantic society of coordinate states, thus suggests a distinct complementarity of sources of strength. However, the promise implicit in this regional alignment is not as near fulfillment as that pervading the African realm, for example; for the existing organizational framework still lacks the spirit or momentum that only culture consciousness can provide.

The attainment of this condition, and therewith the realization of Europe's and America's interlocking destinies, requires a clear perception above all of the role of law in the Occidental value system, and clear-sighted vision here is made difficult for the time being by the semantic confusion in which law-related principles have been caught as a result of their rhetorical diffusion all over the world.[9] Today, precise discernment is greatly facilitated because Africans and Asians have taken the initiative of reinstating their own, culturally convincing, principles of organization in counterpoint to those borrowed earlier from the West, and of correcting, in many instances, the language that describes their normative systems. However, the task of clarifying the relationship between norms and words continues to be impeded by the spurious yet largely uncontested use of the Western vocabulary of law and constitutionalism in the Eurasian

[9] *Supra*, see preceding sections.

region dominated by the Soviet Union where an entirely new syndrome of ideology and system has been relayed from Lenin onward in the legal and political language of the West. The intellectual problems implicit in this convergence upon rhetorical usage emerge clearly from the authoritative restatement of the Communist operational code regarding "Sovereignty and International Duties of Socialist Countries" that was presented at the occasion of Soviet Russia's invasion of Czechoslovakia in 1968.

The following major propositions are here asserted:[10]

Those who speak about the "illegal actions" of the allied socialist countries in Czechoslovakia forget that in a class society there is not and there cannot be non-class laws.

Laws and legal norms are subjected to the laws of the class struggle, the laws of social development.

[10] The statement which appeared in *Pravda* on September 25, 1968, was published in the *New York Times*, September 27, 1968. For text see Appendix. The normative orders of the Soviet Union and the Soviet bloc of satellites are not subject matters of analysis in the present discussion, and the bibliography pertaining to Communism and the organization of the Soviet Union is too rich to be appended here. For a brief but admirably succinct presentation of Soviet renditions of international law see Oliver J. Lissitzyn, *International Law in a Divided World* (New York, 1963), pp. 14ff, and, by the same author, "Western and Soviet Perspectives on International Law: A Comparison," *Proceedings of the American Society of International Law* (1959).

No regionalized organization in the contemporary world is as cohesive and effective as the Soviet bloc, which is held together by a common ideology, greatly similar economic and social structures, and the military might of the Soviet Union.

For a historical survey of Soviet Russia's approaches to the United Nations and a searching analysis of the manipulative uses of established legal concepts and words, see Alexander Dallin, *The Soviet Union at the United Nations* (New York, 1962); also Jan F. Triska, "A Model for Study of Soviet Foreign Policy," *American Political Science Review*, vol. LII, no. 1 (March 1958), where the role of Communist combat ideology and terminology in regional and international relations receives particularly lucid treatment.

These laws are clearly formulated in Marxist-Leninist teaching, in the documents jointly adopted by the Communist and Workers' parties.

Formally juridical reasoning must not overshadow a class approach to the matter. One who does it, thus losing the only correct class criterion in assessing legal norms, begins to measure events with a yardstick of bourgeois law.

The sovereignty of each socialist country cannot be opposed to the interests of the world of socialism, of the world revolutionary movement. Lenin demanded that all Communists fight against small-nation narrow-mindedness, seclusion and isolation.

Formal observance of the freedom of self-determination of a nation in the concrete situation that arose in Czechoslovakia would mean freedom of "self-determination" not of the popular masses, the working people, but of their enemies.

The antisocialist path, "neutrality," to which the Czechoslovak people were pushed, would bring it to the loss of national independence.

Naturally the Communists of the fraternal countries could not allow the socialist states to be inactive in the name of an abstractly understood sovereignty, when they saw that the country stood in peril of antisocialist degeneration.

3 .

International law as it has come to be is a derivative as well as a servant of the following orders of reference, all distinctly Occidental in origin:[11]

11 *Supra*, pp. 35-48.

a) the differentiation between law on the one hand and policy, ideology, or morality on the other;

b) the distinction between war and peace, and the concomitant, essentially moral, conviction that peace is preferable to war;

c) the coexistence of independent, territorially delimited, states;

d) the assumption that states acting through their governments are capable of undertaking voluntary and binding obligations in their mutual relations.

These understandings also inhabit international organization, notably the United Nations, which may be said to represent the institutional aspect of international law.

None of the above-listed propositions commands universal validity today. A review of political systems and cultural realities, together with the behavioral records of governments as accumulated in the last decades, suggests, furthermore, that there are few, if any, other convincing equivalencies between the inner normative orders of the vast majority of states on the one hand, and the substantive concepts of established international law and organization on the other.

States continue to exist officially, but the normative idea they represent is everywhere placed in issue either by the absence of a sense of nationhood, the indeterminacy of territorial boundaries, or the presence of vast empires in the framework of which nominally sovereign states are actually subsumed as dependent, quasi-provincial, units. Since common definitions and requirements for the existence of states are now missing, it is erroneous to assume that the modern world society is perceived accurately as an international system composed of equal

181

sovereign states.[12] Next, it appears clear that real, internationally relevant, political power is no longer represented uniformly by officially functioning governments. In many if not all regions of the world it emanates also, often exclusively, from ideologically conceived international parties, mobile military-political units, and other dissimulated power centers. All of these formations operate across state boundaries and under the surface of existing governments, usually in behalf of structural political designs that are antithetical to the established order.

Contrary to appearances, then, the new era in foreign affairs is marked by movement, revolution, and disorder, rather than by stability, legitimacy, and order; by intense ideological conflicts rather than by moral accords; and by the prevalence of war rather than of peace.[13] Indeed a comparative review of cultural traditions, normative systems, and rival ideologies leads to the conclusion that peace is scarcely a shared value in this century, whereas war is a morally accepted way of life in most cultural traditions as they are now encompassed in representative political systems. It reveals furthermore that the realities of peace, war, and neutrality can no longer be circumscribed authoritatively in the official terminology of international law and international organization. For as the concepts of "the state" and "government" are being

[12] Cp. B. Landheer, "The Situational Approach to International Relations" (prepared for the Fifth Maxwell Institute on the United Nations and International Law, Kasteel Oud-Wassenaar, Holland, August 1968), pp. 31ff for a discussion of various visions of the world society-to-be.

[13] See Adda B. Bozeman, "Normative Thinking, the National Interest and War in a Multi-Cultural Environment," in *Conflict and Subjectivity: Toward New Normative Standards in U.S. Foreign Policy*, ed. Thomas Franck and Edward Weisband (New York, 1971).

eroded, and as combat-oriented internationalist ideologies, proclaiming the principle of "the permanent revolution," "protracted war," or "the just war of liberation" are gaining ground, old distinctions between aggression and defense, civil war and foreign war, and the status of belligerence and that of neutrality are also fast becoming blurred if not defunct, leaving vast regions in the throes of chronic strife, guerrilla warfare, insurgency, or counterinsurgency.

Under the impact of these developments, "war" and "peace" can no longer be viewed as polarized, mutually exclusive conditions, each susceptible of an internationally valid definition. Indeed, the most that can be said of "peace" today—whether contemplated as a concept or as a political reality—is that it denotes a situation where conflict is controlled.

In an epoch, then, in which thought is heavily politicized and in which national and international politics are governed by ideology, law must be expected to recede from the fields of consciousness and perception, all the more so as it had never been developed as a set of separate normative and symbolic references in traditional Asian and African societies. It must be remembered next, in connection with the obvious decline of international law, that all Occidental law is absolutely dependent upon order. That is to say, it cannot be expected to generate the general system of accords within which it is called upon to function as an agent of mediation and control. Present efforts aiming at an extension of international law to the sphere of individual life by drafting, for example, universally valid covenants of human rights, appear in this perspective to be exercises in futility—all the more so as most non-Western governments are not constrained by locally dominant moral

183

orders to assure respect for individual liberties within their respective local jurisdictions. In fact such an accentuation of law is likely to contribute to further discords and divisions in the society of nations, since it is apt to induce a false sense of moral unity. And similar effects may well attend the trust in treaties which stems from the Western disposition to identify meaningful accords more or less exclusively with firm contractual commitments. Here, too, the unity of purpose and the predictability of behavior is likely to be illusory, firstly because this form of obligation is not a transculturally valid norm, and secondly because it is more difficult today than it was in an exclusively Occidental state system to know just what "sovereignty" and "independence" mean, and how credible and durable any accord is likely to be.

The growing distance between the established legal system and reality suggests, in particular, a modified approach to war.[14] Since the modern world is being shaped decisively by war, it is unrealistic to pretend not only that peace is the rule but also that law as the servant of peace can effectively defy force. In this, as in other matters once believed subject to international law, nations would profit, singly and collectively, from a return to the less ambitious Grotian view of the role of international law, in terms of which it was possible to regulate many selected incidents and consequences of war because war as such was accepted as an unfortunate yet common phenomenon of international life. In short, if international law is to have a future in world society,

[14] Cp. Landheer, *loc.cit.*, p. 69 where this issue receives persuasive treatment; see also Stanley Hoffmann, "International Systems and International Law," *World Politics* (October 1961), for one of the most cogent analyses of the problem.

what seems to be called for is a contraction of the domain of law and a de-escalation of legal rhetoric.

The United Nations and related international organizations had been called forth by confidence in the moral unity of mankind and the enduring transnational appeals of law and peace. Today, a quarter of a century later, it is clear that this trust is unredeemable: the United Nations is neither an effective collective security organization nor a morally compelling mechanism. Furthermore and most importantly, the jural order in which the political order was ensconced is crumbling steadily as the Assembly and the Security Council of the Organization continue to take doubtful constitutional steps and to treat their respective decisions as if they had an intrinsic jural validity.[15] This process of severing the international organization from its base in international law, unavowed officially and unchecked by realistic reformist thought, has conduced gradually to the denaturing of the political order of the Charter. Emptied of its fundamental meanings, the latter may well be viewed today as a "nonsystem"[16]—a vacuum in imagery, function, and design that invites the substitution of rival models evoca-

[15] See Maxwell Cohen, "Reflections on Law and the United Nations System," *Proceedings of the American Society of International Law*, 54th Annual Meeting (1960), pp. 243ff, for this line of thinking, an analysis of the work in particular of the Sixth Committee of the United Nations, and comments on the general habit of avoiding resort to the International Court.

[16] This term is used by R.G.A. Jackson, *United Nations: A Study of the Capacity of the United Nations Development System*, 2 vols. (Geneva, 1969), I, Foreword, p. vi, in connection with the argument that the work respectively of the separate U.N. Agencies and of the various U.N. member states summarily comprised in "the third world" is gravely obstructed by the absence of central unifying controls. Inquiries revealed example after example where departmental ministers of state have advocated policies in the governing bodies of the particular Agency which concerned them that were in direct conflict with their government's policies toward the U.N. system as a whole. *Ibid.*, p. v.

tive of the Chinese *wei-ch'i* board[17] on which political players are expected to further their independent destinies by dint of intelligence and diplomacy.

The full implications of such a return to unmitigated power politics under the guise of a legalistic order can be offset in the very context of the United Nations scheme by open recognition that the world society consists of diverse political and diplomatic systems, each an outgrowth of culturally and regionally valid modes of conducting international relations. If these subsystems were recognized explicitly for what they are instead of being overlooked or tolerated as indefinable subrosa forces operative under the mantle of a general law, foreign policies would not have to comply with double standards, confusions in mutual understanding could be averted, and many conflicts might be narrowed to their regional essentials without automatically calling into question the effectiveness or general integrity of the United Nations and its law. Indeed, by focusing on the merits of each particular situation and the cultural and psychological properties of each controversy instead of straining to match each aspect of a given issue with the requisite legal paragraph, an interplay between different approaches to the control of conflict would be set in motion which might, in time, yield new types of meaningful consensus.

17 See *supra*, p. xi, n. 4, p. 157.

APPENDIX

Text of Pravda Article Justifying the Invasion of Czechoslovakia, September 25, 1968.

IN connection with the events in Czechoslovakia, the question of the correlation and interdependence of the national interests of the socialist countries and their international duties acquire particular topical and acute importance.

The measures taken by the Soviet Union, jointly with other socialist countries, in defending the socialist gains of the Czechoslovak people are of great significance for strengthening the socialist community, which is the main achievement of the international working class.

We cannot ignore the assertions, made in some places, that the actions of the five socialist countries run counter to the Marxist-Leninist principle of sovereignty and the rights of nations to self-determination.

The groundlessness of such reasoning consists primarily in that it is based on an abstract, nonclass approach to the question of sovereignty and the rights of nations to self-determination.

The peoples of the socialist countries and Communist parties certainly do have and should have freedom for determining the ways of advance of their respective countries.

However, none of their decisions should damage either socialism in their country or the fundamental interests of other socialist countries, and the whole working class movement, which is working for socialism.

187

This means that each Communist party is responsible not only to its own people, but also to all the socialist countries, to the entire Communist movement. Whoever forgets this, in stressing only the independence of the Communist party, becomes one-sided. He deviates from his international duty.

Marxist dialectics are opposed to one-sidedness. They demand that each phenomenon be examined concretely, in general connection with other phenomena, with other processes.

Just as, in Lenin's words, a man living in a society cannot be free from the society, a particular socialist state, staying in a system of other states composing the socialist community, cannot be free from the common interests of that community.

The sovereignty of each socialist country cannot be opposed to the interests of the world of socialism, of the world revolutionary movement. Lenin demanded that all Communists fight against small-nation narrow-mindedness, seclusion and isolation, consider the whole and the general, subordinate the particular to the general interest.

The socialist states respect the democratic norms of international law. They have proved this more than once in practice, by coming out resolutely against the attempts of imperialism to violate the sovereignty and independence of nations.

It is from these same positions that they reject the leftist, adventurist conception of "exporting revolution," of "bringing happiness" to other peoples.

However, from a Marxist point of view, the norms of law, including the norms of mutual relations of the socialist countries, cannot be interpreted narrowly, formally, and in isolation from the general context of class struggle in the modern world. The socialist countries resolutely come out against the exporting and importing of counterrevolution.

Each Communist party is free to apply the basic principles of Marxism-Leninism and of socialism in its country,

188

but it cannot depart from these principles (assuming, naturally, that it remains a Communist party).

Concretely, this means, first of all, that, in its activity, each Communist party cannot but take into account such a decisive fact of our time as the struggle between two opposing social systems—capitalism and socialism.

This is an objective struggle, a fact not depending on the will of the people, and stipulated by the world's being split into two opposite social systems. Lenin said: "Each man must choose between joining our side or the other side. Any attempt to avoid taking sides in this issue must end in fiasco."

It has got to be emphasized that when a socialist country seems to adopt a "non-affiliated" stand, it retains its national independence, in effect, precisely because of the might of the socialist community, and above all the Soviet Union as a central force, which also includes the might of its armed forces. The weakening of any of the links in the world system of socialism directly affects all the socialist countries, which cannot look indifferently upon this.

The antisocialist elements in Czechoslovakia actually covered up the demand for so-called neutrality and Czechoslovakia's withdrawal from the socialist community with talk about the right of nations to self-determination.

However, the implementation of such "self-determination," in other words, Czechoslovakia's detachment from the socialist community, would have come into conflict with its own vital interests and would have been detrimental to the other socialist states.

Such "self-determination," as a result of which NATO troops would have been able to come up to the Soviet border, while the community of European socialist countries would have been split, in effect encroaches upon the vital interests of the peoples of these countries and conflicts, at the very root of it, with the right of these people to socialist self-determination.

189

Discharging their internationalist duty toward the fraternal peoples of Czechoslovakia and defending their own socialist gains, the U.S.S.R. and the other socialist states had to act decisively and they did act against the antisocialist forces in Czechoslovakia.

Comrade W. Gomulka, First Secretary of the Central Committee of the Polish United Workers party, commented figuratively on this score when he said:

"We tell those friends and comrades of ours in the other countries who think they are upholding the righteous cause of socialism and the sovereignty of the peoples by condemning and protesting against the entry of our troops into Czechoslovakia: When the enemy mines our house, the community of socialist states, with dynamite, it is our patriotic, national and international duty to obstruct this by using the means that are necessary."

People who "disapprove" of the actions of the allied socialist states are ignoring the decisive fact that these countries are defending the interests of all of world socialism, of the entire world revolutionary movement.

The system of socialism exists in concrete form in some countries, which have their own definite state boundaries; this system is developing according to the specific conditions of each country. Furthermore, nobody interferes in the concrete measures taken to improve the socialist system in the different socialist countries.

However, the picture changes fundamentally when a danger arises to socialism itself in a particular country. As a social system, world socialism is the common gain of the working people of all lands; it is indivisible and its defense is the common cause of all Communists and all progressives in the world, in the first place, the working folk of the socialist countries.

The Bratislava statement of the Communist and Workers' parties says of socialist gains that "support, consolidation and defense of these gains, won at the price of heroic effort and the self-sacrifice of each people, represents a common international duty and obligation for all the socialist countries."

What the right-wing antisocialist forces set out to achieve in recent months in Czechoslovakia did not refer to the specific features of socialist development or the application of the principle of Marxism-Leninism to the concrete conditions obtaining in that country, but constituted encroachment on the foundations of socialism, on the basic principles of Marxism-Leninism.

This is the nuance that people who have fallen for the hypocritical nonsense of the antisocialist and revisionist elements still cannot understand. Under the guise of "democratization" these elements were little by little shaking the socialist state, seeking to demoralize the Communist party and befog the minds of the masses, stealthily hatching a counterrevolutionary coup, and they were not duly rebuffed inside the country.

Naturally the Communists of the fraternal countries could not allow the socialist states to be inactive in the name of an abstractly understood sovereignty, when they saw that the country stood in peril of antisocialist degeneration.

The actions in Czechoslovakia of the five allied socialist countries accords also with the vital interests of the people of the country themselves.

Socialism, by delivering a nation from the shackles of an exploiting regime, insures the solution of the fundamental problems of the national development of any country that has embarked upon the socialist road. On the other hand, by encroaching upon the main stays of socialism, the counterrevolutionary elements in Czechoslovakia undermined the very foundations of the country's independence and sovereignty.

Formal observance of the freedom of self-determination of a nation in the concrete situation that arose in Czechoslovakia would mean freedom of "self-determination" not of the popular masses, the working people, but of their enemies.

The antisocialist path, "neutrality," to which the Czechoslovak people were pushed would bring it to the loss of its national independence.

World imperialism, on its part, supported the antisocialist forces in Czechoslovakia, tried to export counterrevolution to that country in this way.

The help to the working people of Czechoslovakia by other socialist countries, which prevented the export of counterrevolution from abroad, constitutes the real sovereignty of the Czechoslovak Socialist republic against those who would like to deprive it from its sovereignty and give up the country to imperialism.

The fraternal Communist parties of the socialist countries were for a long time taking measures, with maximum self-restraint and patience, to help the Czechoslovak people with political means to stop the onslaught of antisocialist forces in Czechoslovakia. And only when all such measures were exhausted did they bring armed forces into the country.

The soldiers of the allied socialist countries now in Czechoslovakia proved by their actions indeed that they have no other tasks than the tasks of defending socialist gains in that country.

They do not interfere in the internal affairs of the country, are fighting for the principle of self-determination of the peoples of Czechoslovakia not in words but in deeds, are fighting for their inalienable right to think out profoundly and decide their fate themselves, without intimidation on the part of counterrevolutionaries, without revisionists and nationalist demagogy.

Those who speak about the "illegal actions" of the allied socialist countries in Czechoslovakia forget that in a class society there is not and there cannot be nonclass laws.

Laws and legal norms are subjected to the laws of the class struggle, the laws of social development. These laws are clearly formulated in Marxist-Leninist teaching, in the documents jointly adopted by the Communist and Workers' parties.

Formally juridical reasoning must not overshadow a class approach to the matter. One who does it, thus losing the only correct class criterion in assessing legal norms, begins to measure events with a yardstick of bourgeois law.

Such an approach to the question of sovereignty means that, for example, the progressive forces of the world would not be able to come out against the revival of neo-Nazism in the Federal Republic of Germany, against the actions of butchers Franco and Salazar, against reactionary arbitrary actions of "black colonels" in Greece, because this is "the internal affair" of "sovereign" states.

It is characteristic that both the Saigon puppets and their American protectors also regard the notion of sovereignty as prohibiting support for the struggle of progressive forces.

They proclaim at every crossroads that the socialist countries, which are rendering help to the Vietnamese people in their struggle for independence and freedom, are violating the sovereignty of Vietnam. Genuine revolutionaries, being internationalists, cannot but support progressive forces in all countries in their just struggle for national and social liberation.

The interests of the socialist community and of the whole revolutionary movement, the interests of socialism in Czechoslovakia demand complete exposure and political isolation of the reactionary forces in that country, consolidation of the working people and consistent implementation of the Moscow agreement between the Soviet and Czechoslovak leaders.

There is no doubt that the actions of the five allied socialist countries in Czechoslovakia directed to the defense of the vital interests of the socialist community, and the sovereignty of socialist Czechoslovakia first and foremost, will be increasingly supported by all those who have the interest of the present revolutionary movement, of peace and security of peoples, of democracy and socialism at heart.

BIBLIOGRAPHY

OF WORKS CITED

Abu-Lughod, Ibrahim. "Nationalism in a New Perspective: the African Case." In *Patterns of African Development: Five Comparisons,* edited by Herbert Spiro. Englewood Cliffs, N.J., 1967.

Acharyya, B. K. *Codification in British India.* Calcutta, 1914.

Aiyangar, K.V. Rangaswami. *Considerations of Some Aspects of Ancient Indian Polity.* Madras, 1916.

Alexandrowicz, Charles Henry, ed. "Studies in the History of the Law of Nations." Grotian Society Papers. In *The Indian Yearbook of International Affairs,* xiii, part ii. Madras, 1964.

————. *An Introduction to the History of the Law of Nations in the East Indies.* London, 1967.

Allott, A. N. *Essays in African Law.* London, 1960.

————, ed. *The Future of Law in Africa.* London, 1960.

Almond, Gabriel A., and Coleman, James S. *Politics of the Developing Areas.* Princeton, 1960.

Anabtawi, M. F. *Arab Unity in Terms of Law.* The Hague, 1963.

Anderson, J.N.D. "The Future of Islamic Law in British Commonwealth Territories in Africa." In *African Law: New Law for New Nations,* edited by Hans W. Baade and Robinson O. Everett. Dobbs Ferry, N.Y., 1963.

————. *Islamic Law in the Modern World.* New York, 1959.

————, ed. *Changing Law in Developing Countries.* New York, 1963.

Andrain, Charles F. "The Political Thought of Sékou Touré." In *African Political Thought: Lumumba, Nkru-*

195

mah, and Touré, edited by W.A.E. Skurnik. Monograph Series in World Affairs, v, 1967-1968. Denver, 1968.

Antonius, George. *The Arab Awakening.* London, 1939, 1945.

Anyaibe, Stephen U. O. "The Wisdom of My People." Manuscript submitted to Bollingen Foundation, 1967.

Apter, David. *Ghana in Transition.* New York, 1963.

Arboussier, Gabriel d'. "L'Evolution de la Legislation dans Les Pays Africains d'Expression Française et à Madagascar." In *African Law: Adaptation and Development,* edited by H. and L. Kuper. Los Angeles, 1966.

Armstrong, Robert G. "The Idoma Court-of-Lineages in Law and Political Structure." In *Selected Papers of the Fifth International Congress of Anthropological and Ethnological Sciences, Philadelphia, 1956,* edited by Arthur Wallace. Philadelphia, 1960.

————. "A West African Inquest." *American Anthropologist,* LVI (December 1959).

Arnold, Sir Thomas. *The Caliphate.* Oxford, 1924.

Arnold, Thurman Wesley. *The Symbols of Government.* New Haven, 1935.

Asante, S.K.B. "Law and Society in Ghana." In *Africa and Law: Developing Legal Systems in African Commonwealth Nations,* edited by Thomas W. Hutchison. Madison, Milwaukee, and London, 1968.

Atreya, B. L. "Indian Culture, Its Spiritual, Moral and Social Aspects." In *Interrelations of Culture: Their Contribution to International Understanding,* UNESCO. Paris, 1953.

Ayrout, Henry Habib. *The Egyptian Peasant.* Translated by John Alden Williams. First published as *Moeurs et Coutumes des Fellahs,* France, 1938. First English translation, Cairo, 1945; new translation, with revisions by author, Boston, 1963.

Babinger, Franz. *Mehmed der Eroberer und Seine Zeit: Weltenstürmer einer Zeitenwende.* Munich, 1953, 1959.

Barkun, Michael. *Law Without Sanctions: Order in Primi-*

tive Societies and the World Community. New Haven and London, 1968.

Basham, A. L. *The Wonder That Was India.* London, 1954.

Bennett, George. "The Myth of Mau Mau." *Journal of African History,* VIII, no. 3 (1967).

Berque, Jacques. *Le Maghreb Entre Les Deux Guerres.* Paris, 1962.

Biobaku, S. O. "An Historical Account of the Evolution of Nigeria as a Political Unit." In *Constitutional Problems of Federalism in Nigeria,* edited by Lionel Brett. Proceedings of a Seminar held at King's College, Lagos, August 8-15, 1960. Lagos, 1961.

Bohannan, Laura, and Bohannan, Paul. *The Tiv of Central Nigeria.* London, 1953.

Bohannan, Paul. *Justice and Judgment among the Tiv.* London and New York, 1957.

————. *Social Anthropology.* New York, 1963.

————, ed. *Law and Warfare: Studies in the Anthropology of Conflict.* New York, 1967.

————, ed. *African Homicide and Suicide.* Princeton, 1960.

Boorman, Scott A. *The Protracted Game: A Wei-Ch'i Inpretation of Maoist Revolutionary Strategy.* New York, 1969.

Bown, Lalage, and Crowder, Michael, eds. *The Proceedings of the First International Congress of Africanists,* Accra, December 11-18, 1962. Bungay, Suffolk, and Evanston, Ill., 1964.

Bozeman, Adda B. "Do Educational and Cultural Exchanges Have Political Relevance?" *Exchange* (publication of United States Advisory Commission on International Educational and Cultural Affairs), Fall 1967.

————. "Normative Thinking, the National Interest, and War in a Multi-Cultural Environment." In *Conflict and Subjectivity: Toward New Normative Standards in U.S. Foreign Policy,* edited by Thomas Franck and Edward Weisbard. New York, 1971.

Bozeman, Adda B. *Politics and Culture in International History*. Princeton, 1960.

———. "Representative Systems of Public Order Today." *Proceedings of the American Society of International Law*, Annual Meeting, 1959. Washington, 1959.

Bretton, Henry L. *The Rise and Fall of Kwame Nkrumah: A Study of Personal Rule in Africa*. London, 1966.

Briggs, Lawrence Palmer. *The Ancient Khmer Empire*. Philadelphia, 1951.

Brogan, Sir Denis W. "Conflicts Arising Out of Different Governmental and Political Institutions." In *The Changing Environment of International Relations*, edited by Brookings Institution. Brookings Lectures, 1956. Washington, 1956.

Brown, D. MacKenzie. *The White Umbrella: Indian Political Thought from Manu to Gandhi*. Berkeley and Los Angeles, 1958.

Buchmann, Jean. *Le Problème des Structures Politiques en Afrique Noire*. Université Lovanium, Institut de Recherches Economiques et Sociales, Notes et Documents, No. 20/SP-1, July 1961.

Burton, Sir Richard F. *A Mission to Gelele, King of Dahome*. 2 vols. Memorial ed., London, 1893.

Busia, K. A. *Africa in Search of Democracy*. London, 1967.

Butt-Thompson, F. W. *Secret Societies in West Africa*. London, 1929.

Cady, John F. *Southeast Asia: Its Historical Development*. New York, 1964.

———. *Thailand, Burma, Laos, and Cambodia*. Englewood Cliffs, N.J., 1966.

Caillié, Réné. *Travels through Central Africa to Timbuctoo; and Across the Great Desert, to Morocco, Performed in the Years 1824-1828*. 2 vols. First French ed., 1830; English ed., London, 1830; new impression, 1968.

Campbell, Joseph. "Human Rights in Oriental Beliefs," *Sarah Lawrence Alumnae Magazine*, xxx (Spring 1965).

Chan, Wing-tsit. *Chinese Philosophy, 1949-1963: An Anno-*

tated Bibliography of Mainland China Publications. Honolulu, 1967.

Chaudhuri, N. C. "On Understanding the Hindu." *Encounter,* XXIV (June 1965).

Chen, Shih-Hsiang. "The Cultural Essence of Chinese Literature." In *Interrelations of Cultures: Their Contribution to International Understanding,* UNESCO. Paris, 1953.

Chu, T'ung-tsu. *Law and Society in Traditional China.* Paris and The Hague, 1961.

Coèdes, Georges. *Les Etats Hinduoisés d'Indochine et d'Indonésie.* Paris, 1948.

Cohen, Jerome Alan. "Chinese Attitudes Toward International Law and Our Own." *Proceedings of the American Society of International Law,* April 1967.

Cohen, Maxwell. "Reflections on Law and the United Nations System." *Proceedings of the American Society of International Law,* Annual Meeting, 1960.

Colson, Elizabeth, and Gluckman, Max, eds. *Seven Tribes of British Central Africa.* London, 1951.

Coulson, N. J. *A History of Islamic Law.* Edinburgh, 1964.

Cranmer-Byng, J. L. *An Embassy to China.* London, 1962.

Dallin, Alexander. *The Soviet Union at the United Nations,* New York, 1962.

Davenport, Guy. "Pound and Frobenius." In *Motive and Method in The Cantos of Ezra Pound,* edited by Lewis Leary. New York, 1954.

Davis, Helen M. *Constitutions, Electoral Laws, Treaties of State in the Near and Middle East.* Durham, N.C., 1947.

Derrett, J. Duncan M. "The Administration of Hindu Law by the British." *Comparative Studies in Society and History,* IV (1961-1962).

————. "Justice, Equity and Good Conscience." In *Changing Law in Developing Countries,* edited by J.N.D. Anderson. New York, 1963.

Dike, K. O. *Trade and Politics in the Niger Delta, 1830-1885.* Oxford, 1956.

199

Dinesen, Isak, pseud. *Out of Africa*. New York, 1938.

Diop, Alioune. "The Spirit of *Présence Africaine.*" In *Proceedings of the First International Congress of Africanists*, edited by Lalage Bown and Michael Crowder. Bungay, Suffolk, 1964.

Doughty, Charles M. *Travels in Arabia Deserta*. With a new preface by the author, an introduction by T. E. Lawrence, and all original maps, plans, and cuts. 2 vols. New York and London, 1923.

Drekmeier, Charles. *Kingship and Community in Early India*. Stanford, Calif., and Bombay, 1962.

Dubs, Homer H. "The Concept of Unity in China." In *The Quest for Political Unity in World History*, edited by Stanley Pargellis. Washington, 1944.

Dumont, Etienne. *False Start in Africa*. Translation of *L'Afrique Noire est mal partie*. New York, 1966.

Duncanson, Dennis J. "How—and Why—the Vietcong Holds Out." *Encounter*, xxvii (December 1966).

East, Rupert, ed. and trans. *Akiga's Story: The Tiv Tribe as Seen by One of Its Members*. London, 1939.

Egharevba, Jacob U. *A Short History of Benin*. 4th ed. Ibadan, 1968.

Elias, T. O. "The Evolution of Law and Government in Modern Africa." In *African Law: Adaptation and Development*, edited by H. and L. Kuper. Los Angeles, 1966.

————. *The Nature of African Customary Law*. Manchester, 1956.

Escarra, Jean. *Le Droit Chinois*. Peking and Paris, 1936.

Evans-Pritchard, E. E. *The Nuer: A Description of the Modes of Livelihood and Political Institutions of a Nilotic People*. Oxford, 1940.

————. *Witches, Oracles, and Magic among the Azande*. Oxford, 1937, 1950.

Fairbank, John K. "China's World Order: The Tradition of Chinese Foreign Relations." *Encounter*, xxvii (December 1966).

200

————. "Tributary Trade and China's Relations with the West." *Far Eastern Quarterly*, i (February 1942).

————. *The United States and China*. Cambridge, Mass., 1948.

Fallers, Lloyd. "Customary Law in the New African States." In *African Law: New Law for New Nations*, edited by Hans W. Baade and Robinson O. Everett. Dobbs Ferry, N.Y., 1963.

Faublée, J. "Madagascar au xixe Siècle: Esquisse d'Histoire Economique et Sociale." *Journal of World History*, v (1959).

Franck, Thomas M. *East African Unity Through Law*. New Haven and London, 1966.

Frobenius, Leo. "Early African Culture as an Indication of Present Negro Potentialities," *Annals of the American Academy of Political and Social Science*, iii (November 1928).

————. *Erlebte Erdteile: Ergebnisse eines deutschen Forscherlebens*. 7 vols. Frankfurt-am-Main, 1928-1929.

————. *Und Afrika Sprach*. Volkstünliche Ausgabe in 1 vol. Berlin-Charlottenburg, 1912.

————. *Und Afrika Sprach*. 4 vols. Berlin-Charlottenburg, 1912-1913.

Frye, Richard N. *The Heritage of Persia*. New York, 1966.

————. "The United States and Iran." In *The United States and Turkey and Iran*, edited by Lewis V. Thomas and Richard N. Frye. Cambridge, Mass., 1951.

Garbett, G. Kingsley. "Spirit Mediums as Mediators in Korekore Society." In *Spirit Mediumship and Society in Africa*, edited by John Beattie and John Middleton. New York, 1969.

Gardet, Louis. "L'Humanisme greco-arabe: Avicenne." *Journal of World History*, ii (1955).

Geertz, Clifford. "The Social-Cultural Context of Policy in Southeast Asia." In *Southeast Asia: Problems of United States Policy*, edited by William Henderson. Cambridge, Mass., 1963.

201

Geiger, Theodor. *The Conflicted Relationship: The West and the Transformation of Asia, Africa, and Latin America.* New York, 1964.

Gelfand, Michael. *Medicine and Custom in Africa.* London, 1964.

George Washington Law Review. *A Symposium on Muslim Law.* Reprint from vol. xxii, October-December 1953. Washington, 1953.

Ghai, Y. P. "Customary Contracts and Transactions in Kenya." In *Ideas and Procedures in African Customary Law,* edited by Max Gluckman. London, 1969.

Ghoshal, U. N. *A History of Hindu Political Theories, from the Earliest Times to the End of the First Quarter of the Seventeenth Century A.D.* London, 1927.

————. "Some Aspects of Ancient Indian Political Organizations." *Journal of World History,* vi (1960).

Gibb, H.A.R. *Modern Trends in Islam: A Critique of Islamic Modernism.* Chicago, 1947.

————. *Mohammedanism: An Historical Survey.* 2nd. ed. Oxford, 1953; reprinted with revisions, 1961.

————. "Social Reform: Factor X. The Search for an Islamic Democracy." *Atlantic Monthly,* October 1956, supplement.

————. *Studies on the Civilization of Islam,* edited by Stanford J. Shaw and William R. Poll. Boston, 1962.

————, and Bowen, Harold. *Islamic Society and the West: A Study of the Impact of Western Civilization on Moslem Culture in the Near East.* i, *Islamic Society in the Eighteenth Century.* Oxford, 1951, 1957.

Gledhill, A. "Fundamental Rights." In *Changing Law in Developing Countries,* edited by J.N.D. Anderson. New York, 1963.

Gluckman, Max. *The Judicial Process Among the Barotse of Northern Rhodesia.* Manchester, 1955.

————, ed. *Ideas and Procedures in African Customary Law.* London, 1969.

Goldenweiser, Alexander. *History, Psychology and Culture.* New York, 1933.

Goodhart, Arthur L. *Law of the Land.* Charlottesville, Va., 1966.

Gordon, Bernard K. *The Dimensions of Conflict in Southeast Asia.* Englewood Cliffs, N.J., 1966.

Gordon, Jay. "African Law and the Historian." *Journal of African History,* VIII (1967).

Gower, L.C.B. *Independent Africa: The Challenge to the Legal Profession.* Cambridge, Mass., 1967.

Granet, Marcel. *La Pensée Chinoise.* Paris, 1934.

Griffith, Samuel B. *The Chinese People's Liberation Army.* New York, 1967.

―――. *Peking and People's Wars.* New York, 1966.

Griffiths, Sir Percival Joseph. *The British Impact on India.* 1953; reprint, Hamden, Conn., 1965.

Groslier, Bernard, and Arthaud, Jacques. *The Arts and Civilization of Angkor.* New York, 1957.

Grotius, Hugo. *The Rights of War and Peace, including The Law of Nature and of Nations.* Translated by A. C. Campbell. Washington and London, 1901.

Grundy, Kenneth W. "Ideology and Insurrection: The Theory of Guerrilla Warfare in Africa." Prepared for presentation to the Annual Convention of the International Studies Association, San Francisco, March 1969.

Haas, William S. *Iran.* New York, 1946.

Hadeed, M.F. Abou. "Psychology and the Arabic Language." *Middle East Journal,* VI (Winter 1952).

Hair, P.E.H. "The Enslavement of Koelle's Informants," *Journal of African History,* VI (1965).

Hakim, Khalifa Abdul. *Islam and Communism.* 1951; reprint, Lahore, 1953.

Halpern, Manfred. *The Politics of Social Change in the Middle East and North Africa.* Princeton, 1965.

Hamady, Sania. *Temperament and Character of the Arabs.* New York, 1960.

Han Fei Tzu. *Basic Writings*. Translated by Burton Watson. New York, 1963.

Hannigan, A. St.J. "The Imposition of Western Law Forms upon Primitive Societies." *Comparative Studies in Society and History*, IV (1961).

Harbison, Frederick. "Human Resources and Development." In *Economic and Social Aspects of Educational Planning*, UNESCO. Paris, 1964.

Hargreaves, John D. *A Life of Sir Samuel Lewis*. London, 1958.

Hart, H.L.A. *The Concept of Law*. Oxford, 1961.

Harvey, William B. *Law and Social Change in Ghana*. Princeton, 1966.

Heine-Geldern, Robert. "Conceptions of State and Kingship in South East Asia." *Far Eastern Quarterly*, II (November 1942).

Herrmann, Albert. *An Historical Atlas of China*. Rev. ed., Chicago. 1966.

Herskovits, Melville J. "The Culture Areas of Africa." *Africa*, III (1930).

——. "Anthropology and Africa: A Wider Perspective." Lugard Memorial Lecture for 1959. *Africa*, XXIX (1959).

Hevi, Emmanuel John. *The Dragon's Embrace: The Chinese Communists and Africa*. New York, 1967.

Hodgkin, Thomas. "A Note on the Language of African Nationalism." In *African Affairs: Number One*, edited by Kenneth Kirkwood. St. Antony's Papers, Number 10. London, 1961.

——, ed. *Nigerian Perspectives: An Historical Anthology*. London, 1960.

Hoffman, Stanley. "International Systems and International Law." *World Politics*, XIV (October 1961).

Holdsworth, William Searle. *Some Lessons from Our Legal History*. New York, 1925.

Holland, J. F. *Elements of Jurisprudence*. Oxford, 1880; new ed., 1928.

Holleman, J. F. *Shona Customary Law*. London and New York, 1952.

Horton, Alan W. "The Charter for National Action of the UAR." *American Universities Field Staff Reports Service*, North Africa Series, IX (1962).

———. "Search for Popular Support." *American Universities Field Staff Reports Service*, North Africa Series, IX (1962).

Hourani, Albert. *Arabic Thought in the Liberal Age, 1798-1939*. London, 1962.

———. *A Vision of History: Near Eastern and Other Essays*. Beirut, 1961.

Hovet, Thomas, Jr. *Africa in the United Nations*. Evanston, Ill., 1963.

Hucker, Charles O. *The Traditional Chinese State in Ming Times (1368-1644)*. Tucson, Ariz., 1967.

Huntingford, G.W.B. *The Nandi of Kenya: Tribal Control in a Pastoral Society*. London, 1953.

Hurewitz, Jacob Coleman, ed. *Diplomacy in the Near and Middle East: A Documentary Record*. 2 vols. Princeton, 1956.

Hussayn, Tāhā. *The Future of Culture in Egypt*. Translated from Arabic by Sidney Glazer. Washington, 1954.

Huxley, Julian. *Africa View*. London and New York, 1931.

Ibn Khaldûn. *The Muqaddimah: An Introduction to History*. Translated by Franz Rosenthal. Bollingen Series XLIII. 3 vols. New York, 1958.

Iqbal, Sir Muhammad. *The Mysteries of Selflessness: A Philosophical Poem*. Translated by A. J. Arberry. London, 1953.

———. *The Restoration of Religious Thought*. Lahore, 1958.

Isaacs, H. R. "Group Identity and Political Change: The Role of Color and Physical Characteristics." *Daedalus*, XCVI (Spring 1967).

Issawi, Charles. "The Arabic Language and Arab Psychology." *Middle East Journal,* v (Autumn 1951).

Jabavu, Noni. *Drawn in Colour: African Contrasts.* London, 1961.

Jackson, R.G.A. *A Study of the Capacity of the United Nations Development System.* 2 vols. Geneva, 1969.

Joset, P. E. *Les Sociétés Secrètes des Hommes Léopards en Afrique Noire.* Paris, 1955.

Kaunda, Kenneth. *Zambia Shall Be Free.* African Writers Series 4. London, Toronto, and Ibadan, 1962.

Kenyatta, Yomo. *Facing Mount Kenya.* London, 1938.

Kerr, Malcolm. *The Arab Cold War 1958-1967: A Study of Ideology in Politics.* Chatham House Essays. 2nd ed. London and New York, 1967.

Keuning, J. "The Study of Law in African Countries." *Higher Education and Research in the Netherlands,* VII (1963).

Khadduri, Majid. *The Law of War and Peace: A Study in Muslim International Law.* London, 1940.

———. *War and Peace in the Law of Islam.* Baltimore, 1955.

———, and Liebesny, Herbert J., eds. *Law in the Middle East.* 2 vols. Washington, 1955.

Khalil, Muhammad. *The Arab State and the Arab League.* 2 vols. Beirut, 1962.

Kluckhohn, Clyde. "Values and Value Orientations in the Theory of Action." In *Toward a General Theory of Action,* by Talcott Parsons *et al.* Cambridge, Mass., 1951.

Kuper, H., and Kuper, L., eds. *African Law: Adaptation and Development.* Los Angeles, 1966.

Lamb, Alastair. *The China-India Border.* Oxford, 1964.

Lambert, H. E. *Kikuyu Social and Political Institutions.* London, 1956.

Lambton, Ann K.S. "The Spiritual Influence of Islam in Persia." In *Islam Today,* edited by A. J. Arberry and Rom Landau. London, 1943.

Lammens, Henri. *Islam: Beliefs and Institutions.* Trans-

lated by E. Denison Ross. London, 1929; reprinted, 1968.
Landheer, B. "The Situational Approach to International Relations." Prepared for the Fifth Maxwell Institute on the United Nations and International Law, Kasteel Oud-Wassenaar, Holland, August 1968.
Lasswell, Harold D., *World Politics and Personal Insecurity.* New York, 1935.
———. "The Relevance of International Law to the Development Process." *Proceedings of the American Society of International Law*, Annual Meeting, 1966.
———, and McDougal, Myres S. "The Identification and Appraisal of Diverse Systems of Public Order," *American Journal of International Law*, LIII (January 1959).
Lawrence, T. E. *Seven Pillars of Wisdom.* New York, 1935.
Lee, J. M. *African Armies and Civil Order.* Studies in International Security 13, The Institute for Strategic studies. London, 1969.
LeMay, Reginald. *The Culture of South-East Asia: The Heritage of India.* London, 1954.
Leng, Shao-chuan. "Pre-1949 Development of the Communist Chinese System of Justice." *China Quarterly* (April-June 1967).
Lerner, Daniel. *The Passing of Traditional Society: Modernizing the Middle East.* New York, 1958.
Leroy-Gourhan, André, and Poirier, Jean. *Ethnologie de L'Union Française.* Vol. 1, *Afrique.* Paris, 1953.
Levenson, Joseph R. *Confucian China and Its Modern Fate.* 3 vols. Berkeley and Los Angeles, 1958-1965.
Levin, Julius. *Studies in African Native Law.* Capetown and Philadelphia, 1947.
Lewis, Bernard. *Istanbul and the Civilization of the Ottoman Empire.* Norman, Okla., 1963.
———. *The Middle East and the West.* Bloomington, Ind., 1964.
Little, Kenneth. "African Culture and the Western Intrusion." *Journal of World History*, III (1957).
———. *The Mende of Sierra Leone.* London, 1951.

Little, Kenneth. "The Political Function of the Poro." *Africa*, xxv (October 1954), and xxxvi (January 1966).

Lissitzyn, Oliver J. *International Law in a Divided World*. New York, 1963.

————. "Western and Soviet Perspectives on International Law—A Comparison." *Proceedings of the American Society of International Law*, Annual Meeting, 1959.

Livingstone, David. *Missionary Travels and Researches in South Africa*. New York, 1958.

Lloyd, P. C. *Africa in Social Change*. Harmondsworth, Middlesex, 1967.

Luethy, Herbert. "Indonesia Confronted." *Encounter*, xxv (December 1965); xxvi (January 1966).

Lugard, Captain F.D. *The Rise of Our East African Empire*, 2 vols. Edinburgh and London, 1893.

Lusignan, Guy de. *French-Speaking Africa Since Independence*. New York, Washington, and London, 1969.

Lybyer, Albert Howe. *The Government of the Ottoman Empire in the Time of Suleiman the Magnificent*. Cambridge, Mass., 1913.

McClelland, Charles A. "The Function of Theory in International Relations." *Journal of Conflict Resolution*, iv (1960).

McClelland, David. *The Achieving Society*. Princeton, 1961.

Macdonald, Duncan Black. *Development of Muslim Theology, Jurisprudence and Constitutional Theory*. London and New York, 1903; reprinted, New York, 1965.

————. *The Religious Attitude and Life in Islam*. Haskell Lectures on Comparative Religion delivered before the University of Chicago in 1906. Chicago, 1909.

MacDonald, Robert W. *The League of Arab States: A Study in the Dynamics of Regional Organization*. Princeton, 1965.

McIlwain, Charles. *Constitutionalism Ancient and Modern*. Ithaca, N.Y., 1940.

McKay, Vernon. "The Arab League in World Politics." *Foreign Policy Reports*, xxii (November 15, 1946).

————, ed. *African Diplomacy: Studies in the Determinants of Foreign Policy*, New York, 1966.

Mackenzie, W.J.M., and Robinson, Kenneth E., eds. *Five Elections in Africa*. Oxford, 1960.

Mahassani, Sobhi. "Muslims: Decadence and Renaissance, Adaptation of Islamic Jurisprudence to Modern Social Needs." *The Muslim World*, XLIV (1954).

Maine, Sir Henry Sumner. *Dissertations on Early Law and Custom*. New York, 1883.

————. *Lectures on the Early History of Institutions*. New York, 1888.

————. *Village-Communities in the East and West*. New York, 1880.

Mair, Lucy. *Primitive Government*. Harmondsworth, Middlesex, 1962.

Majumdar, R. C. *Corporate Life in Ancient India*. Calcutta, 1918.

Malinowski, Bronislaw. "The Problem of Meaning in Primitive Languages." In *The Meaning of Meaning*, edited by C. K. Ogden and I. A. Richards. New York, 1955.

Manning, C.A.W. *The Nature of International Society*, London, 1962.

Mao Tse-tung. *On Guerrilla Warfare*. New York, 1961.

————. *Selected Works*. 4 vols. London, 1954; new ed., 1958.

Maudūdi, Abul A'lā. *The Islamic Law and Constitution*. 2nd ed. Lahore, 1960.

Maung Maung. *Law and Custom in Burma and the Burmese Family*. The Hague, 1963.

Mazrui, Ali A. "On the Concept: 'We Are All Africans.'" *American Political Science Review*, LVII (1963).

————. *Towards a Pax Africana: A Study of Ideology and Ambition*. Chicago, 1967.

————. "The UN and Some African Political Attitudes." *International Organization*, XVIII (Summer 1964).

McDougal, Myres S., and Lasswell, Harold D. "The Identification and Appraisal of Diverse Systems of Public Order." *American Journal of International Law*, LIII (January 1959).

Meek, C. K. *Law and Authority in a Nigerian Tribe: A Study in Indirect Rule*. Oxford, 1937.

———. *A Sudanese Kingdom*. London, 1931.

Meister, Albert. *L'Afrique peut-elle partir?* Paris, 1966.

Meyer, Alfred G. *Leninism*. New York, 1963.

Middleton, John, and Winter, E. H., eds. *Witchcraft and Sorcery in East Africa*. London, 1963.

Migeod, Frederick William Hugh. *A View of Sierra Leone*. New York, 1927.

Montague, R. "The Teaching of Democracy in Islamic Countries." *Journal of African Administration*, April 1952.

Monteil, Charles. *Les Bambara du Segou et du Kaarta*. Paris, 1924.

Montesquieu, Charles Louis de Secondat. *De l'esprit des lois*. 1748; Paris, 1869.

Mootham, Sir Orby. "Constitutional Writs in India." In *Changing Law in Developing Countries*, edited by J.N.D. Anderson. New York, 1963.

Murdock, George Peter. *Africa, Its People and Their Culture History*. New York, 1959.

Myrdal, Gunnar, and Associates. *Asian Drama: An Inquiry into the Poverty of Nations*. 3 vols. New York, 1967.

Nadel, S. F. *The Nuba*. London and New York, 1947.

Nasser, Gamal Abdel. *The Philosophy of the Revolution*. Introduction by John S. Badeau. Buffalo, 1959.

Nawaz, N. K. "A Re-examination of Some Basic Concepts of Islamic Law and Jurisprudence." World Rule of Law Series 23. Reprinted from *The Indian Year Book of International Affairs*, 1963. Durham, N.C., n.d.

Needham, Joseph. *Science and Civilization in China*. 4 vols. Cambridge, 1954-1970.

Nelson, M. Frederick. *Korea and the Old Orders in Eastern Asia*. Baton Rouge, La., 1945.

Nkrumah, Kwame. *Consciencism: Philosophy and Ideology*

for Decolonization and Development, with Particular Reference to the African Revolution. New York, 1965.
———. *Dark Days in Ghana.* New York, 1968.
———. *Ghana: The Autobiography of Kwame Nkrumah.* New York, 1957.
———. *I Speak of Freedom: A Statement of African Ideology.* New York, 1961.
Nolte, Richard. "The Rule of Law in the Arab Middle East." *Muslim World,* XLVIII (October 1958).
Ogden, C. K., and Richards, I. A. *The Meaning of Meaning.* New York, 1959.
Ollennu, N. A. "The Structure of African Judicial Authority and Problems of Evidence and Proof in Traditional Courts." In *Ideas and Procedures in African Customary Law,* edited by Max Gluckman. London, 1969.
Ortega y Gasset, José. *History as a System and Other Essays Toward a Philosophy of History.* New York, 1941.
Ostrogorsky, Georg. *Geschichte des byzantinischen Staates.* Munich, 1940. English translation by Joan Hussey, *History of the Byzantine State.* New Brunswick, N.J., 1957.
Panikkar, K. M. "Indian Doctrines of Politics." First annual lecture delivered at the Premabhai Hall, July 22, 1955, Harold Laski Institute of Political Science, Ahmedabad, 1955.
———. *A Survey of Indian History.* Bombay, 1954.
Peaslee, Amos J. *Constitutions of Nations.* Vol. I, *Africa.* 3rd ed. The Hague, 1965.
Perham, Margery, ed. *Ten Africans.* London, 1936; reprint, Evanston, Ill., 1963.
Polanyi, Michael. "On The Modern Mind." *Encounter,* XXIV (May 1965).
Pym, Christopher. *The Ancient Civilization of Angkor.* New York and Toronto, 1968.
Radcliffe-Brown, A. R. "Primitive Law." In *Encyclopedia of the Social Sciences,* IX (1933).
Rahman, F. "Internal Religious Developments in the Present Century Islam." *Journal of World History,* II (1955).

211

Rapson, E. J., ed. *The Cambridge History of India.* Vol. I, *Ancient India.* First Indian reprint, 1955.

Rattray, R. S. *Ashanti.* Oxford, 1923.

——. *Ashanti Law and Constitution.* 1929; reissued, London, 1956.

——. *Religion and Art in Ashanti.* Oxford, 1927.

Redfield, Robert. *The Primitive World and Its Transformations.* 1953; reprint, Ithaca, N.Y., 1958.

Religions Africaines Traditionelles, Les. Proceedings of "Rencontres Internationales de Bouaké." Paris, 1965.

Rencontres Internationales de Bouaké, Proceedings. See *Les Religions Africaines Traditionelles* and *Tradition et Modernisme en Afrique Noire.*

Richards, Audrey I., ed. *East African Chiefs: A Study of Political Development in Some Uganda and Tanganyika Tribes.* London, 1959.

Richards, I. A. *Mencius on the Mind; Experiments in Multiple Definition.* London, 1932.

Robinson's Admiralty Reports. James Humphreys, Philadelphia, Reprints of cases determined in the High Court of Admiralty.

Rosecrance, Richard N. *Action and Reaction in World Politics.* Boston, 1963.

Rosenthal, E.I.J. "The Islamic Law and Constitution." *International Affairs,* July 1962.

——. *Islam in the Modern National State.* Cambridge, 1965.

——. *Political Thought in Medieval Islam: An Introductory Outline.* Cambridge, 1958.

Roth, H. Ling. *Great Benin.* Halifax, 1903.

Rwayemamu, Anthony H., and Brown, Brack E.S. "Federation: An Unfinished Portrait." In *The Transformation of East Africa,* edited by Stanley Diamond and Fred G. Burke. New York and London, 1966.

Sanson-Teran, José. *Universalismo y Regionalismo en la Sociedad Interstatal Contemporanea.* Barcelona, 1960.

Santillana, David de. "Law and Society." In *The Legacy of Islam*, edited by Sir Thomas Arnold. Oxford, 1947.

Sastri, Nilakanta. *Studies in Chola History and Administration*. Madras, 1932.

Saunders, John J., ed. *The Muslim World on the Eve of Europe's Expansion*. Englewood Cliffs, N.J., 1966.

———. "The Problem of Islamic Decadence." *Journal of World History*, VII (1963).

Schacht, Joseph. *An Introduction to Islamic Law*. Oxford, 1964.

———. "Islamic Law." In *Encyclopedia of the Social Sciences*, VIII (1932).

———. *Origins of Muhammadan Jurisprudence*. Oxford, 1950, 1959.

Schaeder, Hans Heinrich. *Der Mensch in Orient und Okzident: Grundzüge einer eurasiatischen Geschichte*. Munich, 1960.

Schapera, Isaac. *Government and Politics in Tribal Societies*. London, 1956.

———. *A Handbook of Tswana Law and Custom*. 2nd ed. London, New York, and Capetown, 1955.

Schecter, Jerrold. *The New Face of Buddha*. New York, 1967.

Schramm, Stuart R. *The Political Thought of Mao Tsetung*. New York, 1963.

Schroeder, Eric. *Muhammad's People: A Tale by Analogy*. Portland, Me., 1955.

Scott, J. B., and Jaeger, W.H.E. *Cases on International Law*. St. Paul, Minn., 1937.

Sen, S. P. "Effects on India of British Law and Administration in the Nineteenth Century." *Journal of World History*, IV (1958).

Senghor, Léopold. *On African Socialism*. New York, 1964.

Sharabi, Hisham B. *Nationalism and Revolution in the Arab World (The Middle East and North Africa)*. Princeton, 1966.

Shamasastry, Rudrahatha, ed. *Kautilya's Arthasastra*. Bombay, 1951.

Sharma, R. S. "L'economie dans l'Inde Ancienne." *Journal of World History*, IV (1960).

Shouby, E. "The Influence of the Arabic Language on the Psychology of the Arabs." *Middle East Journal*, V (Summer 1951).

Singer, H. W. *International Development: Growth and Change*. New York, 1964.

Skinner, Elliott P. *The Mossi of the Upper Volta: The Political Development of a Sudanese People*. Stanford, Calif., 1964.

Smith, Wilfred Cantwell. *Islam in Modern History*. New York, 1957.

———. *Modern Islam in India*. London, 1946.

Snell, G. S. *Nandi Customary Law*. London, 1954.

Spencer, John H. Review of Peaslee's *Constitutions of Nations*, Vol. I, *Africa*. *American Journal of International Law*, LXI (October 1967).

Spengler, Oswald. *Der Untergang des Abendlandes*. 2 vols. Munich, 1923. English translation by Charles Francis Atkinson, *The Decline of the West*. 1 vol. New York, 1932.

Spellman, John W. *Political Theory of Ancient India: A Study of Kingship from the Earliest Times to ca. A.D. 500*. Oxford, 1964.

Spiro, Herbert, ed. *Patterns of African Development: Five Comparisons*. Englewood Cliffs, N.J., 1967.

Sun Tzu. *The Art of War*. Translated by Samuel B. Griffith. Oxford, 1963.

Suzuki, Daisetz Teitaro. *Essays in Zen Buddhism*. Series 1-3. Boston, London, and Tokyo, 1927-1934.

Swarup, Shanti. *A Study of the Chinese Communist Movement*. Oxford, 1966.

Tempels, Placide. *La Philosophie Bantoue*. Paris, 1959.

214

Thiam, Doudou. *The Foreign Policy of African States.* New York, 1965.

Thomas, Lewis V. "The United States and Turkey," in *The United States and Turkey and Iran,* by Lewis V. Thomas and Richard N. Frye. Cambridge, Mass., 1951.

Thompson, Sir Robert. *No Exit from Vietnam.* New York, 1969.

Tinker, Hugh. *Ballot Box and Bayonet: People and Government in Emergent Asian Countries.* Oxford, 1964.

————. *The Foundations of Local Self-Government in India, Pakistan and Burma.* London, 1954.

Tradition et Modernisme en Afrique Noire. Proceedings of "Rencontres Internationales de Bouaké." Paris, 1965.

Trimingham, John Spencer. *A History of Islam in West Africa.* London, 1963.

————. *The Influence of Islam upon Africa.* New York, 1968.

————. *Islam in East Africa.* Report of a survey undertaken in 1961. London, 1962.

————. *Islam in Ethiopia.* London and New York, 1952.

————. *Islam in West Africa.* Oxford, 1959.

Triska, Jan F. "A Model for Study of Soviet Foreign Policy." *American Political Science Review,* LII (March 1958).

United Nations Educational, Scientific, and Cultural Organization (UNESCO). *Interrelations of Culture: Their Contribution to International Understanding.* Paris, 1953.

Vansina, Jan. "A Traditional Legal System: The Kuba." In *African Law: Adaptation and Development,* edited by H. and L. Kuper. Los Angeles, 1966.

Verheist, Thierry. *Safeguarding African Customary Law: Judicial and Legislative Processes for Its Adaptation and Integration.* Occasional Paper 7, African Studies Center, University of California. Los Angeles, 1968.

Vieyra, Christian. "Structures Politiques Traditionelles et Structures Politiques Modernes." In *Tradition et Modernisme en Afrique Noire,* Proceedings of "Rencontres Internationales de Bouaké." Paris, 1965.

Vinogradoff, Sir Paul. *Outlines of Historical Jurisprudence.* Vol. ii, *The Jurisprudence of the Greek City.* Oxford, 1922.

Von Grunebaum, G. E. *Medieval Islam: A Study in Cultural Orientation.* Chicago, 1946.

――――. *Modern Islam: The Search for Cultural Identity.* Berkeley and Los Angeles, 1962.

Vucinich, W. S. *The Ottoman Empire: Its Record and Legacy.* Princeton, 1964.

Wales, H. G. Quaritch. *Ancient Siamese Government and Administration.* London, 1934.

――――. *The Making of Greater India.* London, 1951.

Waley, Arthur. *Three Ways of Thought in Ancient China.* New York, 1939.

Walker, Richard L. *The Multi-State System in Ancient China.* Hamden, Conn., 1953.

Ward, Robert P. *An Enquiry into the Foundation and History of the Law of Nations in Europe from the Time of the Greeks and Romans to the Age of Grotius.* 2 vols. London, 1795.

Weber, Max. *Law in Economy and Society.* Edited by Max Rheinstein and translated by Edward Shils and Max Rheinstein. 20th Century Legal Philosophy Series 6. Cambridge, Mass., 1954.

Wei Yang. *The Book of Lord Shang: A Classic of the Chinese School of Law.* Translated by J.J.L. Duyvendak. London, 1928.

Westermann, Diedrich. *The African Today and Tomorrow.* 1934; reprint, London, 1949.

――――. *Geschichte Afrikas: Staatenbildungen suedlich der Sahara.* Cologne, 1952.

Wheaton, Henry. *History of the Modern Law of Nations.* New York, 1845.

Whitehead, Alfred North. *Adventures of Ideas.* New York, 1933.

Whiteley, Wilfred H. "Political Concepts and Connotations: Observations on the Use of Some Political Terms in Swahili." In *African Affairs: Number One,* edited by Kenneth Kirkwood. St. Antony's Papers, Number 10. London, 1961.

Wigmore, John Henry. *A Panorama of the World's Legal Systems.* 3 vols. Washington, 1936.

Wilson, Ronald K. *Anglo-Muhammadan Law.* 2nd ed. London, 1903.

Worsthorne, Peregrine. "Trouble in the Air—Letter from Ghana." *Encounter,* XII (May 1959).

Wright, Arthur F. *Buddhism in Chinese History.* Stanford, 1959.

——. "Buddhism and Chinese Culture: Phases of Interaction," *Journal of Asian Studies,* XVII (November 1957).

——. "The Indianization of China." Paper read at the Annual Meeting of the Far Eastern Association, Spring 1949.

——. ed. *Studies in Chinese Thought.* Chicago, 1953.

Wright, Richard. *Black Power: A Record of Reactions in a Land of Pathos.* New York, 1954.

Youlou, Fulbert. *J'accuse la Chine.* Paris, 1966.

Zartman, I. William. *Government and Politics in North Africa.* New York, 1963.

——. *International Relations in the New Africa.* Englewood Cliffs, N.J., 1966.

Ziadeh, Farhat J. *Lawyers: The Rule of Law and Liberalism in Modern Egypt.* Stanford, 1968.

Zimmer, Heinrich. *The Art of Indian Asia: Its Mythology and Transformation.* Completed and edited by Joseph Campbell. 2 vols. Bollingen Series XXXIX. New York, 1955.

——. *Philosophies of India.* Edited by Joseph Campbell. Bollingen Series XXVI. New York, 1951.

INDEX

219

DATE DUE

30. '81	
6. 15. '82	
DU